The Road to Co-operation

Writing a book is an act of pure anti-social selfishness which impacts on all those in close contact with the writer, requiring their enduring indulgence and support. I am extremely grateful to have had Eileen's generous support in writing The Road to Co-operation, *as I have had with all my other projects.*

The Road to Co-operation

Escaping the Bottom Line

GORDON PEARSON
Keele University, UK

GOWER

Gower Applied Business Research
Our programme provides leaders, practitioners, scholars and researchers with thought provoking, cutting edge books that combine conceptual insights, interdisciplinary rigour and practical relevance in key areas of business and management.

Published by
Gower Publishing Limited
Wey Court East
Union Road
Farnham
Surrey, GU9 7PT
England

Ashgate Publishing Company
Suite 420
101 Cherry Street
Burlington,
VT 05401-4405
USA

www.gowerpublishing.com

British Library Cataloguing in Publication Data
Pearson, Gordon J., 1939-
  The road to co-operation: escaping the bottom line.
  1. Corporate governance. 2. Free enterprise. 3. Social
  responsibility of business.
  I. Title
  658.4-dc23

ISBN: 978-1-4094-3202-9 (hbk)
ISBN: 978-1-4094-4830-3 (pbk)
ISBN: 978-1-4094-3203-6 (ebk)

Library of Congress Cataloging-in-Publication Data
Pearson, Gordon J., 1939-
  The road to co-operation : escaping the bottom line / by Gordon Pearson.
    p. cm.
  Includes bibliographical references and index.
  ISBN 978-1-4094-3202-9 (hardback) -- ISBN 978-1-4094-3203-6
  (ebook) 1. Cooperation. 2. Sustainable development. 3. Economics. I.
  Title.
  HD2963.P434 2011
  334--dc23

2011048043

Printed and bound in Great Britain by the
MPG Books Group, UK

Contents

Preface

This book is about freedom. For von Mises, Hayek, Friedman and those of like neoclassical mind, freedom was expressed largely as the absence of state intervention which, for them, led inexorably to centrally planned socialism and thus to the sort of totalitarian government then seen in the Soviet Union and the People's Republic of China and their satellites. Half a century ago such a fear might not have seemed unreasonable.

The free market neoclassical perspective fiercely opposes state intervention wherever possible, relying instead on market forces to direct everything for the best, in the best of all possible worlds: it specifically denies the observed fact that competitive markets, unless regulated to protect and preserve competition, inevitably become monopolistic and open to cornering, fixing and all manner of abuse, to the disadvantage of all but the monopolist.

Moreover, as has been said many times, one man's freedom is another's prison; freedom for some depends on the restraint of others. Hayek's freedom is the freedom to pursue economic growth, accepting the inequitable distribution of income and wealth which results, and explicitly rejecting any attempt at state imposed redistribution. It fails to comprehend that the unlimited freedom for the wealthy depends on the impoverishment of the poor and their captivity in hunger, disease and ignorance. It is the freedom for those who already have, to take from those who have not. And it is an ideology based on false premises.

That is the background to this text. My focus, as in *The Rise and Fall of Management*, is on the management and governance of working organisations where the majority of us spend the most productive and active part of our lives. So organisations are important to us on a personal basis, having a profound effect on how satisfactory we find the whole of our existence. Beyond that, these same working organisations produce the means by which a society provides education, healthcare and social security as well as defence, which protected civilising provisions multiply the human potential and freedom of all people.

The false neoclassical ideology has produced a system of governance which makes all organisations subservient to one interested party: the provider of a particular form of capital. And it has turned management itself into a monstrous caricature of leadership, described by Sumantra Ghoshal as:

> the ruthlessly hard-driving, strictly top-down, command-and-control focused, shareholder-value obsessed, win-at-any-cost business leader.[1]

It is this form of management, and the governance system which facilitates it, which is précised here as 'the bottom line'. Particularly in the Anglo-American economies it has made real economy firms and organisations captive. And it is from that captivity they must escape if we are to survive.

My title, *The Road to Co-operation*, is borrowed impertinently from Hayek's *The Road to Serfdom*. The roads lead in different directions: Hayek's concern was to warn against centrally planned totalitarian socialism, while my focus is to avoid the clearly disastrous outcomes of laissez faire capitalism and in particular to identify necessary preconditions for a sustainable future to which the management and governance of organisations in the real economy might contribute.

Part I, Coercion by Ideas, is concerned with identifying the limitations, omissions and clear falsehoods which the neoclassical ideology comprises, as well as the eccentricity of its adoption of mathematical procedures to model human behaviour. Hayek himself described coercion as, '*when one man's actions are made to serve another man's will, not for his own but for the other's purpose*'.[2] The neoclassical dogma has become so pervasive that the 'madmen in authority', as well as 'practical men' and scholars, have been coerced into its acceptance.[3] The governance and management of industrial for-profit organisations, which the ideology sets up as the ideal type on which all organisations should be modelled, have conformed to its corrosive imperatives. The real economy has been coerced to serve the purposes of the financial sector and its monopolistic machinations.

---

1   Ghoshal, S. (2006), Bad Management Theories Are Destroying Good Management Practices, *Academy of Management Learning and Education*, Vol. 4, No. 1, p. 85.
2   Hayek, F.A. (1960), *The Constitution of Liberty*, Chicago: University of Chicago Press, p. 133.
3   Sensitivity to gender bias was clearly not as finely honed in Keynes' day as it is now, and any offence was doubtless unintended.

Part II, The Unsustainable Context, identifies the practical outcomes of economies so coerced, against a background of a rapidly rising global population, which over the next four decades seems likely to approach its sustainable limit. The neoclassical ideology motivates the manic pursuit of economic growth and the externalising of costs wherever feasible. Thus, it drives pollution, the careless depletion of finite resources and the destruction of the earth's climate. These topics are only briefly referenced, being thoroughly covered elsewhere. Equally unsustainable is the continually widening gap between rich and poor, both within and between nations, which is encouraged by neoclassical ideology. The inevitable conclusion is that the ideology is itself unsustainable.

Part III, Corporate Governance and Accountability, focuses on corporate governance in different jurisdictions. While the neoclassical approach is given universal lip service, compliance is far from complete. Governance practice is briefly described in the financially dominated, post-industrial economies of Britain and the United States, in the industrial economies of Japan and Germany and the industrialising economies of China and India: in those jurisdictions which fail to comply fully with neoclassical imperatives, the real economies, notably manufacturing, have survived and prospered rather better than in the United States and Britain.

Part IV, Sustainability and Co-operation, identifies alternative economic theories which might produce more sustainable futures. In practice, for governance and management a sustainable future will only be achievable by escaping the current dominance of the financial sector and its fixation on the bottom line. The road to co-operation leads firstly to protection against that parasitic tyranny, and then to varying degrees of co-operative governance and management. The final chapter briefly reviews the many regulatory and fiscal changes that have elsewhere been considered as feasible and which might enable a more co-operative future.

So this book is about freedom. Freedom from the coercion of bad ideas, both within organisations and between them, within economies and between them. Freedom from the neoclassical dogma, freedom from hunger, poverty and ignorance and freedom from a future that is clearly unsustainable.

The year 2012 has been designated by the United Nations as the International Year of Co-operatives, and Secretary-General Ban Ki-moon expressed its purpose as '*a reminder to the international community that it is possible to pursue both economic viability and social responsibility.'* The focus of *The Road to Co-operation* is on economic viability. My contention is that co-operation, in its varying degrees, is not merely compatible with viability, but its essential foundation.

Gordon Pearson
4th January, 2012

A Note on Terminology

Economists are famous for never quite agreeing with each other over anything, and often for being in fundamental disagreement. This difference emanates from detailed differences of approach or analysis, proposed by leading economists, resulting in different 'schools' of thought. If it were a science, it would be like the followers of Galileo, Newton and Einstein discussing with flat-earthers the nature of music. It creates more heat than light.

The past three decades have seen the Keynesian model put on the back burner while different variations of the neoclassical free market model have been dominant. This has given rise to a lot of different categories and descriptors. The attempt here is, as far as possible, to avoid getting drawn into this terminological quagmire. For the present purpose, which is one of simple exposition, economics is treated as starting with Adam Smith's *Wealth of Nations* first published in 1776. For around a hundred years that so-called classical version of economics was dominant, the only root and branch challenge being from Marxian economics which laid the marker down between capitalist and socialist systems.

Classical theory contained much common sense and understanding of how things worked, Smith's examination of the pin-making workshop being an elegant example. But it also contained some arcane detailed theorising which, though neither realistic nor testable, was nevertheless applied to real world situations, with significant conclusions being drawn and policy decisions taken.

The application of mathematics towards the end of the nineteenth century opened up new ways of modelling economic phenomena, for which it earned the neoclassical label. The neoclassical approach didn't appear to change the main thrust of economic thought, which included belief in the power of markets, free from government interference and regulation, to produce the best allocation of resources to achieve maximum wealth creation, full employment and maximum social welfare.

Those beliefs were challenged by the reduction in wealth creation, massive unemployment and inadequate social welfare in the 1930s. Keynes argued that there was no reason why markets would achieve the best allocation of resources and therefore the predicted results. Of particular importance, full employment would be unlikely to happen without the assistance from time to time of government.

Leaving Keynes to one side, as has been done for the past 30 years or so, belief in freedom from government intervention has returned with renewed vigour, resulting in the dismantling of government regulation wherever possible, privatisation of state ownership wherever possible and minimised taxation levied at a flat rate with no redistribution of income and wealth. These various extensions have become the orthodox wisdom by which we have agreed to be ruled. Various terms have been used to describe that reality, or aspects of it, including free market fundamentalism, neo-conservatism, neoliberalism, libertarianism, and so on. But, in this text, those various concepts are all subsumed under the neoclassical label; the unique characteristic of which, defined by the adoption of calculus, is the concept of maximisation.

From the perspective of management, the one major theoretical modification to neoclassical thinking was the change from the assumption of profit maximisation to shareholder wealth maximisation. This was articulated by Milton Friedman in 1962, and was based on several sub-strands of neoclassical argument including agency theory, transaction cost economics and the idea of markets in corporate management. This now dominant version accords the shareholder primacy over all other stakeholders, and has been unchallenged in Anglo-American jurisdictions over the past 30 years.

Thus, the economics terminology that has been adopted here is, firstly, the distinction between capitalist and socialist economics. Within the capitalist version the distinction is made between classical and neoclassical, the latter based on mathematical maximising. The Keynesian approach is a sub-strand of neoclassical theory which rejects the notion that the markets are always right. The latter day Friedmanite notion of shareholder primacy takes the mainstream to where it has been these past three decades. By this simplified categorisation it is hoped to avoid the cacophony of terms, some of them deliberately pejorative, currently in use.

Acknowledgements

I have referenced many illustrious writers, theoreticians and practitioners to whom I am obviously hugely indebted. The text has also been greatly improved through the friendly criticism and advice given by various extremely generous individuals. They notably include Jack Clyde, David Erdal, John Hassard, Malcolm Joels, Phil Johnson (of Sheffield University), Peter Lawrence, David Leece, Terry O'Neill, Martin Parker, Gill Reed, Carolyn Roth, Jackie Sheehan, Philip Whiteley and Yuxin Xiao. I am extremely grateful for their various inputs.

About the Author

This is Gordon Pearson's seventh book related to corporate management issues. His background is equally divided between industry and academia. His practitioner experience was with three different groups of companies, two British and one Australian, having joined the first as a management trainee, gaining experience in marketing, operations and control systems and later being largely engaged in general and strategic management.

His first degree was in Management Sciences at Warwick University, followed 15 years later by a PhD at Manchester Business School, investigating what helped and hindered firms being effective innovators. Subsequent academic research was focused mainly on strategic management, innovation and change, his distinctive focus being on the practicalities of implementation.

He wrote several professional journal articles critical of the 'accounting syndrome'. His first book, *The Strategic Discount*, challenged the accounting practice of loading the required hurdle rates for long term investments with a risk premium, which resulted only in more projects being rejected, thus contributing to what Hayes and Garvin described as a 'disinvestment spiral'. The strategic discount was a reduction of the required hurdle rate for long term investments which satisfied strategic ends, thus resulting in more strategically justified investments being made.

Both *Strategic Thinking* and *Strategy in Action* were focused on the practice and theory of strategic management, written primarily for post-graduate, post-experience students of management.

His doctoral research was published as *The Competitive Organization*. Two clusters of organisational characteristics were identified which helped firms to be effective innovators. The first characteristic was related to strategy: having a clear idea of the firm's position in its industry and the direction in which it was headed, that clear idea being held by all the people in the organisation, rather than just top management. The second characteristic was a progressive culture which enabled and encouraged people in the organisation to contribute to the firm's strategic development. The effectiveness of implementation depended on management being seen to act with integrity to all stakeholders, the subject matter of *Integrity in Organizations*.

A focused strategy and progressive culture are exactly counter to the command and control, shareholder focused, short term maximising, demanded by neoclassical economic theory and reinforced by the accounting emphasis on the bottom line.

The Rise and Fall of Management viewed the current plight of management practice and theory in its long term historical context, drawing conclusions regarding the dysfunctional impact of economic theory, and how those effects might be reversed.

The Road to Co-operation considers further how Anglo-American industrial management might escape its coercion by bad ideas and contribute to a more co-operative and sustainable future.

Related blogsite is at www.gordonpearson.co.uk

PART I
Coercion By Ideas

> *Economics ... ignores facts as irrelevant, bases its constructs on axioms arrived at a priori, or 'plucked from the air', from which deductions are made and an imaginary edifice created. It inhabits a world of purely economic phenomena, of universal validity yet, or because of this, without history; therefore subject to mathematical treatment, its variables and constants unaffected by the passage of time. Man and society are stripped of their attributes, as if they could exist without psychological, political, legal, historical or moral dimension. Thus verification is both impossible and regarded as unnecessary. In effect, then, orthodox economics becomes a matter of faith and, ipso facto, immune to criticism. (Routh 1975: 26)*

Routh identified more than a score of leading economists who to a greater or lesser extent shared the critique quoted above. He of course included Marx who rejected the most fundamental premise of capitalism, and Keynes who treated as naïve the basic idea that markets would automatically produce the best outcome. But he also identified leading orthodox economic thinkers who recognised the limitations of theory and the simplistic rules of thumb that resulted and which were adopted by policymakers and practitioners alike.

As far back as Adam Smith, it was understood that industrial progress, though improving the lot of most people, was unfair in its distribution of surpluses, producing great wealth for the owners of the means of production, while for others it produced only poverty and forms of work and working conditions which destroyed the human spirit. Within the industrial company this dichotomy was reflected in the 'us and them' culture which was common experience from the beginning. Exceptions to this confrontational mainstream resulted only from the enlightened professionalism of individual entrepreneurs and managers. The mainstream of economic theory has tended to accept unfairness as a necessary evil if progress is to be achieved, focusing more on the provision of explanations and justifications of the unequal outcomes, rather than seeking to mitigate or reverse them.

Though he had many antecedents, Adam Smith's *Wealth of Nations* is here taken as the opening statement of modern economic theory. Smith set out many common sense and practical ideas based on his own observations and experience. He recognised the importance of the self-interested artisan such as the butcher, baker and so on, and the working of the price mechanism and competition to bring supply and demand into equilibrium. His pin factory was the source of wealth creation based on the division of labour which achieved huge reductions in cost and increases in productivity. He recognised these benefits could only be maintained by the access to markets which were growing or by increasing access to new markets. It was the expansionary process, rather than large but static markets, which provided the innovationary dynamic, justifying continued investment in new methods and processes. Government interference and regulation could only serve to restrict both access and continuing growth.

These ideas, human self-interest, the price mechanism, competition, the wealth creating industrial unit and the enabling contribution of free and growing markets were all developed through observation of real economic activity, and remain today as foundational to its understanding.

Marx's revolutionary alternative acknowledged the economic success of industrial capitalism, but focused on correcting the gross inequalities it created by means which now appear, in the light of more recent experience, to be utopian and unworkable.

By the late nineteenth century, classical economists such as Alfred Marshall had recognised the departure of economic theory from the practical realities of economic life. Labour was treated as 'a commodity', which it clearly was not; the laws of supply and demand, 'a much more mechanical and regular action than is to be found in real life'; and their so-called laws regarding 'profits and wages that did not hold even for England in their own time'. (Marshall 1890: 762) This departure from reality was taken a critical step further with the adoption of mathematical modelling by the neoclassical economists of whom, ironically, Marshall was among the first at the end of the nineteenth century. Their focus on maximisation, whether of profit or utility, opened up new possibilities for the development of theory, but further removed it from real practicalities.

The General Theory of Keynes was an amendment of the classical/neoclassical interpretation:

Our criticism of the accepted classical theory of economics has consisted not so much in finding logical flaws in its analysis as in pointing out that its tacit assumptions are seldom or never satisfied, with the result that it cannot solve the economic problems of the actual world. (Keynes 1936: 378)

Keynes accepted that it was the moral duty of economic policymakers to mitigate the unfairness of economic progress by, among other things, achieving and maintaining full employment. Critically, the Keynesian theory rejected the classical and neoclassical idea that full employment was the natural result of unregulated markets. The Keynesian approach, supportive of Roosevelt's New Deal in the United States, was less enthusiastic for the post-war British Labour government's initiatives such as public ownership of strategic industries. Nevertheless, it remained largely dominant in Britain through to the 1970s, when it was beset by a combination of economic stagnation and wages led inflation.

Keynesian policy-making was brought to a close around 1980 by the return to mainstream neoclassical economics with, initially, a focus on controlling inflation through control of the quantity of money circulating in the economy. The results of this approach were subsequently noted by Milton Friedman, its leading theoretical advocate, as disappointing. The monetarist emphasis then evolved into a more fundamentalist focus on free market ideology. The aim was to reduce government involvement in the economy through mass privatisation, markets freed from regulation and control and minimised state provision with low and non-progressive taxation. That ideology still dominates business and politics as well as the public understanding in both the United States and in Britain, though it is under increasing attack.

The great divide between socialism and capitalism, so fundamental to twentieth century economic development, is now largely a matter of history. The Friedmanite free market extreme of neoclassical ideology, its victory considerably boosted by the failure of the socialist alternative in 1989, has yet to be rejected, despite the revelations of the 2007–8 financial crisis.

Economic ideas have become progressively more influential in Anglo-American jurisdictions. It has become an increasingly important component of teaching in universities and business schools. Succeeding generations of business people and politicians, as well as academics, have been led to some understanding of economic theory and its practical application. But whereas in the past there was plurality in the teaching of economics, the victory of free market neoclassical ideology has been so complete that alternative approaches to research and teaching came to be regarded as deviant. Its dominance became a form of coercion by ideas which have acted, and still act, on academics, politicians and business people. It became difficult, even career threatening, to dissent from that mainstream perspective, which is what J.K. Galbraith referred to as the 'institutional truth', that is, not a truth at all, but an overarching lie to which one must subscribe if one's career is to prosper.

Now, those dissident political economists who persisted, are beginning to be heard again, as exampled by the 2009 Nobel laureate Elinor Ostrom, awarded for her work on common pool resources and economic governance. Behavioural economics and Galbraith's ideas about social balance may yet moderate the free market extreme.

These first four chapters provide a brief assessment of the neoclassical mainstream of economic ideas as they affect the governance and management of industry and organisation. They are written from the perspective of management, and particularly relate to management as it is affected by 'the market', the privately owned corporation which economists refer to as 'the firm', which is the engine of economic progress, and the people who own, manage and work in those organisations.

Neoclassical ideas exhibit little knowledge, understanding or even concern for real markets, real firms or real people. The primary focus of economics has been to develop a field of intellectual study, independently of practical realities. But it is this intellectual study which has influenced governments and firms and the millions who work in them, and which is largely responsible for bringing the developed world to the position it now occupies.

References

Keynes, J.M., (1936), *The General Theory of Employment Interest and Money*, London: Macmillan.

Marshall, A., (1922), *Principles of Economics*, 8th edition, London: Macmillan.

Marx, K., (1867), *Capital*. (Page numbering refers to the 1995 edition, Oxford: Oxford World Classics.)

Routh, G., (1975), *The Origin of Economic Ideas*, London: Macmillan.

1

Ideas About the Economy

The final paragraph of Keynes' *General Theory* includes the following much quoted warning:

> *…the ideas of economists and political philosophers, both when they are right and when they are wrong, are more powerful than is commonly understood. Indeed the world is ruled by little else. Practical men, who believe themselves to be quite exempt from any intellectual influences, are usually the slaves of some defunct economist. Madmen in authority, who hear voices in the air, are distilling their frenzy from some academic scribbler of a few years back. … it is ideas, not vested interests, which are dangerous for good or evil. (Keynes 1936: 383)*

That works today, even more powerfully than in Keynes' day. More than ever before, protection is needed from the 'madmen in authority'. But since it is ideas that are so powerful and dangerous, the need is even more for protection from the ideas and those who promulgate them.

Economic theory directly shapes the development of economic policy, which was traditionally defined as being of the left or right, depending on the economic ideas which were dominant in its formation. Theory also directly influences economic actors such as the entrepreneurs, managers and business people who lead the firms and industries on which the economy depends. They, and the government policymakers, are both indoctrinated through their contacts with university departments and business schools which formulate, develop and publish the theoretical ideas, which then become an almost unassailable economic orthodoxy. But unlike scientific ideas, in economics nothing is certain. A theory, no matter how dominant it might become, remains a theory. There are no certain laws in economics.

Towards the end of the nineteenth century, economists started to use calculus to solve the sort of problems calculus can solve. It could be used to calculate maximum and minimum points on two dimensional curves. So models were defined with objective functions which would fit the limitations of calculus. The two dimensions could be set to represent the prices and quantities of products, reflecting costs and revenues and thus to calculate profits, and in particular, to calculate the prices and quantities which would generate maximum profit. From this it was a short step to express the objective of the firm as being to maximise profit and to calculate it by analysing very small changes in the variables being modelled. For example, profit would be maximised when a marginal change in quantity produced, either an increase or decrease, would result in an increase in cost and therefore a reduction in profit. The shape and content of such models were wholly determined by the imperatives of differential calculus. They had nothing to do with decision-taking in the real world.

The adoption of marginal analysis to focus on maximisation using calculus was a most decisive development in economic theory. Its importance was recognised in the adoption of the new label, 'neoclassical', to distinguish it from the prior 'classical' approach. The development of quantitative models, equations and formulae, which emphasised the apparently almost scientific objectivity of approach to the subject, opened up new and highly fertile areas for academic publication, but was disastrous for practical application.

The mathematics of neoclassical economics may have been immaculate, demanding high-level specialist knowledge and understanding. The models themselves might seem sometimes interesting and their results even on occasion surprising, suggestive of new insight. And the ideas embodied might be expressible in the form and language adopted by the leading academic journals which existed as vehicles for the promotion of academic careers. But the notion of maximisation required underlying assumptions which oversimplified and misrepresented real markets, real firms and real people, marking further the departure of economic theory from any claim to be dealing with the messiness of real situations.

These quantitative theories and models were taught to succeeding generations of political, industrial and business leaders without their real world relevance ever being tested. These are the ideas, untested and mostly untestable, which still drive governments and firms and have become the orthodox wisdom of the age, seemingly immune to challenge, till such a time as now when their failure and the consequent build-up of discontents and annoyances might finally topple them.

Economic ideas are challenged by opposing and consenting scholarship. The challenge to high theory is generally mounted with alternative high theory to failed mathematical models by untried alternatives. These arguments and counter-arguments are generally not accessible to the non-specialist, but distillations from the resulting victorious argument and its mathematical representations are imposed as ideology on real world policymakers and practitioners.

The approach here is more pragmatic, the main tools being common sense and the experience of industrial practice.

The Development of Economic Ideas

Adam Smith published his *Inquiry into the Wealth of Nations* in 1776 when a major concern of the British government had long been to counter the national wealth of a belligerent Spain which was accruing from the precious metals it acquired through its South American conquests. In the absence of a comparable British source of gold, apart from that which was stolen from the Spanish, it was argued that national wealth could be acquired equally well through the achievement of a trade surplus with other nations. Thus, a system of subsidising exports and imposing tariffs and quotas on imports was established, which Smith referred to as 'mercantilism'. The effect of the tariffs and quotas, together with the international responses they elicited, though they may have added to the treasury, certainly reduced the amount of trade and thus the ultimate size of markets. This then set limits on the productivity that could be achieved in manufacture through the division of labour and the application of capital. Thus, a very simple anti-mercantilist argument was clearly made for the freeing of trade from governmental interference.

Smith and the classical economists Ricardo, Malthus, Say, Mill and others were influential from the eighteenth century industrial revolution onwards. Their general idea was that industry, so long as it was not constrained by government regulation and interference, would generate the economic growth which would raise the standard of living of the whole population to unprecedented levels. Say argued that supply would create its own demand and therefore so long as government kept out of it, the economy would stabilise at the level of full employment. The detailed argument to support this idea included explanations of why the theory was not realised in real world experience with its frequent periods of high unemployment.

Ricardo's labour theory of value, a development of Smith's less fully worked through version, suggested profit was rightfully the wage earned by labour in the production of capital goods, but which was expropriated by the provider of capital. This esoteric theory, later adopted by Marx, appeared to be innocent of the true nature of 'profit'. It explained in abstruse theoretical detail what was an obvious common sense fact: the distribution of the benefits from industrialisation was inequitable, producing great wealth and great poverty. It was that obvious inequity, not the esoteric theory, which produced powerful counter-arguments. In the nineteenth century the 'utopian idealists' such as Robert Owen and the Quakers established model villages and management practices which treated workers with some fairness and respect. Their example also supported the movement for legislation to protect the workers from exploitative employers, and to the formation of trade unions and political representation of worker interests as well as the later experiment of co-owned and co-operative enterprise.

In the twentieth century the more economically advanced world became divided between Marx inspired revolutionary communist states, and those that broadly followed the classical/neo-classical free market model. The latter were first in real crisis with the 1929 Wall Street Crash, followed by the Great Depression which was only solved by weighty governmental involvement and regulation and ultimately the demands of total war. Free markets appeared to need government intervention from time to time.

Keynes provided the theoretical explanation of the flaws in the classical economic model. In his opening paragraph he explained his use of the word 'general' (in his title *The General Theory of Employment, Interest and Money*) was to contrast his 'arguments and conclusions with those of the classical theory'. They had argued that a stable state of full employment was the natural outcome of a free economy, whereas for Keynes that was just a special case of the general economic model which was inherently unstable and might settle, if it did at all, at unpredictable rates of involuntary unemployment and might therefore, from time to time, need some extraneous intervention to stimulate the economy to achieve full employment, which was what he envisaged as a prime moral responsibility of government.

A potential problem with maintaining full employment was that organised labour, already enjoying extensive legal protections, might become too powerful and seek to dominate and exploit the other factors of production for their own benefit, just as the robber barons had done in their time, with obvious detriment to the economy as a whole. Keynes recognised this possibility as a problem for politicians. For him its solution lay beyond the realm of economic theory. This, it could well be argued, was a rather too convenient side-step of a fairly fundamental issue, the avoidance of which led in due course to the displacement of the whole Keynesian project.

Keynes' concerns were born out in the stagflation of the 1970s, combining economic stagnation with inflation, the latter driven by the combined effects of apparently powerful trade unions beginning to flex their muscles, driving up wages, and the explosive rises in world oil prices forced by the Organization of Petroleum Exporting Countries (OPEC) cartel.

In due course the politicians, Reagan in the United States and Thatcher in Britain, dealt with that problem, confronting and defeating militant unions by allowing, if not encouraging, unemployment to rise. At the same time, reduced oil consumption resulted in some crumbling of OPEC's ability to control oil prices. The politicians were emboldened to undo various statutory union protections and reverse industrial relations and employment legislation so as to reduce the power of organised labour. In this, they had recourse to the then burgeoning strand in economic thought, originating from the Austrian School of Mises and Hayek and popularised by Friedman and colleagues at Chicago. It is that strand of fundamentalist free market ideology which replaced the Keynesian approach and which has spawned many supportive movements, think tanks, andlobbyists, amply financed by private corporate sources both in America and Europe. Keynes may have underestimated the potential dangers of vested interests: he did not see the vast sums being sunk in politically motivated lobbying to subvert democracy and convince people to vote against their own interests.

This brief outline of the trajectory of economic ideas suggests that though there may be some fundamentals which do not change, there is an ebb and flow of ideas which address the situations and problems of particular times. Ideas have swung from mercantilism to free trade, to socialism, to the general theory of Keynes and latterly to the more fundamentalist free market neoclassical ideology. With each change of direction there appears, initially at least, to have been great benefit, but that gain gradually diminishes and disappears, prompting a new change of direction. The initial opening up of markets by the withdrawal of tariffs and subsidies caused a substantial increase in trade and consequent productivity gains from division of labour. Subsequently, governmental acceptance of responsibility for full employment initiated substantial improvements in the fairness of income and wealth distribution. Later, the defeat of militant trade unionism enabled the return to free markets with an initial gain while ever there were new markets to address. The process of globalisation of markets opened up opportunities in the real economy to their maximum. Then as growth opportunities in the real economy started to decline, new financial markets were developed, guided by the same free market ideology which had been applied in the real economy. The bust of 2007–8 and the subsequent economic downturn with the unstable exaggeration of differentials between the wealthy and the poor across the globe, is prompting the reappraisal of the current free market capitalist orthodoxy.

This ebb and flow of ideas and their application is a common phenomenon in the area of political economy. The breaking down of a monopolistic market to create competition has a substantial initial benefit. But the natural result of a competitive market is the establishment of monopolistic dominance and the benefit is progressively lost. The natural result of monopoly is the rise of new competition, and so the ebb and flow is established between two simply identified ideal states, the real world always existing in the messy difficult to define hinterland.

Similarly, in the ebb and flow between the relatively easy to define states of socialism and capitalism. When communism collapsed, capitalism was taken to unsustainable extremes, having to be bailed out at huge public expense which could only be truly identified as a form of socialism. The extremes are ideal types not found in the real world, which exists in the ill-defined intermediate territory.

Jurisdictions similarly ebb and flow between providing fundamentally free markets and being more or less regulated by government. Deregulation invariably provides an initial economic stimulus which slowly dissipates while continued deregulation leads inevitably to market abuse and excess, producing bubbles which burst, leading to re-regulation.

Probably the most significant dichotomy facing the world economy today is that between globalised markets and national markets protected from global competition. The initial benefits from globalisation, such as the availability of lower cost goods, may be approaching the stage when they are outweighed by the diseconomies of high national rates of unemployment which will only be reduced by forms of protection which may become viral.

Against this dynamic background, the simplistic maximising models of neoclassical economics with, as Routh put it, 'their variables and constants unaffected by the passage of time', are hopelessly inadequate to provide any real understanding. Nevertheless, as Keynes suggested, 'the world is ruled by little else'.

Economic Alternatives

The ideas on which that free market neoclassical model is based were developed at a time when the old world seemed to be threatened by socialist and national-socialist, totalitarian regimes, and the Anglo-American alliance stood up for freedom and individualism. Fears that the values of liberty and democracy might be overwhelmed by one totalitarian system or another were real enough. The threat persisted, though in less extreme forms, till the 1980s. And though now not so potent, except perhaps in the United States, the ideas and arguments deployed for its defeat still persist in the minds of civil servants and politicians, the 'madmen in authority', as well as 'practical men' and academic scholars.

Mises supported Adam Smith's case for free market capitalism. It enabled the further division of labour and private investment in specialised capital to achieve the greatest prosperity. Government intervention could only limit the size of markets and so frustrate that achievement. Even more importantly, for Mises, government intervention would be a first step down the road which led irreversibly to a centrally planned socialist economy, which would be both coercive and economically disastrous. If it was desired to avoid this terrible outcome, it would be essential not to take that first step along the road.

Friedman echoed the same point:

> *Fundamentally, there are only two ways of co-ordinating the economic activities of millions. One is central direction involving the use of coercion – the technique of the army and of the modern totalitarian state. The other is voluntary cooperation of individuals – the technique of the market place. (Friedman 1962: 13)*

Thus, it was a simple matter of choice. Either the government allowed its people the freedom to make their own voluntary decisions in co-operation with other individuals through the workings of the market, or the government could take upon itself all decision-making and coerce individuals into compliance.

Hayek defined socialism as not merely 'espousing the ideals of social justice, greater equality and security', but also encompassing the particular means by which those ideals might be achieved:

> ... socialism means the abolition of private property, of private ownership of the means of production, and the creation of a system of "planned economy" in which the entrepreneur working for profit is replaced by a central planning body. (Hayek 1956 iii)

Those means, and the ends to which they were dedicated, were, for Hayek, inseparable. He believed that even the espousal of social justice, or the aim of greater equality, must lead inevitably to the full-on centrally planned, socialist dictatorship. Such intentions, which many fervent non-socialists might regard as indications of a civilised society, were to be firmly rejected since they led inevitably to coercion and totalitarian government.

The stated prime aim of the free market economists was to guarantee man's personal freedom, which they defined as the absence of coercion.

Hayek asserted that:

> To follow socialist morality would destroy much of present humankind and impoverish much of the rest. (Hayek 1988: 7)

Mises had similarly argued that if we wished to save the world from 'barbarism' we would have first to 'conquer Socialism' (Mises 1951: 52). Government intervention of any kind was recognised as the prime evil, seeming to ignore the fact that the gold standard was itself an intervention of unequalled scale and importance.

They did not shrink from using immoderate language in expressing, what was for them, the essential dichotomy in economic ideas between voluntary co-operation on the one hand, or coercion and barbarism on the other. Their linguistic flair no doubt helped bring their ideas to prominence, but it is their more substantial content which has sustained them through the last decades of the twentieth century and into the present era.

Centrally Planned Socialism

The necessity for detailed central planning in a socialist economy, emphasised by the Austrian critique of socialism, was far from central to the Marxist project. It was more of an unintended consequence of public ownership. The impracticality of central planning was no doubt unforeseen, but in the end it was crucial and a prime cause of communism's failure.

Marx's focus was on the unequal struggle between on the one hand, the labouring class and unemployed 'industrial reserve army' which he saw as the victims of industrialisation, and on the other, the wealthy bourgeoisie who tried to exploit the workers at every opportunity. The only chance he saw of correcting that unequal struggle was for the workers to combine and act in concert. His focus was thus on the worker class.

He accepted Adam Smith's analysis of human behaviour, expressed in the famous dictum:

> *It is not from the benevolence of the butcher, the brewer or the baker that*
> *we expect our dinner, but from their regard for their own self-interest.*
> *(Adam Smith 1776: 22)*

But whereas Smith was content to make use of that self-interest, Marx, the idealist, sought to change it, so that people would give up being acquisitive for their own ends, in the interests of the greater good for the greater number.

He expressed the lack of fairness resulting from industrialisation in direct terms:

> *Accumulation of wealth at one pole is therefore at the same time an*
> *accumulation of misery, agony, of toil, slavery, ignorance, brutality*
> *and mental degradation at the opposite pole. (Marx 1867: 22)*

He sought to redress the unfairness which resulted from the wage negotiation, which defrauded workers of part of their just reward, by adopting the argument of classical economist Ricardo, which demonstrated the theft of wages by the owner of capital. The resolution of this unfairness, proposed in *The Communist Manifesto*, involved, amongst other things, free-for-all education and other social services, progressive abolition of private property, heavily progressive income tax, abolition of child labour in industry, abolition of inheritance rights and the central control of industry, agriculture, banking, communications, media and transport.

Marx recognised that government was needed primarily to protect private property, whereas under the communist system, without private property, the acquisition of wealth would no longer need policing and there would be no need for intrusive government. The ultimate aim was a classless society. Marx, the supreme 'utopian idealist', was aiming, just as the Austrian School was, for the ultimate laissez faire system. But, first the capitalist bourgeoisie would have to be dispossessed of their ill-gotten wealth.

These were ideas which lay behind the Russian Revolution which brought into being the communist states which, in mid-twentieth century, appeared a serious challenge to the neoclassical orthodoxy of non-communist countries. The extent to which these communist states followed, or even intended to follow, the guidelines set out by Marx himself is unclear. The communist system which actually emerged, clearly failed. Its main industries fell behind the West in terms of economic output and technological development and with them the standards of living of their populations. Eventually, and despite the immense and demonstrable coercive power of its totalitarian regimes, the communist system was, in most cases, forcibly rejected by its own people.

The reasons for this failure are no doubt many and various. On the political front, the communist regimes were never sufficiently confident to allow a genuinely democratic choice as to the nature of their government. The Party's retention of power was therefore dependent on means which would not be regarded as legitimate in the free West such as the sometimes violent repression of dissident expression, manipulation of communications and the media, heavy policing and social control and through the corrupt use of local centres of power.

On the economic front the reasons for failure were both institutional and individual. The central allocation of resources across broad fronts was clearly envisaged as a necessary and indispensable part of the socialist state and was also perfectly feasible. Moreover, without the complicating participation of private organisations, broad allocations could be made effectively and efficiently. Free state provision of education and healthcare clearly benefited. Vestiges of such advances are still apparent today, for example, in the disproportionate contributions Cuba is able to make with its medical professionals to the relief of victims of natural disasters. Such broad reallocations may well have contributed to a fairer, more egalitarian society.

The central planning of industrial and agricultural production however was quite a different matter. With state ownership of the means of production came trillions of relatively minor decisions as to the quantity and quality of production, the sourcing in appropriate quantities and qualities of raw materials and subcomponents and the distribution of finished output. The complexity of a modern economy, even one stuck in the early twentieth century, was such that central planning of all these decisions was impossible to accomplish with any reasonable efficiency. Cock-ups multiplied. Even agriculture, with its limited product range, relatively stable demand for its products, broadly predictable and slow moving seasons was beyond efficient central planning as is demonstrated by the many accounts of the Russian famine of 1921–2.

The inevitable result of the attempt to centrally plan production was the creation of a vast bureaucracy overseeing decision-making, both regionally and at individual production units, the loss of flexibility and speed in decision-making and therefore in innovation, notably technological innovation, and the creation of many middle ranking posts where the incumbents were in positions of local power and vulnerable to making illicit and corrupt decisions. Moreover, the commitment to maintain full employment and a tight limitation on the inequality of earnings reduced the incentive for workers to contribute beyond a bare minimum. Such ineffectiveness, inefficiencies, corrupt practice and demotivation, being readily apparent, were a source of alienation among the working people, which might only be overcome by the efforts of exceptionally competent and dedicated local management (Kelemen & Bunzel, 2008). In the Soviet Union and its satellites there was clearly an insufficient supply of such priceless individuals to make up for the deficiencies of the system.

It may well be that the impossibility of central planning was the prime cause of failure of the socialist system, which was what Mises and Hayek had predicted and warned against. The Marxist ideal of no private property, no government, and so on, has so far proved unachievable. First had to come the revolution to dispossess the bourgeoisie. After the revolution, the proletarian leaders would be expected to gradually recede as peace and harmony took over. This was never likely. The many outcomes from what can now be regarded as practical experiments in centrally planned socialist economy serve merely to show that central planning of a whole economy appears unworkable. And there is little reason to expect that it could ever in future be made to work, though this would not necessarily invalidate other aspects of a socialist economy.

Free Market Capitalism

The classical economists focused on the individual rather than a collective, such as the working class, and sought to provide conditions where the individual might exploit his or her freedom and flourish economically, and in so doing, benefit the whole of society.

A laissez faire economy, such as Marx had set as the ultimate goal of socialism, is one where government is no longer needed to intervene. Classical economists shared this aim but recognised the need for government to oversee the rule of law which was primarily designed for the protection of private property.

Mises had argued that the programme of liberalism:

> if condensed into a single word, would have to read: property (Mises own emphasis), that is, private ownership of the means of production. (Mises 1962: 19)

Thus, even for the Austrian School's version of laissez faire, government would be required to protect property rights. But in an ideal world, government would be needed for precious little else.

Mises published his exposition of the ideas of classical liberalism in 1927, two years before the Wall Street Crash. He opened the preface to the first English language translation in 1962 with the following words which explain some of the appeal of the free market philosophy to all sections of the community:

> The social order created by the philosophy of the Enlightenment assigned supremacy to the common man. In his capacity as a consumer, the 'regular fellow' was called upon to determine ultimately what should be produced, in what quantity and of what quality, by whom, how, and where; in his capacity as a voter, he was sovereign in directing his nation's policies. In the precapitalistic society those had been paramount who had the strength to beat their weaker fellows into submission. The much decried "mechanism" of the free market leaves only one way open

to the acquisition of wealth, viz, to succeed in serving the consumers in
the best possible and cheapest way. (Mises 1962: v)

Mises' appeal was for the 'regular fellow' to determine production and to be 'sovereign in directing his nation's policies'. This was not so different from the aims of Marx. But the appeal was to the free individual, whereas Marx's appeal was to the collective class. And Mises' 'regular fellow' was to exercise his power through the mechanisms of the market and the ballot, rather than through direct control.

In 1940 Mises had left his job in Switzerland, being threatened by Nazi Germany, and had emigrated to New York. Subsequently, in the aftermath of the Great Depression and the Second World War, vestiges of Roosevelt's New Deal were still evident in continuing state involvement in the American economy. It was considerably further advanced in European economies with extensive public ownership and provision of social welfare. True laissez faire was limited.

Mises' fear that any step away from the free market ideal would end in full-on communist totalitarian government is still voiced by libertarians, notably in the United States, and supported even by those patently disadvantaged by the laissez faire system.

Mises' stated aim of economic and political freedom for the individual citizen was, he wrote, to be achieved through 'free trade in a peaceful world of free nations'. No doubt this expressed a wish which was universally held, especially in the aftermath of world war. It was not the aims which were disputed, but the means to their achievement.

The Austrians' perspective on economic history was to note the remarkable fact that societies developed in ways which people generally appreciated, at least to some extent, without anyone having planned them that way. The family unit, basic property rights and early forms of money were all fundamental institutions of modern society which were called into existence by inherent necessity. The individual, working solely for the increasing benefit of himself and his dependents, would generate economic growth which in aggregate would benefit the whole population. This happened spontaneously as a result of the application of human nature, man being the proverbial perpetually wanting animal. It required no central planning. Indeed, central planning could only slow down and frustrate processes as well as sucking scarce resources from productive activity into essentially non-productive bureaucracy.

The idealised model of a laissez faire economy would be one of open borders with unrestricted trade between nations; of industries similarly open for competitors to enter and exit at will, with organisations within industries not only free to compete with each other, but established on an equal competitive footing to provide the customer with the best offering of product attributes and price. Such an economy, working efficiently without frictions or interference of any kind, would stabilise at full output and full employment, with maximum benefit to the population. The role of government in such an idealised version would be minimised, limited to maintaining the law.

The classical economists from Smith down through to the mid-twentieth century, while they supported the fundamental logic, were aware of some problems with this idealised model, the most pressing of which being the inequitable distribution of the benefits derived from economic growth. In the real world these tended to be distributed on the basis of economic strength: those with strength took more, those without were given less. In newly industrialised economies the inequalities between those with wealth and those without were stark. Moreover, unless there was some extraneous regulation by government, these inequalities would continue to widen until social unrest would become inevitable, with the probable outcome being some retribution and a realignment of inequalities.

Smith had advocated attending to the education of workers to counteract the stultifying effects of the work which was created by the division of labour and the application of capital. He also advocated paying for that education by taxing the rich more than proportionately to their income. Progressive taxation and the state provision of some basic social services remained part of the classical economists' ideology, despite the laissez faire ideal, until the Austrian School became dominant. Subsequently, under Friedman's guidance a flat rate minimum tax, wholesale privatisation and minimised government became the driving objectives adopted by politicians.

Apart from the unfairness of practical outcomes, the laissez faire approach had other demonstrable shortcomings, not least its apparent inability to avoid booms and busts and its dependence on state intervention to save it from its worst extremes. Keynes' explanation of this problem, which had been clearly evident ever since industrial economies took off in the nineteenth century, was simply that there was no natural equilibrium state at full employment. Instability was an inherent part of a laissez faire economy. Booms and busts were inevitable without the stabilising involvement of government.

Marx himself had accepted that the 'capitalistic' system had created greater productive forces than had all previous generations put together (Marx & Engels 1847). He had addressed himself to the misery and degradation caused by the busts and the unfair distribution of benefits created in the booms. Keynes, recognising the vitality of the free market system and the economic progress it encouraged, sought to explain and redress the causes and outcomes of booms and busts. Had Keynes' general theory accommodated within it the power dynamics of organised labour, it might have rescued the free market neoclassical philosophy from its worst excesses.

The pure free market economy is an unreal concoction, and if it ever was fully realised, it would be no more likely to work than the centrally planned socialist economy. However, it may be that a modified free market model could achieve most of the theoretical positives of laissez faire, while mitigating its practical negatives. But for this to be so, the Austrians must have been wrong when they argued that any step away from the free market ideal would lead inexorably to totalitarian socialism. A centrally planned socialist state has never been, and could not be, achieved by incremental steps. It requires revolution. Small steps in the direction of social justice do not lead to revolution; just the reverse. It was the small steps towards some semblance of social justice in nineteenth century British mill towns that mitigated the horrendous conditions described by Engels, and so defused revolutionary fervour in England.

The achievement of a free market capitalist system, though never realised in full, is also established, as far as it ever has been, by incremental steps such as the passing of laws and repeal of others, by government deregulation and by disposal of publicly owned assets. Though the laissez faire, free market ideal type is unachievable, its line of direction is decisive. A step in the direction of laissez faire makes further steps in that same direction more probable and steps in the opposite direction less easy. Reversing that direction of travel, ahead of the inevitable direction changing crisis, would require a fundamental shift in the minds of economists, political philosophers and practical men, as well as the 'madmen in authority'.

A Third Way

The dichotomy between free market capitalism and centrally planned socialism has been kept alive, albeit in simplistic form, despite the fact that the real world exhibited examples of neither extreme. Central planning systems were able to provide healthcare, education and jobs for all, but in an economy which always in the end proved dysfunctional. Free market capitalist systems have been more successful in providing economic growth from which health, education and jobs could be provided for most individuals, but the unequal distribution of benefits is unacceptable to many, and the final end result might prove even more dysfunctional than that which befell central planning. The need to avoid those dysfunctional outcomes has resulted in recurrent consideration of the possibility of a third way.

Half a century ago the British Conservative Party professed what became known as 'one nation Toryism', a form of conservatism largely accepting of the welfare state and the public ownership bequeathed them by the immediately post-war Labour administration. This approach to Conservatism was disinherited by the free market Thatcher government which dominated the trade union funded Labour opposition. That Labour inheritance was disavowed by the New Labour governments of the turn of the century which followed the free market line. These various changes in apparent allegiance conform to the broad direction defined by the free market ideology, but with verbal support for middle-of-the-road social democratic values. The 'third way' appeared to have attractions for the British electorate, as well as elsewhere in Europe.

In the United States any policies which might suggest that first fatal step towards socialism were firmly rejected. This may be the result of either the 'rugged individualism' of old America, or a successful lobbying system, funded by, and protective of, new corporate America, to the detriment of its working, and not working, poor. The current Obama administration appears to be trying to break this mould, having achieved some small 'third way' success with the acceptance of a much compromised healthcare bill, despite more than $500million of corporate funding spent lobbying against it (Tomasky 2010).

Attempts to define a third way had a clear and simple intention: to capture the economic benefits to be gained from free market forces, while distributing the benefits more equitably, so that the least advantaged members of society gain more than proportionately. Academic definitions such as those offered by sociologist Anthony Giddens, among others, were expressed as the New

Labour government came to power in Britain. Considerations included 'reform of the welfare state', 'the structures of government', 'living in a multi-cultural society', 'the gender revolution' and 'how you approach risk scenarios' (Giddens 1999). These largely incoherent ideas failed to change the trajectory of the New Labour government from consolidating and advancing much of the Thatcherite ideology.

The core values which underlie the third way are common to many political philosophies. They include the pursuit of peace, an inclusive society, some limits on inequality, basic provisions of education, healthcare for all and care for the elderly and vulnerable. There is little that is distinctive in these laudable aims.

The defining characteristic of the third way is that it should lie somewhere between the two extremes. But there is no definitive economic model or theory to describe a distinctive position and route. There is no mathematical abstraction which describes intermediate points: there is only mess which can never be coherently modelled as are the two non-existent ideals.

There is, in theory and in practice, a continuum of economic ideas with the alternative aspects of each extreme being used as descriptors: from individualism to collectivism; from liberalism to communism; and from capitalism to socialism and so forth. But the practicalities of real situations mean modifications, from time to time, in a thousand or more practical ways between the two extremes. There is no single coherent third way, no new grand highway, but a million or more different routes, each defined through pragmatic groping for ways of avoiding the worst excesses which have so far been endured.

Conclusions

Theoretical ideas about the economy contain many flaws. The real world shows no examples of pure free market capitalism, nor full-on centrally planned socialism. Real world economies fall between these two ideal types.

The Austro-Chicago fear that any step away from the free market ideal would end with an irrevocable commitment to socialism was expressed at a time when the world seemed headed in that direction. Retaining that perspective today appears largely neurotic, though it is promulgated at huge expense by vested interests.

The free market ideal found its political application through what became known as Reaganomics and Thatcherism. The orthodox argument that markets, freed from governmental regulation and interference, achieve most economic growth appears largely valid though not permanent. The problem is that it produces an increasingly inequitable outcome which is unlikely to be tolerated indefinitely by the mass of people.

Clearly both the socialist and free market ideals are problematic, so that a route between the two extremes needs to be identified. There is no single definitive third way, but an infinite number of variations. The challenge for economics is to identify practical ways forward.

The following chapters take this perspective further, looking at markets, organisations and people, considering the application of the currently dominant free market ideology, and comparing the application of its outputs with those of a more pragmatic interpretation of how things really work.

References

Friedman, M., (1962), *Capitalism and Freedom*, Chicago: University of Chicago Press, p. 13. (A 40th Anniversary edition was published by Chicago in 2002 with an additional preface, page numbering refers to that edition.)

Giddens, A., (1999), Interview by Nyta Mann for BBC News Online, 19th March. (See http://news.bbc.co.uk/1/hi/uk_politics/298465.stm)

Hayek, F.A., (1956), *The Road to Serfdom*, first published in 1944 by London: Routledge. (This quotation is from the preface to the 1956 paperback edition published by New York: Routledge, pp. iii.)

Hayek, F.A., (1988), *The Fatal Conceit: The Errors of Socialism*, London: Routledge, p. 7.

Kelemen, M. & Bunzel, D., (2008), Images of the model worker in state socialist propaganda and novels: the case of Romania, *Culture and Organization*, vol. 14, no. 1, 1–14.

Keynes, J.M., (1936), *The General Theory of Employment Interest and Money*, London: Macmillan, p. 383.

Marx, K., (1867), *Capital*, Oxford: Oxford World Classics.

Marx, K. & Engels, F., (1847), *The Communist Manifesto.* (Page numbering refers to the 2002 edition with an introduction and notes by G.S. Jones, London: Penguin Classics.)

Mises, von L., (1951), *Socialism: An Economic and Sociological Analysis.* English translation by J. Kahane, New Haven: Yale University Press. (Page numbering refers to that edition.) Originally published in German 1922.

Mises, von L., (1962), *The Free and Prosperous Commonwealth*, translated by R. Raico (ed.), A. Goddard, New York: Van Nostrand Co.

Smith, A., (1776), *An Inquiry into the Nature and Causes of the Wealth of Nations.* A selected edition with introduction and notes by K. Sutherland was published in 1993. (Page numbering refers to this edition Oxford: Oxford World's Classics, Oxford: Oxford University Press.)

Tomasky, M., (2010), The money fighting health care reform, *The New York Review of Books*, vol. LVII, no. 6.

2

Ideas About 'The Market'

Since prehistory, man has always traded produce and goods in order to get the wherewithal for living, with such exchanges taking place for convenience in certain places at certain times, that is, in markets. Prior to industrialisation, markets were local with food markets often serving just village populations, and non-food markets for items such as building materials for shelter, textiles for clothing and fuel for heating, still limited. The difficulties of transporting heavy goods, such as coal, restricted the area that could be served and thus the number of customers that could be attracted to a market. This then limited the size of production operations. Coal extraction, for example, was generally carried on in workings employing no more than a dozen colliers. There was therefore not much opportunity for specialisation of work – most were pick-and-shovel men. Nor was there much use for machinery, had any been available. Nor was extraction much below the surface ever a paying proposition.

Markets were originally established spontaneously without the need for any official intervention. They sprang up in locations where they would attract sufficient buyers and suppliers to make them worthwhile. Where they attracted a larger number of customers, they then attracted a larger number of suppliers and where they lost customers, the suppliers would migrate to adjacent villages or towns where the markets were more prosperous. Thus, competition existed between markets as well as between suppliers within markets.

Adam Smith recognised the immense power of competition to work for the benefit of the customer and the common good. He exposed the inefficiencies and bureaucracy which had become established in the monopolies which the government had granted to the overseas trading companies of his day. Inefficiency was inevitable, he suggested, since the managers were looking after other people's money, rather than their own, and could not therefore be expected to look after it with 'the same anxious vigilance' (Smith 1776: 506).

The monopolies were inefficient precisely because they lacked competition. The explicit aim of setting tariffs and subsidies was to manipulate overseas trade to inhibit foreign competition. Its consequence was to restrict trade and thus the size of markets.

Smith also argued against government interference in domestic markets. With his pin factory example, he demonstrated the productivity gains that could be achieved through the division of labour. Whereas one man working on his own could only make a few pins a day – 'certainly could not make twenty' – by the division of labour, ten men could make 'upwards of 48,000 pins in a day' (Smith 1776: 12). The cost of producing pins that way would obviously be much reduced. The only problem was whether there was a market for that many pins at a price that would make it worthwhile to produce. The bigger the market, the more pins could be produced and the more labour could be specialised to further reduce costs to create an even bigger market. The only limitation to this virtuous cycle was the ultimate size of the market.

Interference and regulation by government could only inhibit access to markets and thereby reduce their size, and thus the potential surpluses that might be achieved through the division of labour. This would then restrict the creation of wealth and consequent advances in standards of living, which was the implicit object of economic activity.

This powerful argument for free markets remains potent and has guided the opening up of international trade since the Second World War, initially under the auspices of the General Agreement on Tariffs and Trade (GATT), and since the mid-1990s the World Trade Organisation (WTO). The liberalisation of markets has been further promoted by the International Monetary Fund (IMF), making its support for nations in need conditional on adoption of the same economic philosophy. While it has seen a substantial increase in global wealth, it has also seen a widening of the gap between the rich and poor, both within and between nations. The argument is not without dissenters. Countries which have rejected the ideologically based requirements of WTO and IMF, such as Malaysia in the 1990s financial crisis among the Asian tigers, have done so with considerable benefit. The free trade argument is perhaps not as straightforward as was once supposed.

Keynes argued that market liberalisation was not an unalloyed benefit. In many markets there was little comparative advantage to be gained. Manufacture of automobiles, for example, could be accomplished more or less equally well, anywhere in the world. It would be better, he argued, for a country to make cars which were not necessarily the best value in the world, than not to make cars at all. Where the labour cost in a product is significant, low wage countries have a comparative advantage. And where that advantage is exploited, the associated technology, know-how and expertise will be developed and strengthen the initial comparative advantage. A dominant global position might thereby be established which could be to the detriment of other economies. In this circumstance, as Keynes argued, some limited protection might not be a bad thing. His view was at least partly coloured by his wartime experience and his fear that freed international trade could lead to war as national economic interests clashed. Today's globalisation of markets would have caused Keynes considerable concern, for example, in the potential for hostilities between the United States and China, caused by the now rising conflict of interests.

Local, regional, national and global markets facilitate economic production at those various levels. So long as those markets are competitive, they are likely to work for the benefit of their customers. Whether they also always work for the common good is less clear.

Competitive Markets

For industrial practitioners there are problems enough defining what the real market is that they actually serve: where its boundaries lie, who its potential customers are and who its possible suppliers, as well as precisely which competitors compete on what basis. But such practical difficulties are side-stepped by the theoretical idea of 'the market'. Without such a concept as 'the market', unrealistic though it is, it would not be possible to model mathematically how markets might be expected to work.

The textbook explanation of 'the market' is that of a competitive system for bringing the supply and demand for any product into parity through operation of the price mechanism, much as happened in the pre-industrial local produce markets. If demand for a product rises, it will have the effect of causing its price to rise and thus increase the amount that will be produced and at the same time reduce the amount that will be purchased. Similarly, if more of a good is available than people want, its price will fall and as a result less will be produced and at the lower price more will be purchased. This all happens automatically as a result of competition between participants buying and selling things with the intention of making a sufficient surplus from which to purchase the needs and wants of what Keynes referred to as 'the good life'. So much is no more than common sense.

The adjustments to changes in demand for a product are damped down by the practical realities of production. It takes time to build new capacity to produce more. The initial adjustment to an increase in demand would be by a price increase, but the price increase would be limited by the knowledge that in due course additional capacity would be brought on stream and more product would become available when the price would then be likely to fall again. Similarly, in a downturn in demand, it would take time to reduce capacity. Initially, stocks would build up and the price would fall, until it became clear that there was too much production capacity and some of it would be closed down. This delayed adjustment of physical capacities to changes in demand has the effect of damping down movements in prices. It may reduce the efficiency of market operations, but the resulting stability more than compensates for the loss of efficiency.

Where there is no adjustment of physical capacity, there is less stability as changes in demand have to be fully accommodated by changes in price. In the famous seventeenth century case of tulip mania, demand had little to do with the intrinsic merits of tulip bulbs, but everything to do with expectations of future tulip bulb price movements. This then became a speculative market, quite different in character from normal product markets for which demand rested on the needs and wants of people in their normal lives. Speculative markets are discussed in a following section.

Competition is the key characteristic of free markets, resulting in every participant striving to produce the best offering for the customer in terms of price and product attributes. At a common sense level, this can be simply stated as competition is good because it benefits the customer and potentially the whole economy.

However, the mathematical model of competitive markets, unlike the common sense idea, requires a number of unreal conditions to be met. For example, there have to be so many competitors in the market that none of them can have any influence on market prices. Every competitor has to produce and sell the same undifferentiated product which they produce at the same cost. There have to be no barriers to exit from, and entry to, the industry. And every participant in the industry, producers and consumers alike, has to have the same complete knowledge of all market conditions.

Economists, of course, recognise that no such market exists. Participants always vary in size and the larger they are, the more likely they will be to influence prices: competitors invariably try to differentiate their product from others, through one product attribute or another; they are most unlikely to have exactly the same costs; and no-one has perfect knowledge of the market and knowledge such as it is, is never universal.

The reality is that market competition is restricted by these various factors. Moreover, as Adam Smith noted, industry participants conspire to raise prices, by cartel arrangements and other monopolistic practices. These various restrictions on competition are all damaging to the free market idea.

In a highly competitive market, if any one competitor managed to achieve a competitive advantage, as is obviously their intent, then the whole theoretical system collapses. That successful competitor could reduce its price a little, thereby increasing its sales volume. Economies of scale would thus be achieved, further increasing its competitive advantage. So, in due course, that competitor would become dominant, setting prices at levels at which the others could not make a profit. Unless it was prevented, the dominant competitor would, according to the theory, in due course, take over the whole market and become the monopoly supplier working, to maximise its own utility, rather than the customers' and the greater good. Thus, the natural result of competition would be monopoly, unless prevented by extraneous regulation.

Market Efficiency

The theoretical importance of competition goes far beyond the benefits to the customer. The theory is that all markets compete for the consumer's scarce resources and so, with no external regulation, money is spent so that it provides the customer, all customers, with the greatest satisfaction. This allocation of resources, between and within markets, would be the optimal for the economy as a whole, the efficient market. Any alternative allocation would result in a reduction of consumer satisfaction. That would, of course, be the inevitable result were government to interfere with any market in any way.

The allocation of scarce resources such as land, labour and capital is the key role of 'the market' in economic theory. The efficient allocation maximises economic production. If an alternative allocation of resources would result in an increase in output, then participants in 'the market' would seek out and produce that revised allocation. It is in this sense that 'the market' is said to be efficient.

This theoretical concept of efficiency applies across all markets. If in any market an increase in allocation of any resource would produce more than it is producing from its current allocation, then 'the market' would enable the transfer of that resource from the existing sector to the new, more productive one. Thus, 'the market' is efficient when all factors of production are allocated to achieve maximum production. The theory is that this is the natural equilibrium state for an economy, so long as it is allowed to run free without regulation or interference.

Thus, if, for example, labour could earn more producing bicycles than butter, some quantities of labour would transfer from butter to bicycle production in order to increase their income, and in so doing would increase the economy's overall production. This theoretical idea is facilitated by the assumption that labour is a 'homogeneous commodity'. If anything were to interfere with the free market forces, then efficiency would be impaired and overall production decreased. For example, if labour refused to respond to reduced demand in one industry, perhaps because the relevant trade union refused to accept a cut in wages in that industry, then the allocation of resources would be to that extent inefficient and overall production reduced. Similarly, labour might not respond to the possibility of earning more in a different industry, simply because of the different skills, training and education required in the different industries. Moreover, markets are not static so the theoretically most efficient allocation of resources will be continually changing, making significant reallocations less viable.

The theoretical result of an overall efficient market would be the generation of maximum wealth and social utility for the whole economy. That is the mathematical feasibility, rather than a practical possibility. In practice it would be neither possible to determine such an allocation, nor to know whether such an allocation had resulted.

Nevertheless, the concept of efficiency is an important component of neoclassical theory, which still engages with the old and once discredited idea, referred to as Say's Law, that supply creates its own demand.[1] In this theoretical account an efficient market would naturally stabilise at full employment. If

---

1   Jean-Baptiste Say (1776–1832) argued that any increase in supply and therefore the income of those employed supplying, would lead to an increase in demand because of the increased

unemployment was experienced in free markets, it would only be temporary and could only be caused by extraneous shocks to the market. However, if inefficiency did persist in one market, as in practice it does, then that inefficiency would impact on other markets. Under those circumstances the benefits from efficient markets would be lost, and any practical value of such a theoretical idea would evaporate, as is clearly the case in the real world.

Monopolistic Markets

Not only is market efficiency unobtainable, but competition itself is a fragile state. Marx had predicted that a Mr Moneybags – his personalised version of the bourgeois capitalist – would come in due course to monopolise every industry. For Marx, monopoly was the natural and inevitable result of free market competition, with the monopolist company in the ownership of a single individual. He did not foresee the degree to which company share ownership would be fragmented among large numbers of individuals and financial institutions, such as pension funds, supposedly acting in the interests of large numbers of individual members.

Mr Moneybags was a nineteenth century creation which was never fully realised; though some of the late nineteenth century American 'robber barons' came close. The mathematical model of the perfectly competitive market clearly supports Marx's contention that the natural result is monopoly.

Monopoly markets are controlled by a single supplier who is therefore able to fix the price of product and the quantities supplied. The monopolist is, like any other economic actor, assumed by economic orthodoxy to be a profit maximiser. By restricting supply, prices can be raised and profits increased above the levels that could be achieved in a competitive market. Thus, according to the theory, monopoly results in an inefficient allocation of resources, benefiting the monopolist rather than the customer.

However, the fact that monopoly is a bad thing in theory is not necessarily conclusive regarding its role in the real world. A monopolist is likely to enjoy potentially lower costs than a competitive producer. As the sole producer, it could achieve both economies of scale in its operations and lower prices from its suppliers. These benefits could be passed on to customers. On the other

---

income with which to pay for goods. There would therefore never be any shortage of demand and never any reason, within a free market, for there to be any unemployment.

hand, mainstream economic theorists argue a monopolist lacks the competitive spur to perform, and may consequently permit costs to rise higher than in a competitive market.

The position is similarly indistinct in terms of technological innovation, a measure of how an industry is progressing over time. On the one hand, monopolists would be more likely to innovate than competitive firms: a) because their innovations are not going to be copied and the resulting profits competed away; and b) the profits retained from innovation are available to be invested in further Research and Development (R&D) for further technology improvements. But again, the economic theorist argues that the monopolist feels no pressure to innovate and is likely just to sit back and enjoy the extra profits it can make as monopolist.

Thus, the final evaluation of monopoly is inconclusive. It may seem surprising that the economic arguments against monopoly are behavioural, rather than mathematical. Mainstream theory tends to denigrate the lack of scientific method in what is called 'behavioural economics'. However, the fact is that the most 'scientific' looking models of economic behaviour are fundamentally based on assumptions about human behaviour, albeit assumptions specifically made to enable mathematical modelling, rather than necessarily to reflect observed reality.

The non-behavioural arguments appear to favour monopoly, at least as to its potential. The problem with monopoly is how to ensure that its potential benefits are realised for customers and for the greater good. Achieving this would only be likely if the monopoly was controlled by some public authority. That would pose a wholly different set of issues to do with the most effective means of management and governance of such a public authority. The dominance of neoclassical Friedmanite ideology has led to the myopic belief that public sector management and governance can only be effective if it adopts private sector norms and criteria. However, it is clear that where such have been adopted, as in the case of British privatised organisations, they have invariably failed to live up to expectations.

The most effective management and governance of a monopoly is likely to vary according to whether the monopoly in question was a natural monopoly such as gas, electricity, water and so on, a monopoly granted by law or an industry which had developed towards monopoly as it matured.

The empirical evidence on the virtue, or otherwise, of monopoly in practice is limited, not the least because real monopoly is so rare. British experience of privatisation has offered interesting cases of state owned monopoly industries being converted into privately owned pseudo-competitive industries. By pseudo-competitive is meant not merely that the industry is not perfectly competitive, but that the attributes of competition have had to be artificially created. This creation, which has necessarily been accompanied not just by central government regulation, but by the bureaucratic on-costs involved in targeting, monitoring and supervision, is a far cry from the free market ideal. Empirical studies of these exercises have not so far demonstrated consumer welfare gains in the industries affected. Keynes said he could see no reason why a government should become involved in owning a railway, but the result of privatising British Rail and trying to open it to competition, suggests Keynes may have been short-sighted.

Full-fledged, explicit, controlled monopoly may, or may not, be an effective market construct. Friedman's assertion that it cost a government twice as much as a privately owned for-profit company to do anything, though likely to court populist support, was not, and has never been, supported by empirical evidence. Monopoly industries are so few that conclusive empirical evidence may be unlikely. It is an example of where an untested economic theory has become the self-fulfilling orthodox wisdom.

The monopolistic tendency is at the root of many problems with competition. Monopoly by stealth is an ever present danger in all markets. The effects, if not the aims, of such covert trespass are invariably damaging to both the customer and the common good. From time to time it may be the clear aim to exploit the customer, and the public, for as much money as possible.

In some cases the possibility of monopolistic tendencies, distorting market forces, has been an explicit concern. For example, 'the labour market' has been the target of much legislation over centuries to limit the monopolistic power of trade unions, then to liberate unions from those constraints, then to remove some of those freedoms deemed to be excessive. The 'madmen in authority' have been extremely sensitive to monopolistic tendencies in labour markets.

It is clear that monopolistic forces would interfere with market efficiency. In particular, the potential for maximising social utility would be inhibited, while its equitable distribution would be wholly frustrated with the strong exploiting the weak both within and between markets.

In other cases, for example financial markets, monopolistic tendencies have been largely ignored by those in authority. Financial monopoly, even though it may be covert and surreptitious, is advanced, dangerous and, furthermore, well understood by those in authority. Nevertheless, it has remained largely uncontested.

The Competition – Monopoly Continuum

The real world is made up of markets which are neither perfectly competitive nor yet monopolistic, but lying in between these two ideal types as imperfectly competitive or oligopolistic. Competition creates a dynamic and challenging business environment which is under continual assault from market participants seeking to achieve a competitive advantage so as to acquire some monopolistic power. So competition requires protection if that monopolistic tendency is to be restrained.

Though pure monopoly is no more feasible in reality than is perfect competition, the direction of travel is clear and stages along the route are widely recorded and comprise one of the more basic ideas in the orthodox business school teaching of strategic management. Porter's *Competitive Strategy* (1980), for example, categorises industries as fragmented, emerging, mature and global, each of these categories being some measure of the degree to which an industry has concentrated over time in its progress along the continuum from being competitive to monopolistic.

Porter describes a fragmented industry as one which exhibits, to a greater extent, competitive characteristics. His strategic prescription for a business in such an industry is to break free from conforming to the competitive characteristics by, for example, achieving economies of scale, or by differentiating products or making acquisitions to achieve critical mass. The strategy is thus aimed specifically at reducing competition and achieving a more monopolistic position.

Porter's industry categories explicitly define stages between competition and monopoly. Newly emerging industries quickly attract a large number of competitors with, typically, several different approaches to providing the best solution. The development of the market for personal computers was an example of this progression. When PCs first emerged there were many different manufacturers/assemblers adopting several different hardware and software technologies. During the period of high growth, technological innovation continued apace and gradually a standard approach emerged, with most producers that had opted for different solutions being forced to change or drop out of the industry. Gradually, the emphasis of technological development began to focus more on cost reduction and less on technical features, since the generally most effective technology was settled, though subject to continual improvement. As the industry matured, the number of significant competitors reduced through business failure, industry exit, mergers and acquisitions. When the industry goes into its decline phase, most manufacturers will have moved on, leaving a very small number of assemblers still producing old-fashioned desktop or laptop PCs.

The migration from competition towards monopoly has to be regulated effectively if the interests of customers and the general population are to be protected. Statutory regulation, supported by established processes and regulating bodies, has in the past offered effective protection of competition. More recently in Anglo-American markets such initiatives have been reduced in the face of the neoclassical orthodoxy.

The Friedmanite argument is that anti-trust regulation has generally done more harm than good, in terms of consumer welfare, by protecting inefficient firms. The resulting minimalist approach to regulation is that it should focus solely on such explicit abuses as price fixing cartels, monopoly creating mergers and predatory price fixing by dominant competitors (Bork 1993). However, such limited regulation suggests competition will continue to be threatened. As well as the hostile natural forces already noted, competition is also restricted by many other deliberate and covert attempts to corner, fix and abuse markets for the benefit of the producer or other vested interest, and against the interests of the consumer and the general population. These attacks would need to be defeated for competition to flourish.

The protection and maintenance of competitive conditions is a major challenge for free market advocates who have a choice to make: either competitive markets or markets free from regulation. They can't have both, at least, not for long.

Speculative Markets

So far, consideration has been largely restricted to traditional markets for real products or services which economic theorists have taken as the exemplar of all markets. Financial markets, markets in land, labour, company managements and many others are all held by standard textbook theory to be simply markets, with traditional market characteristics: 'What is true of markets for consumer goods is also true of markets for factors of production such as labour, land and capital inputs' (Samuelson 1948: 39). But this is simply not the case. Different markets exhibit radically different characteristics and warrant individual analysis to understand how they actually work. Applying concepts derived from traditional markets to other situations, though explicitly advocated in mainstream literature, is both misleading and dangerous.

The dichotomy between traditional markets in real products and services and speculative markets is fundamental. Mainstream economic theory accommodates speculation mainly as a means of stabilising prices in traditional markets should they become too far out of line with their value based on fundamental criteria. However, in the real world, speculative markets are different in kind from traditional markets and are anything but stable or stabilising.

Speculative bubbles have always punctuated economic history, and no doubt always will. Tulip mania, the South Sea Bubble, canal and railway manias, the 1929 Wall Street Crash, the 1990s dot.com bubble and the bust of 2007–8 all demonstrate the volatility which is endemic to speculative markets. The defining characteristic of a bubble is that it will at some stage burst, and that defines all the famous speculations. They invite analysis of their fairly simple processes to identify what might be done to avoid such disruptions in future. The start, development and end of such speculative markets has been widely studied and explained, for example, by Minsky (1986). There is no mystery about them. They would be readily avoidable, if governments so chose.

Keynes made the distinction between risk which is calculable and uncertainty which is not. He argued that the booms and busts we suffer arise from not having due regard to the importance of uncertainty, especially is this so in financial markets. The reduction of uncertainty may be regarded as the Holy Grail by some, a key step in the fulfilment of perfect information. However, it is uncertainty which enables speculative markets to be so profitable, and so disastrous.

The essence of the speculative market is that its investors are not much concerned with the substance of the assets in which they are invested. Their main concern is the probability that those assets, whatever their intrinsic worth, will be priced at higher (or lower) levels in future and therefore enable a profit to be taken.

Industrialisation and its need for large and long term investment provided a massive stimulus for financial markets and banking. Markets in bonds and shares and insurance expanded massively from this necessity. By raising finance from a multitude of small and widespread investors, financial markets were able to kick-start and maintain the industrialisation process. Banks, which had previously been largely concerned with safe depositing, recognised that, so long as depositors had confidence their money could always be retrieved, they had access to a proportion of depositors' funds to invest in the new industries and so take a share of the profit generated.

Share markets fulfilled a similar purpose, enabling investors to buy into a company's activities, secure in the knowledge they could sell their shares again, should they ever need to do so, though in this case they stood the risk that the shares might fall in value as well as rise, and might even turn out to be worthless. The quantity of issued shares is relatively fixed, rather than varying, in response to changes in demand, which therefore has to be wholly and immediately reflect in changes in price. It is this characteristic which defines markets in shares and other financial securities, as speculative. They are not purely speculative, like a game of roulette; the value of most securities bears some relation to their fundamental values. Moreover, some shareholders retain their investments over long periods of time rather than seeking to maximise short term profit. But the markets themselves are speculative in that prices depend largely on expectations of future prices rather than depending on actual performance or fundamental values, though these may contribute to expectations.

The speculative nature of financial markets has tended to reverse their original role of supporting the real economy. This is most clearly seen in the case of hostile takeovers. Around 80 per cent of the shares in quoted companies are controlled by financial institutions which have no expertise or interest in the products and processes in which they are invested. Lacking commitment to their hosts, these financial institutions seek the extraction of maximum short term value from their investee companies. Value extraction can be achieved by simple asset stripping, by disposal to takeover bidders who are hostile to the investee companies' interest or by the closure and disposal of operations where the short term gain was sufficient to justify that action. The expectation of immediate returns from such activity creates mini bubbles of speculative investment. Moreover, in an environment shaped by the neoclassical ideology, the hostile bidder is enabled to finance their acquisitions from short term borrowing, which can then be loaded as debt onto the acquired business, thus providing large-scale returns from small scale investment, while, in many cases, wrecking the acquired business.

Share prices respond to an increase in demand, even to rumours of an increase in demand, which commonly occurs in relation to takeovers. There is no damping effect as in traditional product markets while production capacities are adjusted to accommodate the revised demand. In the United States, and especially in Britain, there is no equivalent damping, as is apparent in European stock markets, such as Germany, where employees have a significant voice in takeovers and mergers and are enabled to vote against their livelihoods being sacrificed for the benefit of financial speculation. In the American and British markets the share price movement is immediate and, since it is justified by expectations of future movements, can be disproportionate to any assessment of fundamental value.

Speculative markets provide for investment directly in the shares of quoted real economy companies, in commodities and in financial products such as insurance, as well as investment in derivative 'products' which may be combinations of securities which provide different and often opaque risk and return profiles. Investors in these markets may, or may not, be completely free from the disciplines required of publicly quoted companies.

In comparison with the real economy, speculative market returns may be both high and quick. A successful manufacturer might expect to make a return of, say, 15 per cent on capital employed in a good year, whereas a deal in a financial market might achieve many times that return, overnight. There is also downside potential in speculative markets, with the ever present possibility of any particular deal being completely wiped out.

The speculative nature of financial markets does considerable damage to manufacturing and other real economy activities, and has done so notably in Britain and the United States. In Britain financial markets have become so dominant that, from their base in the deregulated and time-zone convenient city of London, they invest in real economy companies all over the globe, and in so doing bring some wealth and taxes back to Britain. This partially compensates for the wealth and taxes formerly generated by the real economy which the financial sector reduced. It also explains the reluctance by successive British governments to regulate and tax speculative markets for fear they would go elsewhere in the world where regulators have not legislated to control speculative market operations.

Speculative markets are decisively different from traditional markets. The assertion of 'the market' as a general explanation is therefore clearly inadequate. Speculative markets may be efficient, as the economic model assumes 'the market' to be, since they lack the frictions which slow down and stabilise real markets. But the downside of that efficiency is that, unlike real markets, they are inherently unstable. Today's prices being dependent on expectations of tomorrow's speculative markets are inevitably subject to sentiment, even hysteria, with irrational booms and busts being intrinsic to market operations.

Conclusions

Ideas about markets are largely based on the abstractions of theory, perfect competition and monopoly and the notion of market efficiency, which is itself unachievable and immeasurable in practice. Real markets do not naturally resolve to a stable equilibrium which maximises economic output and sustains full employment. Prolonged periods of unemployment and misallocation of resources, plus periodic booms and busts, are universal experience. Policy prescriptions based on unrealistic models do not, and are unlikely to, work as predicted by the model.

The distinction between traditional and speculative markets is crucial. Firms in speculative markets have benefited from deregulation and the withdrawal of the state from much economic activity inspired by free market ideology, falsely based on the traditional market model. Thus encouraged, firms in the financial sector have become exploitative of their traditional hosts.

The idea that speculative activity serves to damp down price volatility may be partly true of limited traditional market situations. But speculative activity in financial markets has the opposite effect, making the market itself speculative and all participants necessarily responsive to speculative situations such as hostile takeovers.

The quick returns possible in speculative markets encourage participants to initiate potential speculations opportunistically. While fulfilling the Friedmanite objective of maximising shareholder wealth, speculative markets feed off and exploit, rather than serving the greater good.

The substantial differences between traditional and speculative markets, in terms of their purpose, their operation and their practical effect requires quite different regulation, taxation and controls if they are both to contribute positively to economic wellbeing and the common good.

References

Bork, R.H., (1993), *The Antitrust Paradox* (second edition), New York: Free Press.

Minsky, H., (1986), *Stabilizing an Unstable Market*, New Haven: Yale University Press.

Porter, M.E., (1980), *Competitive Strategy – Techniques for Analyzing Industries and Competitors*, New York: Free Press.

Samuelson, P.A., (1948), *Economics: An Introductory Analysis*, New York McGraw–Hill.

Smith, A., (1776), *An Inquiry into the Nature and Causes of the Wealth of Nations*, (1993), Oxford: Oxford World's Classics.

Ideas About 'The Firm'

3

For economists, 'the market' is still the main focus of attention, with 'the firm' playing only a subsidiary part. This is surprising. Adam Smith recognised the firm, rather than the market, as the prime source of economic progress. The first chapter in *The Wealth of Nations* explains the division of labour in the pin-making workshop, and the role of 'common workmen' in improving methods and devising machinery to increase output. The market played only an enabling role as the title of Chapter 3 confirms: 'That the Division of Labour is limited by the Extent of the Market'. It was the division of labour and consequent use of specialised machinery in manufacturing on which the whole industrialisation project was founded. And it is the inventiveness and productivity of the industrial firm and those employed in it, on which economic health still depends.

Since Smith's time the importance of the firm has been further increased by the huge productivity gains from technological innovation, and the application of capital as well as further specialisation of labour to exploit it, and the ever increasing importance of intellectual capital embedded in the firm. Today the firm is more important than ever, but there is little in economic orthodoxy to suggest any significant comprehension of what the firm is and how it prospers. This theoretical limitation has substantial practical outcomes and is hugely damaging to industrial enterprise.

Attempts to represent the firm in theoretical models of the economy have been simplistic to the point of silliness, sometimes extending to a denial of the firm's very existence. Representing the firm in a reasonable and mathematically tractable form would be extremely complicated if it were possible at all. But economic theory has not so far attempted any such depiction.

Consequently, there is no coherent theoretical connection between the firm and the market. Market regulation, or lack of it, designed to fit the macro context, can therefore take no account of its impact on the micro unit. For example, maximising shareholder wealth, as required by the Friedmanite ideology, cannot be shown within the theory to have the direct effect of destroying real economy firms which are the life blood on which shareholders depend. But that is the real effect.

Business historian Alfred Chandler suggested that Adam Smith's invisible hand of market forces had, by the late nineteenth century, been replaced in America by the visible hand of industrial management, and the modern business enterprise had become 'the most powerful institution in the American economy and its managers the most influential group of economic decision makers'(Chandler, 1977: 1).

Nevertheless, since Smith's depiction of the pin-making workshop, economic theory has largely ignored the realities of the firm. Ideas about it are the most limited and unrealistic of all economic ideas. Some limited behavioural ideas were developed but were drowned by the continued acceptance of neoclassical marginal analysis and the simplistic symbolism of the calculus based models. These would certainly have inhibited any attempt at realism, had any been made.

At an early stage in his career, economic ideas infected practitioner turned academic Chester Barnard, who claimed it was not till he had relegated economic theory to a secondary place that he began to understand organisations or human behaviour in them (Barnard 1938: xi). But the prevention of real understanding is not the main damage done by economic ideas about the firm.

As with markets, the distinction needs to be made between industrial firms which serve traditional markets for products and non-financial services, and firms which are active in speculative markets. The distinction is sometimes made between industry and business, industry being concerned with making and distributing things and with non-financial services, while business is solely concerned with making money.

A further distinction is sometimes made between two types of banking business: traditional banking which is supportive of real economy activity on the one hand, and on the other, so-called investment banking activities which act in speculative markets. These latter also include home loan specialists, private equity funds, pension funds, sovereign wealth funds, securitisation specialists, money market funds, hedge funds, insurance companies and various others.

Different regulatory regimes apply in different sectors, and businesses in one sector often have subsidiaries operating in other sectors to take advantage of lighter regulation.

The essential characteristic of these speculative businesses is that they invest and manage money, either on their own behalf or for their depositors. The scale of such investment is surprising. Lanchester (2010: 64) refers to the international market for swaps and derivatives having been estimated in mid-2008 at '$54 trillion ($54,000,000,000,000), equivalent of many times the value of the world's stocks and shares'. Mostly they have only limited and occasional connection with the provision of finance for traditional investment by industrial companies. Their main objective has nothing to do with supporting industry which is the traditional banking role. However, deregulation allowed banks to engage directly with these highly profitable, if risky, activities and consequently bankers themselves have argued that access to speculative activity is now essential to support their traditional activity supporting industry.

However, the truth is that once extreme profits have been made from speculation, it is difficult to withdraw funds from that activity to support the more mundane needs of, for example, manufacturing. Consequently, in the discussion which follows, traditional banks are categorised along with hedge funds and other purely speculative actors. Only when they are barred from speculative investment would it be coherent to treat them as fulfilling their traditional role supportive of industry.

Legal Basis of the Firm

Originally, overseas trading was established on the basis of individual expeditions with investors paying all the costs, bearing all the risks, which were considerable, and enjoying any surpluses when their ship returned and the contents of its holds were unloaded and sold. The trading companies that organised these expeditions gradually accumulated permanent capital and from the mid-seventeenth century were organised and financed as ongoing businesses with permanent capital, the first examples of joint stock companies, created and protected by royal charter, but lacking limited liability.

Major infrastructural projects of the industrial revolution such as the canals and turnpike roads, required large-scale and long term financing, it being typically up to seven or eight years from commencement of a canal project to the generation of its first income. This scale of investment was enabled through widening share and bond ownership. With the coming of the railways, further progress was required and the 1844 Joint Stock Companies Act made company formation easier and cheaper, dispensing with the need for a royal charter or an act of parliament. Limited liability was added in 1855. Since then various Companies Acts have developed the concept of the company further but the basic idea was settled. The company was established as a legal entity in its own right, with its directors legally bound to act in the company's best interests, rather than their own.

Though this account relates specifically to the British experience, it is not untypical of practice across the globe. The 2006 Companies Act charges company directors 'to promote the success of the company' having regard to 'the likely consequences of any decision in the long term', 'the interests of the company's employees', 'the need to foster the company's business relationships with suppliers, customers and others', 'the impact of the company's operations on the community and the environment', 'the desirability of the company maintaining a reputation for high standards of business conduct', and 'the need to act fairly as between members of the company'.[1]

Other than for sole traderships the limited liability company or corporation is the legal form of firms serving traditional markets, while firms serving speculative markets may take different forms.

Traditionally, professional practices in accounting, the law and so on were not limited companies, but partnerships. A partnership did not enjoy limited liability, the partners being personally liable for the debts of the practice. That responsibility set partners, personally and professionally, apart from company directors in a limited liability company. Traditional partnerships in the financial sector such as stock jobbers, brokers and merchant bankers were founded on the integrity which such personal liability made essential.

Apart from lacking limited liability, partnerships were treated differently from companies in their taxation. The partnership was not taxed as a legal entity, its proceeds being divided between the partners, taxation was levied on them individually.

Partnerships in speculative markets are inherently risky. Partners advising banks and other financial institutions may be subject to large-scale claims

---

1   Companies Act, 2006, Part 10, Chapter 2, paragraph 172.

which might bankrupt them personally, as was notably the case following the bursting of a real estate price bubble in the United States in the 1980s. To resolve this problem, a new legal form, the limited liability partnership (LLP), was established in America in the early 1990s, giving partners the protection of limited liability but retaining the distinctive tax status.

In effect, this was a further stage in deregulation, relaxing the requirement for partners to be personally liable for the actions of fellow partners and for the liabilities of the partnership as a whole. Britain followed suit in 2000, establishing the limited liability partnership as a separate legal entity. This format has since been followed in most other jurisdictions.

These brief notes on the legal basis of firms establish the fundamental point that the firm, and now the LLP, is a legal entity in its own right. Typically, shares in the industrial corporation are widely dispersed among many shareholders, whereas LLP firms operating in speculative markets are owned by their partners who are usually not answerable to outside shareholders. Thus, firms in traditional markets and those in speculative markets not only differ as to their business operations and the markets they serve, but also in most cases as to their legal and taxation status, despite economic theory conflating the two in the theory of the firm.

Production Functions

Even without the complications referred to above, no meaningful economic theory of the firm was ever developed. Mathematical modelling of the firm was so implausible it was argued to be deliberately treating it as an unknown, a black box. The firm was simply a 'production function' within the competitive market which sought to maximise its profits. It was defined in terms such as $Q = f(K, L)$: the quantity of output (Q) being a function of factor inputs, K and L, capital and labour. This production function then served its theoretical purpose by enabling calculations to be made of revenues, that is, Q times P, where P is the price per unit, and profit which is QP minus QC where C is the cost per unit. And, importantly for theorists, it enabled the marginal analysis, using simple calculus, to maximise profit by setting Q at the level at which marginal revenue equalled marginal cost. Maximisation proved to be the ultimate reductionist concept in economics.

It would be possible to waste much space here examining the further development of such unreal ideas. In many cases where economic theory ceases to be grounded in any recognisable reality, it is still possible to deduce some core concept which appeals to a basic intuition or common sense. But in the case of the firm as a production function, there is no such appeal. The price mechanism is still present in the depiction of supply and demand, but other connection with the real world is not even claimed.

Some theoreticians raise the instrumentalist argument in defence of the production function idea. This suggests that it should not be assessed as to whether or not it depicts reality, which it is universally agreed it does not, but by how effective it might be at predicting outcomes. There is no evidence that it does that either. Its predictive power is as limited as its explanatory, both only serving to demonstrate the trivial nature and practical limitations of the theory of the firm itself.

Economists were always sensitive to this apparent weakness, not only in the approach to the firm but also to the market. The profit maximising production function was dependent on the assumptions of perfect competition, which didn't exist. The real world was populated with imperfectly competitive markets in various stages of concentration.

Attempts were made to develop a model of the firm which might explain behaviour in oligopolistic markets, the term which appeared to reduce the real world to a special case. For example, Baumol proposed a model of sales revenue maximisation to explain firm behaviour under conditions of oligopoly (Baumol 1958). It was argued that sales maximising was more realistic than profit maximising as it was more likely to satisfy the self-interest of management decision-makers, who might perceive their 'take' from the firm (salary and perks) being more closely related to the size of the firm than to its profitability. This was a minor development of the calculus driven profit maximising model, but not an adequate response to the fundamental objections, though it did signal an interest, inadequate though it was, in developing more realistic models of 'the firm' which might be applicable in more realistic market conditions.

Behavioural Theory

In their own summary of the basic concepts of their behavioural theory of the firm, Cyert and March pointed out that classical economic 'theory has not been adequate to cope with oligopolistic markets' (that is, the real world). They therefore set out to specify 'an alternative framework and an alternative set of key relations for dealing with the modern 'representative firm' – the large, multi-product firm operating under uncertainty in an imperfect market'(Cyert & March, 1992: Chapter 7). They dropped the inadequate calculus based model and developed a computerised linear programming model which enabled them to specify more nuanced objective functions than simply profit maximisation and make them subject to various minimum levels of achievement in other directions. The computer code was provided as an essential part of the 'Behavioural Theory' when it was first published in 1963.

Behavioural Theory adopted the concept of 'satisficing', which had been first introduced by Simon (1956), instead of maximising. Simon's use of the term was to describe actual behaviour, which was more the product of human limitations, than intent. In reality, humans were unable, given informational, processing and time constraints, to assess all possibilities, remember all assessments and so choose the best option. Thus, humans worked within what Simon referred to as 'bounded rationality'.

Cyert and March's use of the term satificing was rather more subtle, even though it was the result of using the linear programming procedure which required the definition of minimum performance in other directions than the objective function. They suggested that a coalition of individuals such as a company's board of directors who would be key decision-takers in a particular area, might decide a level of aspiration below maximum which would satisfy every coalition members' minimum performance requirements in relation to their particular areas of responsibility. This satisficing might then allow free resource to be allocated in other directions such as in 'organisational slack', stored on one side for the proverbial rainy day. The model introduced concepts which the authors had developed in their studies of organisational learning which were related to observations of real firms. However, it was not modelled in a form that could be readily aggregated to inform neoclassical theory, which remained based on mathematically defined, perfectly competitive or monopolistic markets.

For some, the use of linear and dynamic programming in models of economic activity, made practical by computerisation in the 1960s, appeared to release economic theory from the unrealistic restraints of traditional mathematics. For others, the behavioural theory was an inconvenient reminder of the inadequacy of traditional methods. However, its gestures to the real world were not in the end wholly convincing. It was still constrained to formulation according to the dictates of mathematical procedure which, even with computer maths, set unrealistic constraints, both as to the market and the firm. Surely the market could produce all that was needed or wanted, at least by theoreticians!

Transaction Cost Economics (TCE)

Belief in the extreme power of market forces, so long as they were free from regulation or any other form of interference, apparently led to the curious belief that the market could produce any item at some cost: the costs of transactions in the market. Only if a firm could produce cheaper than the cost of market transactions would the firm be justified in production. This fertile thread of economic theory was originally expressed by Ronald Coase in a 1932 lecture, formalised five years later in an article on the nature of the firm (Coase 1937). The concept was further developed in the 1960s by Oliver Williamson (1964) and others. It challenged the legitimacy of managerial decision-makers, arguing the power of market forces to decide, notably 'make or buy' decisions.

Macher and Richman (2008: 3) in a late review article suggested that:

> the key conceptual move to TCE is to describe firms not in neoclassical terms (as production functions) but in organizational terms (as governance structures). The basic insight of TCE is to recognize that in a world of positive transaction costs, exchange agreements must be governed, and that, contingent on the transactions to be organized, some forms of governance are better than others.

Transaction costs were identified as having three main sources. First, there were costs of planning for an uncertain future. Second, there were costs in reaching mutually comprehensible and acceptable contracts. And third, the difficulty of communicating unambiguous contracts meant all contracts were effectively incomplete and so parties were vulnerable to being misled or cheated, which led to firms choosing institutional arrangements so as to minimise the cost of transactions.

Transaction cost economics, despite its curious logic, has been a productive field of academic publication. The review article quoted above refers to around 900 TCE studies published in academic journals. However, despite being so fertile as a field for publication, practical application has been limited. It is unable to address technological innovation and so misses the point of much of what importantly takes place within a real firm, even one such as a pin manufacturer. It could not have contributed to John Lombe building the world's first large-scale textile mill, or Henry Ford deciding to build the world's first mass-produced automobile. The market simply did not provide cheap pins, silk materials or low cost autos. And since a major part of entrepreneurial effort is explicitly focused on developing products which are differentiated from anything the market already produces, comparison with transaction costs is of limited value.

By depersonalising the alternative source of products as 'the market', the theory ignores competitive relationships. The market actually produces nothing; consequently analysis of the transaction costs sourcing from the market would inhibit consideration of the firm's strategic position. For example, it may be essential for a firm to maintain a competitive position in certain technologies if it is to protect its main product market position. Thus, even if it could not achieve lower costs than the costs of transactions incurred outsourcing, it could still be vital to maintain that production itself. TCE theory cannot accommodate such strategic considerations.

Moreover, it is also incoherent in its treatment of time; there being no consideration of short and long term effects. Not maximising immediate profit would be evidence of irrational behaviour and inefficiency. Such management should therefore be subject to external review and expulsion through the operation of the market in company managements.

This argument was developed concurrently with observation of the asset stripping activities of British companies such as Slater Walker Securities in the late 1960s, and then used to justify the firms engaged in those activities as participants in the market for company managements. Asset stripping was largely funded by the issue of convertible loan stock, the terms of which were deliberately obscure so as to make it difficult to value on the basis of its fundamental characteristics, and thus for its price to be entirely dependent on assumptions about its future value. This kind of stock issue was later referred to as 'junk'.

Williamson argued transaction cost analysis as the key to 'make or buy' decisions. But, in the real world, management already had that comprehensively covered: if a firm could source an item cheaper elsewhere than it could produce itself, the firm should consider its position, bearing in mind not just the immediate costs but any other relevant longer term strategic considerations (Hayes & Garvin 1982). Transaction cost economics made no practical contribution to the calculation of such decisions.

This was a problem for theory, since it meant that decisions might be taken on the basis of the discretion and expertise of managers, rather than by the market. This did not fit accepted theory. Within economic theory, comprehension of management had not progressed, and had probably regressed, since the time of Adam Smith who never lived to see large-scale enterprise. He had acknowledged the role of self-interest among butchers, bakers and brewers in providing his dinner. And he had observed of 'managers' in the eighteenth century trading monopolies that they could not be expected to watch over other people's money 'with the same anxious vigilance' as if it were their own. The free market ideology adds nothing to those crude observations and takes no account of the realities of modern industrial activity.

The theory excludes any notion of professional management, there being no apparent way of accommodating the role within any known economic models. Management was charged with the legal duty of promoting the best long term interests of the company. But the theoretical approaches already noted effectively disregard the firm, despite it being, as Chandler put it, 'the most powerful institution in the American economy'. And they ignore the management role despite managers being 'the most influential economic decision makers'. In this disregard and ignorance, economic theory was also disregarding and ignoring a hundred years or more of business management research and theory which was largely empirically based, which had led to genuine enlightenment on how best to manage industrial enterprise for the benefit of its customers, employees and shareholders, as well as its local community and the wider environment.

Some dissident groups of academic theorists continued to seek effective behavioural models of the firm, while the increasingly dominant Friedmanite free market mainstream continued to disregard it, addressing the issue of firm management by adoption of the legal idea of agency.

Ownership, Control and Agency

Through the nineteenth and early twentieth centuries technological innovation led to more capital-intensive production methods, justifying greater economies of scale and ever larger firms. The financing needs of these new big businesses were satisfied by wider dispersion of share ownership and the increasing separation of that ownership from the control of the firm.

Berle and Means studied this divergence of interest and identified three distinct functions: 'business ownership', 'business control' and 'participation in action on behalf of the business'. They noted that in the nineteenth century the owners fulfilled the first two and hired managers fulfilled the third:

> *the owners … were in a position both to manage an enterprise or delegate its management and to receive any profits or benefits which might accrue. The managers on the other hand … operated an enterprise, presumably in the interests of the owners. (Berle & Means 1932: 119)*

With the growth of firms, the position of owners was reduced and management advanced. For Berle and Means, owners had three main interests:

> *first that the company should be made to earn maximum profit compatible with a reasonable degree of risk; second that as large a proportion of these profits should be distributed as the best interests of the business permit …; and, finally, that his stock should remain freely marketable at a fair price. (Berle & Means 1932: 121)*

These interests were couched in measured terms. There was no simplistic assertion that the company should maximise profit or dividend payments or shareholder wealth without regard to other factors. Nor was there any explicit assertion of the interests of management, though they did conjecture about their possible interest in personal profit, or in prestige or power or perhaps in the gratification of 'professional zeal'.

This separation of ownership from control identified by Berle and Means became one of the key foundations of neoclassical ideology which flowered in the 1980s. The connection was made between that separation and the relationship between principal and agent, which had a long legal provenance dating back to the earliest overseas expeditions. In those days the ship's captain was deemed to be the agent of the ship's owners, and therefore enabled to enter legally binding agreements on their behalf, at the same time being required at all times to act professionally in their best interests. This agency relationship has a very wide relevance, but has more recently been misused to justify a spurious management–shareholder relationship. It has proved to be another fertile ground for academic publication which in this case has achieved remarkable practical damage.

Since 1844 in Britain, company law has held directors to have a duty to act in the best long term interests of their employing company, which was then established as a separate legal entity, capable of entering legal contractual arrangements with directors acting on its behalf and in its best interests. Various Companies Acts have since spelled out these duties in some detail. Company directors are thus agents of the company, which is the principal in that relationship.

Shareholders engage in a quite separate arrangement with the company, based on their purchase of share certificates which entitle them to a potential receipt of dividends as well as capital growth, both of which are at risk. Beyond that, shareholders are established with the right to appoint directors (or confirm their previous appointment, or not, at a company general meeting) and are enabled to vote for resolutions raised at company general meetings. They owe no duty to the company or its employees or customers, having discharged it in full when they paid for their share certificates. Thereafter, the relationship between the shareholders and the company is one largely defined by risk and reward.

In the 1970s the legal aspect of the firm was addressed in a limited way by some economic theorists still in denial as to the real nature of an industrial organisation. Alchian and Demsetz (1972: 778) expressed the firm as a 'centralised contractual agent in a team productive process'. Deliberately or not, this depicted the firm as an agent, rather than the principal. Jensen and Meckling also defined a model which was in direct opposition to the law. It was an essential prerequisite for them to side-step the inconvenient fact that the company was a legal entity and the principal in contractual arrangements. This, Jensen and Meckling did with the following statement in a frequently cited paper:

> It is important to recognize that most organisations are simply legal fictions which serve as a nexus for a set of contracting relationships among individuals. (Jensen & Meckling 1976: 309)

Attention was thereby focused on the contracting relationships, and Jensen and Meckling focused specifically on the relationship between directors and shareholders, claiming falsely that the directors were agents of the shareholders and therefore bound to act at all times in the shareholders' best interests. A footnote against the first mention of 'legal fictions' reads:

> By legal fiction we mean the artificial construct under the law which allows certain organisations to be treated as individuals. (Ibid: 310)

This would appear to remove meaning from the term 'legal fiction', but did not signal a retreat from what they themselves acknowledged was in contravention of the law, that directors were agents of shareholders.

This false argument, sometimes referred to as agency theory, pits management against shareholder, disposing entirely of any meaningful idea of the firm beyond the 'set of contracting relationships'. Jensen and Meckling pointed out that the theory of the firm was limited and had frequently attracted criticism from leading economists. Nevertheless, they clung to the simple maximising model and identified the 'agency problem' which prevents maximisation:

> Since the relationship between stockholders and manager of a corporation fits the definition of a pure agency relationship, it should be no surprise to discover that the issue associated with the "separation of ownership and control" in a modern diffuse ownership corporation are intimately associated with the general problem of agency. (Jensen & Meckling 1976: 309)

As already noted, the relationship between stockholder and manager certainly does not fit the pure agency relationship as argued by Jensen and Meckling. The truth is there is no direct relationship between a firm's management and its shareholders, both relate to the firm itself. Nevertheless, agency theorists adopted the maximising objective that followed naturally from depiction of the shareholder as principal: to maximise shareholder value rather than profit. Thus, 'shareholder primacy' became a foundational part of neoclassical ideology and has become so widely accepted that the law itself, despite being restated many times, has been quite overcome.

The neoclassical defence of the spurious agency relationship is quite strident. The problem is to dispose of the inconvenient fact that the company is a legal entity in its own right which exists between the firm's management and its shareholders: hence Jensen and Meckling's denial, with their assertion that the firm is a legal fiction. A last ditch defence has even claimed that:

Though it is a separate legal person, the corporation is, however, a slave.
(Sternberg, 2004: 37)

This curious assertion, denying the legal entity basic human rights, is a rather desperate attempt to justify the application of agency. It is also a justification of the concept of corporate ownership. If a company's most important asset is its people and, since slavery was abolished people cannot be owned, then it follows that the company cannot be owned in the normal sense of that term, even without considering how limited liability changes the nature of ownership.

Agency theory, as adopted by economics, has proved a fertile area for academic publication, notably in relation to the so-called agency problem. The problem is that the agent, that is, management, cannot be relied on to achieve maximum shareholder wealth or, being totally self-interested, even to try. Consequently, there are costs involved in the model. Firstly, it is necessary to offer incentives to management to persuade them to maximise shareholder wealth. Secondly, management behaviour has to be monitored, for example by the appointment of external independent directors, to ensure that management tries to maximise shareholder wealth. And finally, some management might nevertheless get away with what Jensen and Meckling, and their many followers, referred to as 'shirking' – the sort of behaviour in which slaves might be expected to indulge given half a chance.

The agency model of the firm is an intrinsic part of the free market ideology, supporting Friedman's contention that management had 'no other social responsibility than to make as much money as possible for shareholders'. The lack of any time relation disguises the fact that, like all maximisation models, the focus is short term, if not immediate. This is in stark contrast to the notion that management's clear responsibility is for the company's survival and long term prosperity.

The difference between these two perspectives is stark for a company director faced with a profitable but destructive takeover bid. That is an increasingly common predicament, with predatory bids being both the cause and effect of failing industrial production and growing financial markets.

The Firm in Traditional Markets

The theoretical models of the firm, referred to above, are inadequate representations of firms in traditional markets as they have developed over the past two and a half centuries. Understanding of the true nature of such firms and behaviour in them started to accrue in the mid-eighteenth century, but for over a century little of it was written down or taught. The first stirrings of an industrial management literature date back to the late nineteenth century with Fayol's contribution based on his long experience managing a French coal mining company. Mining for coal was dirty, dangerous work, involving the use of a pick and shovel, human sweat and not much else. Fayol's management problem was how to get large numbers of unskilled and largely ill-educated people to do fundamentally unpleasant and dangerous work, as efficiently as possible, in return for wages set low enough for the company to make a sufficient return in order to survive and prosper. Some argue that work was not a whole lot better on Ford's mass-production lines of the 1920s.

But management's problem has changed since then: technology has progressed and with it, understanding of human behaviour and the various socio-technical systems making up the modern industrial organisation. The management problem today is more to do with 'how to recruit, retain and develop highly skilled and educated people, working in smaller numbers with a high degree of autonomy and their rates of pay no longer the main cost drivers, but their individual and team contributions crucial to organisational survival and prosperity, and at the same time, to engender a "true spirit of co-operation between employer and employee"' (Pearson 2009: 131).[2] That change in the management problem obviously required a fundamental change in management.

In the early twentieth century, contemporary with Fayol, work study-based scientific management was introduced by F.W. Taylor (1910). Scientific management, enthusiastically adopted by Ford and others, is sometimes simplistically considered to be a means to control and exploit workers. Taylor recognised the workers' distrust of their employers which resulted in what he referred to as 'soldiering', the deliberately limiting of output by workers because the surplus resulting from their labour was not fairly distributed. Taylor's

---

2   The quotation is from a letter by trade union leader George Preston, writing about the ill-effects of Taylor's scientific management, which he said would destroy the true spirit of co-operation between employer and employee. The letter is archived by the Samuel C. Williams library of the Stevens Institute of Technology, Hoboken, New Jersey.

approach, defining in great detail how jobs should be done, could produce substantial gains in productivity and he himself intended that the resulting gains be distributed on such a basis that would engender trust and so reduce 'soldiering'. The famous case of Schmidt handling pig iron resulted in a 276 per cent rise in output and a 60 per cent rise in Schmidt's income. The widespread and often incompetent adoption of Taylor's methods produced a further substantial loss of trust between employer and employed, which inevitably resulted in an increase in 'soldiering', which was not properly understood till the mid-twentieth century when industrial psychologists studied what actually happened in organisations and its effect on human behaviour. Then, based on their understanding of human relations at work, ways of managing were developed which were more attuned to that understanding and to the modern industrial organisation.

It was recognised that there was no one best way to manage a firm, the most appropriate course being contingent on individual circumstances. This knowledge and understanding of firms, and human behaviour in them, was taught across the globe in universities and business schools. Then, around 1980, the field began to be invaded by the simplistic neoclassical ideology which increasingly overwhelmed management theory and practise, turning them into a top-down, hierarchical, command and control, shareholder wealth maximising cliché. That broad approach, Taylorism without benign intent, has been widely taught in business schools and universities ever since. The neoclassical ideology makes a virtue out of ignoring individual circumstances such as the professional expertise, intellectual capital and resources necessary to produce products or services which satisfy customers' needs and wants.

The economic model of the firm, typified by the considerations already outlined in transaction cost economics and agency theory, suggests no understanding of the real firm in traditional markets and little interest in the most effective management approaches. But it may have some resemblance to the firm in speculative markets.

The Firm in Speculative Markets

The origin of firms in speculative markets was to provide finance in support of traditional activity in the real economy. These were not risk-free investments, but the shares or bonds represented known investments, the safety and progress of which were reported at regular intervals. The change of financial markets from that essentially supportive role, to one which is fundamentally exploitative of the real economy, can be illustrated by taking a brief look at how the practice of mergers and acquisitions has developed.

Firms are required to publish reports on their affairs at regular intervals so that investors, existing and potential, can understand the company's business standing and decide whether or not to buy, sell or hold investments in the company. The annual accounts are required to provide a true and fair picture of the company's position and auditors are required to certify that it is so, or to refuse to certify as such. In the 1960s it was common for quoted firms to carry undervalued assets, especially property, on their balance sheets. This was mainly the result of property price inflation and the accountant's commitment to prudence, which meant that they would only include property on the firm's balance sheet at the last professional valuation. Since professional valuation was expensive this was carried out infrequently. Thus, for most firms the real value of their assets was greater than the value included on the balance sheet, which would influence the value of the firm's shares on the stock market. Not unnaturally, this encouraged financially oriented firms to initiate a wave of asset stripping acquisitions which got under way in the early 1970s.

Financing such acquisitions was only a short term problem. Borrowing to acquire the shares in a takeover could be repaid by selling the assets of the acquired firm. Alternatively, it might be possible to float off substantial parts of the acquired firm having stripped it of any surplus assets and loaded it with as much debt as feasible, including the borrowings incurred to achieve the acquisition. Moreover, it was quickly discovered that opaquely labelled loan stock could give ready access to cash while a firm was growing rapidly from this sort of acquisition, the stock being valued on the basis of its assumed future value when converted, rather than on the basis of its fundamental worth.

Prior to the 1986 'big bang' computerisation and deregulation of the London stock market, various roles involved in the purchase and sale of securities were controlled as closed shops. The two prime roles, jobbing and broking, were effectively eliminated by computerisation. Jobbers were members of the stock exchange who were licensed as traders, operating on the floor of the exchange and dealing in securities in their own right, remunerated from the profit they could make between the purchase and sale prices. Jobbers could sell to other jobbers or to brokers, and they generally specialised in certain securities, developing expertise in specific market areas. Brokers were also members of the stock exchange who traded with the jobbers, buying and selling securities on behalf of outside clients and being remunerated through a brokerage fee.

Stock exchanges always worked as purely speculative markets. Before deregulation, merchant banks made money speculating within account periods as well as exercising call and put options which enabled them to gear up their dealing and to make large sums from price movements whether they were up or down. Short selling, associated today with hedge fund speculation, is a variation of the put option, the result being the same: if the price declines as predicted, profit is made from the difference between the price when the deal was struck and the price when the stock has to be purchased.

The promise, 'my word is my bond' between members of the stock exchange, was essential to enable the old system to work with reasonable efficiency, but it did not mean the system was transparent, nor its integrity assured. One leading merchant banker from that era admitted that when bills were settled at the end of an account period, that was when they decided whether purchases and sales had been made on behalf of a client, and if so, which, or in the bank's own name.

Financial markets were in an advanced stage of maturity before deregulation and, as in most mature markets, competition had declined with a few large players achieving price-making monopolistic power. The market for government bonds, for example, was dominated by just two firms. Two other firms provided some competition in equities, but industry concentration had gone about as far as it could without the market becoming entirely monopolistic.

This decline in competition had seen London lose share of international financial markets, but computerisation and deregulation reversed that decline. The stock exchange floor was replaced by remote screen connections and was accompanied by extensive deregulation. Closed shops were eliminated with the former jobbers and brokers being mainly taken over by investment banks, many of them foreign firms attracted to London for the first time.

High Street banks were allowed to engage with investment banking activity and this unleashed a prolonged period of mergers and acquisitions within the financial sector, with all the High Street banks acquiring jobbers, brokers or merchant or investment banking arms. There was further consolidation among merchant banks, with new foreign firms coming to London via acquisitions, making it a leading financial centre in the world, out of all proportion to the size of Britain's real economy.

Deregulation enabled the creation and expansion of new financial institutions such as private equity funds, hedge funds, state owned sovereign wealth funds, securitisation specialists and money market funds, all with large sums of money at their disposal, their role being focused entirely on speculative gain for its own sake, rather than to support investment in real economy companies. By the time of the 2007–8 bust these financial institutions controlled almost three quarters of all quoted equity on the London market. They sought growth substantially beyond the capacity of the real economy, with innovative, new, deliberately opaque derivative securities adding to the size of the speculative market which was approaching the size of the planet's GDP (Lanchester 2010: 64).

Computerisation focused traders' attention on the simple matter of growing the fund for which they were responsible as fast as possible, so that they progressed up the fund management league table. Automated investment decision systems had been introduced in 1986, and had become progressively more sophisticated and lower cost. By 2010 Reuters reported that 'tumbling technology costs have opened potentially lucrative ultrafast trading strategies to tiny start-up players'.[3] It was estimated that ultrafast trading then accounted for around 80 per cent of the Wall Street trades with London catching up fast. These 'ultrafast', or 'high frequency' systems, using fast hardware to beat other investors to profitable trades, were capable of placing trades on the basis of news reports or rumour circulating in the financial underworld. Readily available, high-tech, low cost, high frequency trading software was encouraging new entrants to the markets. The Reuters' report, referred to above, quoted one broker CEO as saying 'venture capitalists are giving money to guys coming straight out of MIT (Massachusetts Institute of Technology) and setting up desks'. It was also noted that such traders could enter the market without the requirement for a licence to trade, a situation that had attracted the attention at least of European regulators.

The financial institutions involved in speculative markets seem to fit well with the free market idea of the firm. Their essential infrastructure consists of office space with computer software and hardware. They are specialised organisations, their employees largely comprising traders whose main speciality is mathematical. They are not engaged in real economy activities,

---

3   See http://www.reuters.com/article/idUSTRE6363VE20100407

and consequently have no need to combine the skills and expertise of different specialised groups of people in pursuit of organisational aims.

Such a firm could, with some truth, be described as a 'nexus of contractual relations'. Typically, they are limited liability partnerships with the main decision-makers being partners, and the workforce made up of traders with responsibilities for the application of certain funds and focused on particular market situations with little opportunity to exercise any social responsibility. Their focus is simply on maximising returns for their investing clients and themselves. That complies with the agency theory conception of how a firm should act.

Conclusions

Smith depicted the firm as the key driver of the industrialisation project and the source of increasing economic wellbeing. The importance he ascribed to the firm in 1776 has only increased as industry and technology has advanced. It is surprising therefore that economics has had so little coherent to say about the firm. What Keynes referred to as 'academic scribble' has been largely incoherent in its treatment of the market, but even more so about the firm.

The only firm which is conjured with any degree of coherence is the firm in speculative markets such as the hedge fund or its equivalent, with a small number of individuals taking educated guesses as to which trades to make. The rich complexity of firms, employing the mass of people in the real economy, is ignored.

Doubtless, this inadequate representation of the firm arises at least in part because of the difficulty of integrating any realistic model of the firm within a theory of the market or the economy as a whole. Part of the problem no doubt lies in the inadequate theoretical depiction of the market. And partly, it might be the inconsistency of theoretically modelling a speculative firm to fit in a traditional market.

The inadequate and wrong depiction of the firm within economic theory is important because of what Ghoshal referred to as the double hermeneutic. Whereas in natural science a theory will not affect actual outcomes, in social science and in particular in economics, a theory whether right or wrong, if accepted by sufficient numbers, will shape behaviour. Thus, a false theory such as agency theory which focuses 'corporate officials' on maximising shareholder wealth, adopted as the orthodox wisdom, has the effect of diverting management efforts from pursuit of the firm's best long term interests onto maximising shareholder value.

Agency theory reduces the firm to the interplay between two separate actors, management and shareholders. Both are graced with the personal characteristics of economic man, being amoral maximisers of their own personal utility, minimising their give, maximising their take and 'shirking' wherever and whenever possible and therefore needing to be heavily monitored and 'incentivised'. These are the characteristics which are currently held to explain and justify the behaviour of business management.

This personal characterisation lies at the heart of economic theory, explaining, justifying and encouraging destructive behaviour, and earning economics the common description as the dismal science.

References

Alchian, A.A. & Demsetz, H., (1972), Production, information costs, and economic organisation, *American Economic Review*, vol. 62, 778.

Barnard, C.I., (1938), *The Functions of the Executive*, Cambridge Mass: Harvard University Pree, pxi.

Baumol, W.J., (1958), On the Theory of Oligopoly, *Economica*, vol. 25, no. 99, 31–43.

Berle, A.A. & Means, G.C., (1932), *The Modern Corporation and Private Property*, New York: Macmillan.

Chandler, A., (1977), *The Visible Hand: The Managerial Revolution in American Business*, Cambridge Mass: Belknap Press of Harvard University.

Coase, R., (1937), The nature of the firm, *Economica*, vol. 16, no. 4,. 386–405.

Cyert, R.M. & March, J.G., (1992), *A Behavioral Theory of the Firm*, Oxford: Blackwell.

Hayes, R.H. & Garvin, D., (1982), Managing as if tomorrow mattered, *Harvard Business Review*, (May/June).

Jensen, M.C. & Meckling, W.H., (1976), Theory of the firm: managerial behaviour, agency costs and ownership structure, *Journal of Financial Economics*, vol. 3, 305–360.

Lanchester, J., (2010), *Whoops! Why Everyone Owes Everyone and No One Can Pay*, London: Allen Lane.

Macher, J.T. & Richman, B.D., (2008), Transaction cost economics: an assessment of empirical research in the social sciences, *Business and Politics*, vol. 10, no. 1.

Pearson, G., (2009), *The Rise and Fall of Management: A Brief History of Practice, Theory and Context*, Farnham: Gower.

Simon, H.A., (1956), Rational choice and the structure of the environment, *Psychological Review*, vol. 63, no. 2, 129–138.

Sternberg, E., (2004), *Corporate Governance: Accountability in the Marketplace*, The Institute of Economic Affairs.

Williamson, O.E., (1964), *The Economics of Discretionary Behaviour: Managerial Objectives in a Theory of the Firm*, Englewood Cliffs NJ: Prentice Hall.

4

Ideas About People

The shortcomings of neoclassical theory in its modelling of economies, markets and firms stem, at least in part, from its misconceptions about people and how they behave. Much of this inadequacy seems to stem from the application of mathematical procedures which necessarily impose their own constraints and structures on what can be depicted and how. Thus, markets are depicted as a two-dimensional model of supply and demand with all other variations assumed away, or at least to be constant. This would be no use to an industrial marketeer, and it is not immediately clear to whom it might be useful. Similarly, the two-dimensional model of the firm as a production function showing just price and quantity: certainly such a model would be of no use to a firm manager, nor would any of the other variations on the theory of the firm.

Their purpose is neither to represent reality, nor to be useful to those who deal with the reality. They are devised to be theoretical, objective and 'scientific'. As such, they are important components in the neoclassical infrastructure that has developed as an ideology which, paradoxically, affects the reality of human behaviour.

The economic model of human behaviour is most simply expressed in a single dimension: self-interest. Smith expressed it as a fairly broad concept, but it was sharpened by neoclassical analysis and turned into a maximising model which had profound implications for the misunderstanding of human behaviour and even more profound impacts on that behaviour.

The adoption of mathematical procedures to model economic phenomena was prompted by the intent to be objective, empirical and as 'scientific' as possible. But the ambition to use quantitative methods seemed to overwhelm the analysis of where such procedures might be valid or useful. Quantitative analysis of human behaviour is notoriously problematic and the simplistic model at the base of neoclassical theory is perhaps the most fundamental problem in its analysis.

Classical Economic Man

The concept that became known as 'economic man' stems from Adam Smith's simple idea that it was from the self-interest of the butcher, the brewer and the baker, that he expected his dinner, rather than from their benevolence. No doubt aware of the negative connotations of this assertion, Smith reinforced and justified it, suggesting that:

> By pursuing his own self-interest he frequently promotes that of the society more effectually than when he really intends to promote it. (Smith 1776: 22)

This notion of self-interest was foundational to economic study right from the beginning. It was made operational, as with markets and firms, by use of the price mechanism by which interests are priced and the usual laws of supply and demand operate. The butcher's regard to his own interest might be expressed as his aim to provide a continuing living for himself and his dependents, based on his experience and understanding of butchery, and of the very 'real risk of ending up with an impoverishing deficit, and the need, the absolute need, to avoid this loss' (Drucker 1950: 52).

As chief breadwinner, he would not be in it for a quick buck. He was in it for life and his family depended on him. He would consequently be concerned to satisfy his customers and deliver them genuine value so they stayed with him. His sure intention was to conduct an ongoing business with regular transactions in lasting relationships with customers and suppliers. Such a relationship could not be based on the one party seeking to exploit the other by charging the maximum price or supplying the lowest quality of product, or by the other delaying or denying payment. If such behaviour were to punctuate the relationship it would surely not last long, with either party seeking alternative arrangements at the first opportunity. The butcher's aim would be to develop lasting relationships with all significant entities on which the butchery might depend. Surely, so much is no more than common sense.

It was not based on any idea of maximisation. The idea of maximising profit was not introduced till more than a century after Smith's time. The distinction between being self-interested, as depicted by Smith, and seeking to maximise self-interest is crucial but it is not a distinction that is often made. The introduction of maximisation corrupted explanations of human motivation.

Moreover, Smith was clearly concerned with the interests of 'society' as well as those of the butcher and colleagues. His perspective on mankind was not half as dismal as his successors appear to suggest. He did not present his butcher, brewer and baker as fly-by-night opportunists. The needs to earn a sufficient living and avoid an impoverishing deficit are the financial imperative of all business activities. That is the idea embedded in company legislation over the past century and a half and is retained to this day. Such needs and duties should largely determine the behaviour of law abiding management decision-makers as they promote the survival and long term prosperity of their firms with consideration for the interests of all stakeholders.

Self-interest is the important foundation of economic man. The specific denial of any altruism or generosity of spirit was not initially essential to the concept. It was an amoral concept simply to exclude any complicating ethical or moral values from consideration. This was not to suggest the pursuit of self-interest was necessarily wholly single-minded, merely that the economic man as butcher, brewer or baker was to be focused on the job in hand, rather than also engaged in promoting the interests of society. For classical economists, that social aspect of business was to be overseen by government ensuring a fair distribution of the surpluses from economic activity. Smith argued that it was:

> not very unreasonable that the rich should contribute to the public expense, not only in proportion, but something more than in that proportion. (Smith 1776: 451)

He also recognised the 'mental mutilation' of industrial workers caused by the boring, repetitive jobs which resulted from the division of labour. He argued that in 'every improved and civilised society' it was the moral duty of government to compensate these ill effects by providing education for working people (Ibid: 429).

The original idea, from which economic man was derived, was clearly a more balanced concept than the cliché which became widely accepted in the later nineteenth century when mathematics invaded the common sense of Adam Smith's economics.

Neoclassical Economic Man

By the mid-nineteenth century the miserable living standards of the new industrial mill towns of northern England had become apparent. The reality of economic man was seen in the way many mill owners exploited their workers. Access to the industrial reserve army of unemployed paupers only strengthened the owners' position. Marx expressed the developing idea of economic man succinctly in his assessment of the self-interested amoral model of human behaviour:

> *The bourgeoisie, wherever it has got the upper hand, ... has left remaining no other nexus between man and man than naked self interest, than callous cash payment.... It has resolved personal worth into exchange value. (Marx & Engels 1848: 222)*

By the late nineteenth century Alfred Marshall, one of the last of the classicists and first of the neoclassicists, not only recognised the threat posed by the developing one-dimensional economic man, but also the departure from reality of many economic theorists:

> *... Ricardo and his followers often spoke as though they regarded man as a constant quantity ... This same bent of mind ... caused them to speak of labour as a commodity without staying to throw themselves into the point of view of the workman; and without dwelling upon the allowances to be made for his human passions, his instincts and habits, his sympathies and antipathies, his class jealousies and class adhesiveness, his want of knowledge and of the opportunities for free and vigorous action. They therefore attributed to the forces of supply and demand a much more mechanical and regular action than is to be found in real life; and they laid down laws with regard to profits and wages that did not hold even for England in their own time. (Marshall 1922: 762–3)*

The more balanced understanding expressed by Marshall was to be overridden by the neoclassical adoption of marginal analysis, using calculus to advance economic man's aims from making a continuing living to maximising his own utility. It was a crucial, though unheralded change. It had the most widespread impact, both theoretically and as theory came to dominate practice, in the real world as well.

It is apparent, for example, in the neoclassical adoption of agency theory, which depicts people being assumed to be seeking to maximise their own utility, and therefore 'shirking' at every opportunity, unless they could be monitored, coerced and punished, or bribed with financial incentives. It betrays a more primitive view of human nature even than that in Fred Taylor's scientific management concept of 'soldiering'.

The neoclassical shift to maximising sought to establish a more quantitative, clinical and objective model of economic activity, including human behaviour. But its real effect was to replace a common sense set of assumptions about human behaviour and motivation with the most fundamentally cynical and self-destructive set of value judgments about human motivation and behaviour. And once established, the neoclassical approach pursued its simplistic assumptions, via calculus, to their logical conclusion, despite the many real world indications of their falsity and inadequacy.

Landlords, Entrepreneurs, Labourers and Managers

The three categories of people with which economic theory was traditionally concerned were the landlords, entrepreneurs and labour, the owners of the three factors of production. As examples of economic men, they were all equally possessed of self-interest and were competing against each other both in their production activities and as consumers.

Thus, landlords were presumed to want to charge as much rent for their property as they could. Entrepreneurs, the providers and managers of capital, were to make as much of a surplus as they could between the payment for land, materials and labour and the price they could achieve for their finished products. Labour was assumed to seek to earn as much wage as they could per unit of input. But as stakeholders in an ongoing business, each had an interest in achieving levels of payment over the long term, rather than achieving the greatest one-off receipt.

Clearly, in their competing pursuit of self-interest, the three categories were far from evenly matched. The landlords, and later the capitalist–entrepreneurs, were not only wealthier than labour, but more politically powerful, largely determining the law of the land which was focused on the protection of their private property. Empirical studies of the pursuit of self-interest by these competing constituencies demonstrate the unfairness which was meted out from time to time to the weakest group, the working labourer and still more to the unemployed.

The law has never effectively prevented combinations among employers, but was successful in repressing worker combinations till the mid-nineteenth century, and from then on has been inconsistent and ambiguous, granting and then repealing workers' rights, encouraging and then repressing their expression of political progress. Nevertheless, recognition of the interdependence of the three groups has persisted and, by and large, has resulted in progressively improving conditions of employment for working people, though the gain has been substantially less than for the other two categories.

Economic theory holds up the entrepreneur as the hero of industrialisation, providing both the technical innovations essential to economic progress and the risk bearing role associated with the input of capital. The very real risk bearing role of other employees is largely ignored. The entrepreneur combined the roles of ownership and control of the firm. But when firms developed into large-scale businesses with widespread share ownership, the shareholders enjoying limited liability, the roles of ownership and control became separated. Only in small businesses were ownership and control both still held by the entrepreneur. In larger businesses control was exercised by the new, autonomous category of management which was independent of both capital and labour.

The category of managers was never adequately reflected in economic theory, and its separateness never incorporated till the development of agency theory which completely overwhelmed the legal position of managers as agents of the firm as denoted in their contracts of employment. Though managers, or directors, were charged with the legal duty of promoting the firm's best long term interests, this was not recognised by the other categories. The leaders of labour largely accepted the agency theory argument that managers were simply the agents of the owners, that is, the tools of capital. The theory led shareholders to believe that managers, being neoclassical economic men, would seek to pursue their own interests, rather than those of shareholders.

Latterly, even managers themselves came to believe they were simply the agents of the shareholders, with a legal duty to act only for shareholders' best short term interests. While management might take the interests of employees and others into consideration, where those interests were in conflict with the interests of shareholders, as for example in the case of a hostile takeover bid, managers were led, falsely, to believe themselves to be bound to pursue shareholders' interests, which were exclusively financial.

Maximising and Impoverishing

The neoclassical revolution, with its adoption of mathematics as the source of economic explanation and prediction, opened up vast new fields for economic publication. Over a century later the impact is still live, with massive publication in leading academic journals on obscure topics expressed with mathematical precision in terms which are entirely closed to the non-specialist reader. The preponderance of quantitative publication gives theory the appearance of substance. Without the supportive maths, economic ideas might appear quite trivial; with it, their application to real situations has become the norm, so that indeed, 'the world is ruled by little else'.

Differential calculus established the maximising principle. Every production function would seek to maximise its profit. Within each production function there would be a group of executives, separated from ownership, who were themselves maximisers seeking to maximise their own utility, thus giving rise to the 'agency problem'.

In an interview regarding 'the corporation', Noam Chomsky (2004) highlighted what he referred to as a very lively, independent working class press in mid-nineteenth century America. It was run by young women from the farms, factory girls, Irish immigrants and so on. They bitterly condemned what they referred to as 'the new spirit of the age: gain wealth, forgetting all but self'. They argued, in Chomsky's words, it was degrading, dehumanising, destructive of culture, of independence and of freedom and they described themselves as being subjects of a monarchical, feudal system, losing their rights as Americans. Such expressions paralleled the descriptions by Engels of the capitalist system at work in England.

The neoclassical perspective explained and justified maximisation, that is, 'gain wealth, forgetting all but self'. The economic system was made up of such maximising units – markets, firms and people – not just amoral and self-interested, but seeking to maximise that self-interest. The difference was crucial since maximising has an often overlooked downside. Maximising is only half the story; the impoverishment of everything else is the other half.

At a company level this downside is well understood with the emphasis on short term maximising profit being detrimental to the long term prosperity of the firm. But it also impacts the most personal relationships. For example, a couple with two children, a girl and a boy, having limited resources to invest in their children's education, decide they would like to maximise the boy's education and so invest all their discretionary resource in him. The consequence is that the girl's education is neglected. That is the general effect of maximising behaviour. Maximising led to man's inhumanity to man, previously exercised only by the inhumane becoming the indoctrinated custom and practice among all economic actors. Conscientious dissidents, who continued to behave according to some notion of equity and fairness, were treated by the theory as irrational exceptions.

The neoclassical version of economic man was not just amoral, calculating and self-interested, which the classicists accepted and which caused such angst among the socially minded and 'utopian idealists', including Marx. But in addition, neoclassical economic man was a maximiser and therefore also an impoverisher.

If Smith's butcher had been a maximiser he would have impoverished his suppliers and customers in the short term and inevitably himself in the long term. The defence of maximising is therefore frequently made that it refers to long term maximising. On the face of it this is a perfectly sound defence. But it has no mathematical expression and so resolves to simple common sense. The mathematics of maximisation sets up a relationship between variables, and resolves what values would produce the maximum, or minimum, value in the dependent variable. The model is not capable of incorporating timescale. So if profit maximising was deemed to refer to the long term, any concern with neoclassical mathematics could be completely set aside. Moreover, the idea of long term profit maximising in the real world lacks any coherent meaning. In the long term there are a million and one ways of increasing profit, not just a single route to maximising.

As a generalised common sense expression, long term profit maximising could mean anything. It is not as useful a target as Drucker's suggestion of making sufficient profit to survive and prosper, that is, to avoid 'an impoverishing deficit, and the need … to avoid this loss by providing against the risks' (Drucker 1950: 52). Provision against the risks means accruing some surplus resource within the firm that could be deployed in times of need.

Even long term maximisation would be incapable of accommodating such a proposition.

For all its manifest flaws and shortcomings, maximising has nevertheless prevailed through economic theory. It led to the economic man idea becoming an extreme of brute self-interest tamed only by 'the market' if such existed. Moreover, if the market was competitive, the amoral maximising unit would seek, in order to maximise its own utility, to corner, corrupt or abuse that market so as to reduce the level of its competitiveness. Being conditioned to impoverish as well as maximise, such amoral activity was readily adopted, the test of legality being the only constraint.

The final tweak to the maximising/impoverishing behaviour of neoclassical economic man was the misapplication of the agency idea to justify the conversion of the firm's objective from profit maximising to shareholder wealth maximising (Friedman 2002: 133). This not only authorised the impoverishment of the firm for the sole benefit of shareholders, but also the impoverishment of all other stakeholders, including employees, customers, suppliers, the local community and the environment (as proxy for future generations).

Motivation, Corruptibility and Coercion

People in speculative market firms work under some pressure, logging price movements, trend data and formulae calculations and so on to provide inputs to buy, hold and sell decisions, with the timing of those trades being critical. Such activity appears unlikely to offer great fulfilment in the working lives of intelligent people. It has no other dimension to it than the achievement of a deal which offers a financial surplus; the greater the surplus, the greater the achievement. The provision of monetary incentives for such work is therefore widely held to be essential to the achievement of satisfactory performance.

Traditionally, monetary incentives, such as piecework systems, used to be applied to shop floor work which could be, as Smith identified it, 'mentally mutilating'. Piecework was thought to provide the motivation to perform such tasks, though Wilfred Brown (1962) demonstrated the inadequacy of that approach half a century ago. Incentivisation was also applied to work which was essentially unsupervisable, such as the travelling salesman who could easily 'shirk' unless paid commission on sales. However, the claimed necessity for payment by results at higher levels of organisation is a more recent phenomenon.

Money may compensate for the narrowness of a financial trader's working experience and support conspicuous consumption and waste as part compensation. But the scarcity of any life enhancing experience as well as the mindless pressure of working days results in many leaving the speculative activity at a problematic stage in their careers. Staying in for 'just one more bonus' is a common cry.

Peter Drucker commented to *Forbes Magazine* in 1997 regarding the exorbitant executive salaries that free market fundamentalist maximisation had enabled:

> *Few top executives can even imagine the hatred, contempt, and even fury that has been created – not primarily among blue-collar workers who never had an exalted opinion of the 'bosses' – but among their middle management and professional people. (Beatty 1998: 82)*

Drucker had suggested that top salaries could be no more than twenty times that of the average hourly paid worker 'without injury to company morale'. By 2005 that ratio had in fact reached 262 times (Mishel 2007), and by 2010 was estimated at more than 300 for companies in the FTSE100 index, and the hatred, contempt and fury had been made evident over the bonuses the bankers and traders habitually paid themselves.

The maximising effects of financial sector activity are clear in the continuing development of bubbles. The impoverishing impacts of a bust are also clear enough as they hit the general population in job losses, heightened insecurity and increased poverty. During intervening periods of stability the financial sector impoverishes the real economy by seducing talented people away from more socially useful activity.

Smith suggested that though the economy depended on people being self-interested, he also argued that 'frugality' was the strongest motivator. By frugality he meant the 'prudence and parsimony' which would result in one:

> *becoming the proper object of this respect, or deserving and obtaining this credit and rank among our equals … our anxiety to obtain the advantages of fortune is accordingly much more excited and irritated by*

> *this desire, than that of supplying all the necessities and conveniencies,*
> *of the body which are always easily supplied. (Smith 1790: 213–4)*[1]

Smith's explanation was a richer account of human motivation than the diminished version provided by neoclassical economics. He expected people would act in their own interest, but in the context of his *Theory of Moral Sentiments*, which he opened with the following:

> *How selfish soever man may be supposed, there are evidently some*
> *principles in his nature, which interest him in the fortune of others, and*
> *render their happiness necessary to him, though he derives nothing from*
> *it, except the pleasure of seeing it. Of this kind is pity or compassion,*
> *the emotion which we feel for the misery of others, when we either see*
> *it, or are made to conceive it in a very lively manner. (Smith 1759: 3)*

It may be that the bankers, traders and bosses of the current age would prefer to be proper objects of respect, deserving and obtaining credit and rank among their equals, rather than the hatred, contempt and fury they clearly obtain today. Achieving such a change in their standing would be well within their own power, but such higher motivations appear to have been crowded out by the monetary incentives to which they are subject.

So pervasive has the maximising model become, that any other behaviour than maximising one's own monetary utility, particularly in a professional or business capacity, has come to be regarded as not just irrational, but even irresponsible, since it would inhibit the market working its magic. Economists might not deny people have the internal motivations identified by Smith, but since they cannot be included in their mathematical models, they have to be disregarded.

Frey (1997: 20) points out that external interventions, especially monetary rewards, have been shown to have the 'crowding out' effect. They crowd out and undermine any intrinsic motivations which individuals may have. For example, paying a child for doing household tasks may push them from doing those tasks 'to help the family' to doing them simply for the reward, so that if the reward is withdrawn the child may resist doing the tasks. He quotes Hirsch, arguing that such monetary incentives debase:

---

1   This quote is an addition to the 1790 edition of *The Theory of Moral Sentiments*, published fourteen years after publication of *The Wealth of Nations*. The sentiment must have been seen by Smith as integral to self-interest.

moral values such as 'truth, trust, acceptance, restraint, obligation' and
tend to reduce the intrinsic motivation to perform. (Hirsch 1976: 143)

The crowding out effect, which destroys intrinsic motivation, has mostly been studied from the perspective of how the effect can be avoided, and intrinsic motivations maintained, despite the provision of extrinsic incentives.

Ellerman (2006), for example, recommended changing the World Bank's approach to development assistance. He noted the disincentive effects on the receiver of the orthodox mode of providing development assistance. This was caused by the receiver losing autonomy and self-respect, being required to perform according to externally specified regulation. This destroyed the receiver's intrinsic motivation. Ellerman advocated offering aid indirectly, so that the receiver's autonomy was respected and they were helped to help themselves. In that way the crowding out effect might be minimised or eliminated altogether.

With few exceptions, all human beings are susceptible to having their higher motivations crowded out by extrinsic, especially monetary, rewards; all, with few exceptions, are essentially corruptible. There may be a hierarchy of human needs, as expressed by Smith himself, showing the structure of motivation: starting with hunger and thirst, heat and cold as the most basic needs, 'other wants and fancies' such as clothing, housing, furniture and personal ornament, at a higher level, with the highest need being the 'frugality' already referenced (Smith 1776: 152). Maslow's hierarchy (Maslow 1943) was based on similar ideas which were further developed and refined through the 1960s and 70s, as outlined elsewhere (Pearson 2009). These analyses suggest that while man is indeed perpetually wanting, motivation is by intrinsic needs which may be modified by the need also to satisfy an intrinsic sense of justice and equity.

What they do not adequately confront is the idea of corruptibility. At any point on the hierarchy, monetary incentives can subvert intrinsic motivations. Any desire for respect and credit from among our equals, or any motivation to self-actualise, can be side-tracked by the availability of monetary incentives to act in some other way than to satisfy those higher level needs.

Though the great majority of people clearly do have social consciences and expectations of justice, if expectations are not met, their intrinsic feelings may be crowded out and replaced with an 'if you can't beat them, join them' philosophy. Economic man would be unlikely to be a war hero, or motivated to achieve great craftsmanship or to take pride in any sort of work for its own sake. But real people are naturally like that.

The neoclassical ideology, far from seeking to minimise the crowding out of intrinsic motivation, deliberately uses monetary incentives to convert any personal intrinsic motivations to those which are indicated from outside. For example, managers being identified as the agents of shareholders, but not directly controlled by shareholders, being in control of the firm, might work to achieve quite other ends than the maximisation of shareholder wealth. Any intrinsic motivation such as to work for the long term, autonomous prosperity of the firm, must be overridden if they would work to maximise shareholder wealth. The only means to achieving this, available within economic theory, is by the offer of monetary incentives. In this case that monetary incentive can be provided in the form of share options which has the convenient co-effect of actually converting managers into shareholders. Such incentivising is hardly distinguishable from a deliberate bribe, its aim being explicitly to coerce managers to serve the ends theory misleadingly dictates.

Empirically based studies of behaviour at work, going back as far as the human relations inputs from the 1930s on, demonstrate considerable knowledge and understanding which utterly discredit the economic man model. Ellerman illustrated the point, using McGregor's dichotomy between Theory X and Theory Y which was first published in 1960. Theory X assumes that people at work are lazy and will avoid work if they can; they dislike taking responsibility, prefer to be directed, have little ambition and only want security. Consequently, they must be coerced, controlled, directed and threatened in order to get them to contribute to organisational goals. Such an approach to management results in people being managed conforming to the Theory X stereotype. The modern economic man approach is pure Theory X.

Theory Y, on the other hand, assumes people enjoy and seek responsibility, most have the capacity to be creative and imaginative in pursuit of organisational goals given half the chance, but that in much of their working life they are not given the opportunity. Moreover, that working towards goals to which they are committed is natural, and external threats and punishment are not the most effective means of gaining co-operation, commitment stems from the rewards associated with achievement, and in most circumstances, intrinsic rewards are more effective motivators than extrinsic monetary rewards (McGregor 1960).

Real understanding of human behaviour at work has been crowded out by the dominant neoclassical shareholder primacy ideology. Bankers, traders and bosses are persuaded to see themselves as economic men seeking to maximise their own utility, and therefore having to be incentivised. Otherwise, they'll either 'shirk' or leave. Any other consideration lies beyond the scope of the economic model. Higher motivations have been crowded out and the individuals concerned corrupted.

This is not new. Smith himself indicated 'the man inside' judges what others would think if they saw his act of theft. Whether the theft was picking up a £10 note on the street and pocketing it, or taking a multi-million pound bonus for doing something which has little social worth, it matters what others think. They would prefer others to think well rather than ill of them. Only when they know others think irredeemably ill, do they no longer care. There is then nothing to lose, so they themselves become lost, isolated among sycophants who permit them to delude themselves, the ultimate exemplars of neoclassical economic man.

Neoclassical Culture

The term culture is used here in the sense in which it is applied to organisations, though here it is intended to relate to a whole economy or even global understandings. White (1984: 14) defined culture as:

> *The behaviour patterns and standards which bind a social group together and which are built up over many years and is a unifying philosophy, ethic and spirit.*

Schein (1984: 4) broadly concurred with this definition:

> *Behaviour, beliefs, values and learned recipes.*

Bower (1966: 22–41), former McKinsey CEO, had famously expressed it as 'the way we do things around here', though he referred to it as company philosophy rather than culture. The concept of culture suggests how economic ideas can become so important. The dominant economic man idea is what determines the behaviour, beliefs, values and learned recipes which, for better or worse, determine the way we do things around here.

But organisational culture is not simply homogeneous. It is more the sum of many subcultures, each of which contributes its own nuances of meaning and its own rituals and images. Although culture is often regarded as 'the glue that binds organisation together', it is equally clear that it can in fact be divisive, just as easily as cohesive, with the various subcultures in conflict with each other. On occasion this conflict may become overt and sometimes highly dysfunctional, but more usually the conflict will be bubbling below the surface. It has been described as a 'melange of cross cutting subcultures', continually reacting against each other in some more or less cohesive, or divisive, not necessarily stable, equilibrium (Gregory 1983: 76).

At the level of society as a whole, economic man describes the dominant set of shared beliefs and behaviour patterns. By combining maximisation of self-interest with the impoverishment of everything else it, not surprisingly, also justifies and encourages the increasing divide between the rich and poor, between the top earners and the bottom. In this its impact is almost wholly negative, as demonstrated by Wilkinson and Pickett (2009): the more unequal societies are bad for almost everyone living in them, not just the poor. The less equal a society is, the more likely it is to suffer ill-health, violence, drugs, mental illness, big prison populations and so on. The neoclassical economic man philosophy has taught people to behave badly, and it has bred the narrow self-interest which makes the population cynical and suspicious.

The making of that culture is not simply the result of the economic ideas themselves but of the way they have been promulgated over many years. Nineteenth century economic man, though largely rejected during the period of Keynes' dominance in the mid-twentieth century, was never far below the surface. Resurrected with the triumph of neoclassical free market ideology, led by Friedman, it had acquired new depths of self-interested maximisation. Its dominant position at the heart of economic culture has been established among those of influence in academia, industry, business and government.

Replacing that culture with one that is more benign and equitable will not be achieved overnight. However, there have always been alternative perspectives. Veblen (1899) and Galbraith (1958), for example, both flagged up the dysfunction and stupidity of the dominant model of economic behaviour. Keynes provided the most coherent alternative and the more recent failures of the system have highlighted more of its practical shortcomings. The need, the urgent need, for an alternative is beginning to be more widely appreciated.

Conclusions

The application of economic ideas has not been an untarnished success. Achievement has invariably been accompanied by unintended consequences. It is not clear whether there is any benefit to be gained from the application of theoretical economic ideas which is not already available through the application of common sense and hard won practical experience.

The currently dominant neoclassical free market ideology has created a culture which encourages the maximisation of self-interest and the impoverishment of everything else, the consequence of which is an explosion of dysfunctional inequality. It compounds this basic inequity by encouraging and supporting the wealthy in exploiting the already disadvantaged, by whatever means they can, short of breaking the law.

Maximisation of self-interest, profit and shareholder wealth, all being measured in monetary terms, has led inevitably to the focus on purely financial business without the inconvenience of making and distributing physical objects, investing in physical resources or providing large-scale and disparate employment. The maximisation of self-interest has led to the continual search for ways of avoiding rules and regulations and the limitations they set. The freedoms gained have encouraged further growth in speculative markets, which have been seen to endanger the traditional banking sector which existed to serve the real economy.

The cultural impact has been severe. The widely accepted belief is that it is good to maximise one's own self-interest, so long as the law is not contravened. To do otherwise would be irrational, if not insane. But the result is the opposite of what the theory predicts.

Postscript to Coercion by Ideas

The focus of these first four chapters has been on the neoclassical ideology which rules the world and has largely shaped the management and governance of industrial companies, especially over the past three decades.

Neoclassical economics is driven by the demands of the mathematical models and procedures on which it is based, rather than by observation of the real world situations and phenomena which fascinated Adam Smith. The self-interest Smith envisaged was demonstrated by his butcher, baker and so on, whose aims were to survive and prosper so as to provide lifelong support for themselves and their dependents. The neoclassical amendment changed that self-interest to mean something quite different. Profit maximising with its mathematically inherited inability to account for time, enabled a simplistic short term financial orientation to become the norm, focusing almost exclusively on the 'bottom line'.

Economists themselves are in broad agreement that neoclassical models do not accurately describe real situations. Nor do they predict outcomes. Despite being quantitative they are therefore by no means scientific. They provide a crude, inaccurate and simplistic account of real world processes, as discussed in these chapters relating to economies as a whole, to markets, to firms and to people and their behaviour.

Despite these shortcomings, possibly because of its simplicity and acknowledged internal coherence, the neoclassical ideology is widely understood and broadly accepted. It has consequently had a profound impact on the shaping of the economic environment, on management practice in companies and on their governance as well as on human behaviour in all these contexts.

The original driving force behind its replacement of the more pluralistic Keynesian economics was the Austrian School led by von Mises and Hayek. Their great concern was that any step away from the neoclassical free market ideology would end up with the free West being overtaken by totalitarian socialism. Led by Friedman and colleagues at Chicago, the ideology came to dominate academia, industry, business and policy-making, notably in the United States and Britain. From the perspective of industrial management, the Friedmanite/agency sleight of hand which changed the perception of industrial management's prime duty from maximising profit to maximising shareholder wealth has been both crucial and destructive.

The research into, and teaching of, industrial management in universities and business schools has been so corrupted that specialist knowledge and expertise in management, gained over a century of empirical study, has been overtaken by the neoclassical orthodoxy. The result for the management of firms has been the now familiar business leader described by Ghoshal and repeated in the preface to this text.

Coercion by those ideas has damaged Anglo-American industry, ensuring the focus of management is wholly on financial issues such as returns on investment, p:e ratios and shareholder value, rather than products, customers, technologies and the like. With that financial orientation, the management focus is short term, on cutting rather than building and even on encouraging the break-up and disposal of industrial firms if a quick gain can be achieved for shareholders, which it almost invariably can. This is the 'bottom line' orientation from which Anglo-American management must escape if their industries are to recapture their economic role.

But the financial focus of industrial management on the bottom line, giving primacy to shareholders above all else, has even more profound impacts than that. It has contributed to the unsustainable position the world now occupies and which is the subject of Part II of this text.

References

Beatty, J., (1998), *The World According to Drucker*, Orion Publishing Group.

Bower, M., (1966), *The Will to Manage*, New York: McGraw-Hill, Chapter 2, pp. 22–41.

Brown, W., (1962), *Piecework Abandoned*, London: Heinemann.

Chomsky, N., (2004), in The Corporation video based on J. Bakan (2004), *The Corporation: The Pathological Pursuit of Profit and Power*, New York: Free Press.

Drucker, P.F., (1950), *The New Society*, New York: Harper & Bros.

Ellerman, D., (2006), *Helping People to Help Themselves*, Ann Arbour: University of Michigan Press.

Frey, B.S., (1997), *Not Just for the Money: An Economic Theory of Personal Motivation*, Cheltenham: Edward Elgar Publishing.

Friedman, M., (2002), *Capitalism and Freedom*, 40th Anniversary edition, Chicago: University of Chicago Press, p. 133.

Galbraith, J.K., (1958), *The Affluent Society*, London: Hamish Hamilton.

Gregory, K.L., (1983), Native view paradigms: multiple cultures and culture conflicts in organisations, *Administrative Science Quarterly*, September, vol. 28, 75–85.

Hirsch, F., (1976), *The Social Limits to Growth*, Cambridge, MA: Harvard University Press.

McGregor, D., (1960), *The Human Side of Enterprise*, New York: McGraw Hill.

Marshall, A., (1922), *Principles of Economics*, 8th edition, London: Macmillan.

Marx, K. & Engels, F., (1847), *The Communist Manifesto*, (2002), London: Penguin Classics.

Maslow, A., (1943), A theory of human motivation, *Psychological Review*, vol. 50, 370–396.

Mishel, L., (2007), *CEO to Worker Pay Imbalance Grows*, Economic Snapshots web site: www.epi.org/content.cfm/webfeatures_snapshots_20060621

Pearson, G., (2009), *The Rise and Fall of Management: A Brief History of Practice, Theory and Context*, Farnham: Gower, pp. 8–11.

Schein, E.H., (1984), Coming to an awareness of organisational culture, *Sloan Management Review*, Winter, 3–16.

Smith, A., (1759), *The Theory of Moral Sentiments*. (Currently available in the Dover Philosophical Classics Series, New York: Dover Publications.)

Smith, A., (1776), *An Inquiry into the Nature and Causes of the Wealth of Nations*, (1993), Oxford: Oxford World's Classics.

Veblen, T., (1899), *The Theory of the Leisure Class: An Economic Study in the Evolution of Institutions*. New York: Macmillan.

White, J., (1984), Corporate culture and corporate success, *Management Decision*, vol. 22, no. 4.

Wilkinson, R. & Pickett, K., (2009), *The Spirit Level: Why More Equal Societies Almost Always Do Better*, London: Allen Lane.

PART II
The Unsustainable Context

I argue that academic research related to the conduct of business and management has had some very significant and negative influences on the practice of management. These influences have been less at the level of adoption of a particular theory and more at the incorporation, within the worldview of managers, of a set of ideas and assumptions that have come to dominate much of management research. More specifically, I suggest that by propagating ideologically inspired amoral theories, business schools have actively freed their students from any sense of moral responsibility. (Ghoshal 2005: 75)

Something is profoundly wrong with the way we live today. For thirty years we have made a virtue out of the pursuit of material self-interest; indeed, this very pursuit now constitutes whatever remains of our sense of collective purpose. We know what things cost but have no idea what they are worth. We no longer ask of a judicial ruling or a legislative act: is it good? Is it fair? Is it right? Will it help bring about a better society or a better world? (Judt 2010: 1–2)

Smith's 1776 *Inquiry* did not inspire or guide the industrialisation process which caused the sudden and long term rise in the 'wealth of nations'. Lombe's first large-scale textile factory had opened almost 60 years earlier. The transport infrastructure which enabled the opening up of markets and necessitated the development of banking had started in the 1750s, and Arkwright's first cotton mill opened in 1771. By the time Smith's *Inquiry* was published, industrialisation was well under way.

The agrarian revolution had involved the enclosure of agricultural land, dispossessing peasant workers of their strips of land and their access to commons, creating a new army of rural paupers. The industrial revolution multiplied the inequalities between the tenants and entrepreneurs and their dependent labourers, creating both great wealth and great poverty as described by Engels in his studies of the working people in the new mill towns of northern England. This poverty was later moderated by industrial legislation placing some restriction on the exploitation of working men, women and children. While Smith's economic ideas may have explained and justified the industrialisation process, the legislation to limit the inequity of unregulated industry was the result of pragmatic observation of need, rather than the application of any theoretical ideas.

The Wall Street crash of 1929 and the subsequent depression of the 1930s was met by Roosevelt's pragmatic, socially minded and common sense New Deal. The theory only came later, with Keynes' *General Theory of Employment, Interest and Money*, published in 1936, which explained and justified the pragmatic response to the Great Depression.

Similarly, the liberal socialism of post-war Britain, with the establishment of a welfare state and some public ownership, was the practical implementation of social democracy rather than the dogmatic application of theoretical socialist ideas. The necessary conditions for that socialised state had been created by the shared experience of two world wars.

It was not until the free market ideology resurfaced in the 1980s that policy was dominated by the doctrinaire application of theory. Since then, as Ghoshal indicates in the above quotation, it has had a profound impact on the way industrial companies are managed. Over the past 30 years neoclassical ideology has ruled, despite the poverty of its ideas.

The environmental and ecological impacts of industry and resulting consumptions, in the context of finite earth, are well documented elsewhere and only briefly examined here. The scale of those impacts is continuing to accelerate and the imperative to act on them is becoming more widely recognised. Nevertheless, neoclassical orthodoxy maintains its focus on economic growth to provide a still growing population with a continually improving standard of living. These concerns continue to dominate environmental considerations, but are not yet incorporated in any theoretical framework which could guide economic development.

Moreover, it is neoclassical ideology which explains and justifies the new explosion of wealth and income inequality, both within economies and between rich and poor nations.

The resulting rich are not the personalised capitalists who Marx stigmatised for their exploitative negotiations with the possessors of labour and who he predicted would come to be the capital owning monopolists in every market. They were largely prevented by the wide dispersal of company ownership among thousands of small shareholders who neither could, nor wished to, control the corporation. This was referred to by Drucker as 'the post-capitalist society' where wealth was managed by financial institutions on behalf of the ultimate owners such as the members of pension funds and so on. Those financial institutions were managed by employees who, though 'well paid professionals', were, according to Drucker, 'unlikely to be rich themselves'. It is estimated those financial institutions now control over three quarters of all marketable securities on behalf of their ultimate owners.

While Drucker's analysis remained optimistic, he suggested the problem with such massive funds was how to protect them from:

> looters' and 'special-interest groups' that might 'use their political power to divert pension fund money to subsidize themselves. (Drucker 1993: 67)

Those problems proved to be real enough, with the consequence that the investment management professionals, bankers and traders were enabled to convert themselves into the new Mr Moneybags, a wealthy capital owning 'special-interest group' whose focus has indeed been on 'subsidizing themselves' on a massive scale. The system's theoretical apologists argue that it is their duty to pursue self-interest and therefore the interests of the other shareholders they represent. However, the inequitable outcome from which they benefit is actually achieved at the expense of longer term and wider considerations.

This inequity is a short term effect which could be corrected by straightforward political action if there was a will to take it. But environmental impacts are less tractable. Moreover, the underlying economic ideology is long established and its moderation, even of the simplistic free market extreme, is prerequisite to correcting the imbalance of outcomes, both immediate and longer term.

Moderation of neoclassical ideology is also the essential prerequisite for moving the control and direction of industrial companies beyond the myopic fixation on maximising shareholder wealth. Only then would broader considerations, both within the corporation and beyond, be feasible. Displacing the neoclassical dogma would be the first crucial step.

This second part briefly highlights the practical outcomes of the coercion by ideas described in the Part I which have created this unsustainable context.

References

Drucker, P.F., (1993), *The Post-Capitalist Society*, Oxford: Butterworth-Heinemann.

Ghoshal, S., (2006), Bad management theories are destroying good management practices, *Academy of Management Learning and Education*, vol. 4, no. 1.

Judt, T., (2010), *Ill Fares the Land*, London: Allen Lane.

5

Externalities and Sustainability

Thom Watson, late of Warwick Business School, used to challenge the thought that any of his students of management could ever make the smallest contribution to the creation of wealth. This didn't go down too well with the students, since that was what they were there for – to learn their part in wealth creation. Watson's point was that the earth comprised a planetful of potential wealth, and all earth's inhabitants, including his students, could do, would be to convert it into a finished product, and to do so, as with the conversion of energy from one form to another, with varying degrees of inefficiency. Any act of conversion was therefore actually a loss of wealth potential.

Some of earth's resources such as those sunk in the body of the earth are definitely finite. Other resources are practically infinite such as solar, wind and wave energy, though there may be quite severe limitations on the amount of that practically infinite supply that can be extracted per time period. Other resources, biological ones, are neither finite nor yet infinite, but can be grown and developed, or constrained and killed, intentionally or by accident, again with varying degrees of inefficiency in terms of their consumption of finite resource. Moreover, some of these biological resources are recognised as essentially benign, while others are malign, in that they do not contribute to sustainable ways of living on this finite planet, and may in fact prevent it. The biological resource which is both most successful and by far the most damaging is, of course, humanity itself.

Keynes envisaged that within his lifetime it should be possible 'to perform all the operations of agriculture, mining and manufacture with a quarter of the human effort' then required: in other words 'mankind is solving its economic problem' (Keynes 1931: 325). By 2020 he anticipated mankind would be freed to address better and more fulfilling aims in life than simply improving the standard of living or the manic pursuit of money. He imagined the love of money for its own sake:

will be recognised for what it is, a somewhat disgusting morbidity, one
of those semi-criminal, semi pathological propensities which one hands
over with a shudder to the specialists in mental disease. (Ibid: 329)

He may have been right about the rise in incomes, but he seems to have been wrong about people living more fulfilling lives. The pursuit of money is never ending for those who are consumed by it, while the poverty of unemployment still afflicts a too large minority. The economic theory which was intended to fulfil Keynes' hopes has actually resulted in their frustration. In addition, the pursuit of shareholder wealth ahead of all other considerations is driving the destruction of earth's resources and climate.

The decisive facts of population growth, resource depletion, pollution and man's contribution to global warming are surely no longer in serious doubt, though their extent is still uncertain. The connection between these constraints and the economic theory that challenges them is less commonly acknowledged. The connectedness between all these issues presents stark alternatives which demand to be considered and critical decisions agreed as a matter of some urgency.

Population, Resources, Pollution and Climate

Man's habitation of this planet, it is widely argued, is at a critical turning point. The combination of Darwin's theory of evolution by natural selection and the more recently established methodologies for identifying DNA sequencing has made it possible to make informed guesses, based on genetic changes, as to how populations of living organisms have developed over time. This study extends our understanding further back than has been possible by other methods.

A crude summary of the current understanding (about which I'm quite unqualified to express any view) goes roughly as follows. *Homo sapiens* appear to have first emerged as a separate species around 195,000 years ago. Population probably grew at a steady rate till somewhere around 80,000 years ago. During that time people migrated from their Ethiopian origins, across Africa and the Middle East, it is presumed, in search of food supplies to hunt and gather. Then, sometime between 80,000 and 50,000 years ago, the human population appears to have gone into some kind of crisis. According to some, we may have approached extinction, with possibly only around 2000 people in total some 70,000 years ago (Wells 2010: 15). It is assumed this was probably as a result of climate change reducing food supplies. Then, around 60,000 years ago, the population started to recover and gradually spread across the entire globe. Around 10,000 years ago the population commenced a period of consistent growth, from a few million to around a billion by the end of the eighteenth century. It seems fairly certain that the cause of that population growth was the adoption of agriculture which replaced the former hunter-gathering mode of living.

The trends of more recent times are of course known with greater certainty. The population explosion that started around 250 years ago, reaching around 7 billion today, clearly resulted from improved agricultural methods, progress in healthcare and the additional wealth generated by industrial development. Global growth peaked at around 2 per cent per annum in the mid-twentieth century. Population itself has already peaked in some advanced economies: Japan and some countries in Western Europe are already experiencing what is probably the start of a reduction in population. Combined with the concomitant ageing of the population, this creates a new set of challenges. However, global population growth remains positive at slightly above 1 per cent per annum, with expectations that earth's peak population will be around 9.5 billion which will be reached around the midpoint of the present century.

On this analysis, the current era is therefore something of a watershed in the history of human evolution. It is marked by population's collision with finite earth; finite in terms of its resources and its ability to absorb the various forms of human abuse meted out to it. That abuse rapidly accelerated after the Second World War, as witnessed by Schumacher (1973). And it is still accelerating.

These concerns are not new. In the nineteenth century Malthus recognised that population depended on the means of its subsistence, that it would grow when those means permitted, and that it would grow geometrically while food supplies would only grow arithmetically, and that therefore population would ultimately be limited by hunger and starvation, unless previously limited by war, plague, or disease. Innovations in industry, agriculture and healthcare have so far prevented the global catastrophe he feared, but it remains unclear how much more population growth such developments could be made to support.

The fear now is that population growth and its support at increasing levels of affluence is resulting in the too rapid depletion of resources as well as many kinds of pollution. By too rapid is meant depletion ahead of their replacement by resources which could be made permanently sustainable. The result is the extinction of biological species, damage to the ecosystem and rising levels of so-called greenhouse gases, including atmospheric carbon dioxide, which are contributing to global warming. That produces various effects which may well be irreversible such as the melting of the polar icecaps, acidification of the oceans and rising sea levels and temperatures, which may cause the extinction of further biological species, some human habitations and a continuing vicious cycle of adverse effects.

Different regions of the globe experience these various pressures differently. For example, population growth rates are still above 2 per cent in some of the world's poorest countries in sub-Saharan Africa, the Middle East and South America. In some cases populations are having to confront natural disasters such as famines caused by floods and drought, their survival only being achieved through external assistance. If these conditions persist, or increase, those areas will become chronically overpopulated and migration of whole populations, either *en masse* or by stealth, will be inevitable. Either accommodation or resistance will be likely to cause social catastrophe.

These effects are recognised, but the rationale of their cause is not completely understood. There is a persuasive consensus among the relevant expert communities regarding the interconnectedness of these various phenomena. Different perspectives on the supply and demand of critical resources make little difference to the global situation. Finite supply will at some stage be overtaken by continuing and growing demand. Decisive action will then be unavoidable. The sooner action is agreed the less traumatic it will have to be.

The same applies to the many forms of pollution and environmental damage being done to the land mass and, increasingly, to the oceans and the atmosphere. The later corrective action is taken the more fundamental it will have to be.

The prime cause of these pressures on finite earth is the growth of population. But its effects are multiplied many times by the pursuit of economic growth per capita, unquestioned in the developed world and a natural aspiration of the rest.

Economic Growth

Not only does economic growth generally create jobs, reduce unemployment and contribute to an improving standard of living, but it also means tomorrow's tax intake will be greater than today's and substantially more than yesterday's. That enables government to be more benign to the people in the pursuit of its political aims, whatever they are. It also enables government to borrow more, since its ability to repay is continually increasing. The increasing debt can be used to finance even more generosity to the people, or to particular chosen subsets of them. The absence of growth removes all these benefits, while economic contraction or decline reverses the processes and would seem likely, if it persisted, to result in some rebellious populations.

Prior to industrialisation, government in Britain was most concerned to achieve a surplus on its international trade and accrue that surplus in the form of gold bullion to offset the gold wealth achieved by Spain from its South American conquests. The mercantilist system of tariffs and subsidies was designed to support that aim. Industrialisation changed all that. The need for continually growing markets to justify the ever more specialised division of labour to reduce costs of production etc, defined a virtuous cycle of achievement so long as markets continued to grow. The mercantilist system, set up specifically to control and limit markets, had to be replaced by the free trade system in order for new markets to be opened up and therefore to support growth and further industrialisation.

Life in pre-industrial England was, for the vast majority, insecure and fairly short. England'sEnglish population had remained around five and a half million through the first half of the eighteenth century, held there by recurrent famine and disease (notably dysentery, smallpox and consumption). They lived in poverty with infant mortality running at one in fifteen for most of the first half of the century. Then in the four decades from 1760, as industrialisation was beginning, conditions overall improved substantially. More productive agriculture eliminated famine and provided an improved diet for the masses, improved living conditions and hygiene, and medical practice substantially reduced disease, with the result that the population grew by around two thirds to over 9 million by the end of the century, infant mortality fell almost eightfold to one in 118 and life for the majority became progressively less precarious.

That experience was repeated wherever the industrialisation process was established. In the New World these benign outcomes were compounded by the progressive opening up of the sparsely populated, but richly fertile, land to the West which provided one of the factors of production more or less free, apart from the cost of dispossessing the relatively small population of Native Americans. While ever markets were extending and growing, these effects continued, always subject to peaks and troughs around the trend growth. In the twentieth century the process was interrupted by the 1930s Great Depression as well as being stimulated by two world wars. During the last few decades trend growth, which was beginning to slow, was stimulated by the removal of trade barriers and opening of most markets to global competition. This has enabled less developed countries such as China, India, Brazil and others to participate in the industrialisation process and so give the world economy a final growth stimulus as their populations begin to join the consumer society.

Future growth stimuli are likely to be more modest than the great adjustments of the past. There are no new Wild West territories to open up, though there are massive areas of land which are unutilised, especially in Africa. Fertility may be poor, but their natural resources are now being exploited by foreign investors. The impact of China, India and other industrialising nations is restrained, or at least damped down, by their need to support mass populations still close to the breadline.

But there is an alternative scenario. The stimulus of economic growth being both great and essentially uncontrollable, the mass of people in the industrialising nations could succeed in achieving sufficient affluence to become, for example, a car owning middle class. Then, earth's resources would be consumed faster, pollution would multiply and sustainability limits be met sooner and the *impasse* be more painful.

It remains in doubt as to whether those populations will continue to act as a damper or as an explosive source of economic growth and consumption as they climb out of poverty. Subsequent generations of industrialising nations would then be unlikely to have as dramatic an impact on the global economy, which would be approaching its peak rate of growth.

In these circumstances, with markets already largely global, free trade could no longer be relied on to produce ever bigger markets. For the already rich nations this may not be as great a problem as feared. Economic growth and increases in average incomes appear to make little contribution to social wellbeing (Wilkinson & Pickett 2009: 15). Moreover, as Keynes himself had believed, the continued pursuit of growth at all costs through the exercise of free trade between nations, with one nation seeking to take advantage of another, could well have a more belligerent outcome (Keynes 1936: 381–2).

Despite all these problems and disbenefits, current economic orthodoxy requires the continued pursuit of economic growth through unregulated markets. Firms are led to reject the adoption of any social responsibility other than making money for shareholders. Thus, firms are persuaded to neglect all other stakeholder interests wherever possible, including the local community and the environment. They therefore contribute, without restraint, to the careless depletion of finite resources and pollution of all kinds.

The pursuit of growth is therefore likely, in due course, to be self-defeating. An alternative goal needs to encompass the ideas of sustainability and stability, concepts which are not commensurate with the notion of an economic man seeking to maximise his own utility by whatever legal means are available.

The Amoral Externalising Machine

Chomsky referred to 'the corporation' as a great, amoral, externalising machine and its first regulatory body, its board of directors, as an unaccountable tyranny. By externalising is meant the avoidance, wherever possible, of compensating any costs which arise external to the corporation as a result of its activities or existence. The prime example of such an externality is pollution. Since industrialisation started, firms have polluted the atmosphere, the ground and water, and generally managed to avoid compensation to society for that pollution. When the costs of cleaning up or of operating with clean processes can be avoided, in most cases firms will avoid them. According to the free market ideology, it is the duty of corporate officials to accept no social responsibilities beyond making money for shareholders. Paying for externalities is one such social responsibility.

Critical resources that are being depleted at an unsustainable rate tend also to be undervalued by the market, unless they become subject to a speculation. The market systematically undervalues such resources because its focus is short term. Undervaluation of key resources is also an external cost of industrial operations which will need to be compensated in due course.

The ideology decrees that the sole test to which firms should submit is the one of legality. If costs can be legally avoided then corporate officials should ensure they do so. The onus is therefore on society, and its government, to ensure regulations are such that firms cannot avoid compensating those externalities for which they are responsible. The argument might be taken further, that firms should overcompensate in order to finance the development of sustainable processes which would eliminate all such future externalities.

The pursuit of economic growth by these amoral, externalising machines produces the result in terms of resource depletion, pollution and climate change that have already been noted. The unaccountable tyrannies are held to do no more. The boards of directors are led, by the dominant ideology, to believe that they must act in the best interests of their shareholders and not make choices on the basis of their personal values or predilections. Company directors, like everyone else, have it in them, as Chomsky has said, to be saints or to be gas chamber attendants. We are all corruptible, not least by a persuasive economic theory.

Degrees of Inequality

Economic progress has always had the tendency to magnify inequalities between the rich and poor, the employers and employed and between the providers of capital and providers of labour. These inequalities were accepted by some to be a necessary component of industrialisation and elaborate philosophical arguments were raised for their justification. Inequalities became so extreme in the nineteenth century that they motivated protective legislation, regulating working hours and conditions, as well as the rights of workers to combine in their own defence. They also motivated the Communist Manifesto and subsequent revolutions.

The twentieth century saw a move to a more equitable distribution of income and wealth, coincident with two world wars which forced recognition of the fact that all people are truly interdependent. However, since the 1980s, extremes of inequality have again been experienced, as suggested by the quote from the late Tony Judt at the start of this Part: 'Something is profoundly wrong with the way we live today…'

The maximising of material self-interest is fundamental to neoclassical ideology and the pursuit of economic growth. It seeks to minimise payment of taxation and exclude wherever possible any government regulation and control aimed at inhibiting the strong from exploiting the weak. It rejects anything which might have the effect of redistributing income and wealth on a more equitable basis, both within economies and between them. The degrees of inequality between nations will increase as a result of resource depletion, pollution and global warming since it is the poorer nations that will be on the brunt end of such effects.

Up to now, neoclassical dogma has succeeded in frustrating attempts to replace the amoral pursuit of money, with a search for fairness and equity. However, with empirical evidence of its error continually mounting, such initiatives may become irresistible.

Wilkinson and Pickett (2009) showed how dysfunctional inequality can be, not just for its victims but for whole populations: 'Most of the important health and social problems of the rich world are more common in unequal societies'. For example, if a country has relatively poor physical health and life expectancy, it is likely also to experience more teenage pregnancies, larger prison populations, more obesity, lower literacy scores, worse mental health and a bigger problem with antisocial behaviour and violence. The differences, which relate to whole populations not just disadvantaged groups within populations, are substantial, with between three and ten times more problems in unequal societies such as the US and the UK in particular, compared with more equal societies such as Japan and Scandinavia.

Wilkinson and Pickett's research has been subject to much scrutiny and some criticism has been offered. Surveys of statistical data can always be readily challenged by selection of particular statistics which offer a counter-argument. However, the breadth and depth of their work makes it difficult to challenge on anything other than a trivial basis. The broad picture they present seems incontrovertible.

It may not be immediately obvious why these adverse effects of inequality impact on the whole population, including the rich. It might be a simple matter for the rich to insulate themselves entirely. Such insulation was no doubt in Drucker's thoughts when he suggested that top executives could not even imagine the hatred, contempt and fury with which they were regarded for paying themselves exorbitant salaries (Drucker was referring to salaries in excess of 20 times the average). But Drucker may have been mistaken: those top executives, some now paying themselves in excess of 300 times, may have been able to imagine the hatred and contempt only too well. This accords with the rising levels of anxiety experienced in more unequal societies that Wilkinson and Pickett noted, the anxieties particularly relating to how we are seen and how others think of us. It accords also with Adam Smith's suggestion that our highest level of motivation is to become a 'proper object of respect ... among our equals'.

The level of stress arising from this assessment of our worth, both self-assessment and assessment by our peers, has risen markedly over the past few decades as inequality has increased. There is a natural desire to make the social assessment and our own self-assessment consistent, which adds pressure to promote ourselves as being worthy of that respect. Self-promotion has therefore replaced self-deprecation and modesty, and this adds further to the stressfulness of living in the more unequal societies:

> *The best way of responding to the harm done by high levels of inequality is to reduce inequality itself. Rather than requiring anti-anxiety drugs in the water supply or mass psychotherapy, what is most exciting about the picture we present is that it shows that reducing inequality would increase the wellbeing and quality of life of all of us. Far from being inevitable and unstoppable, the sense of deterioration in social wellbeing and the quality of social relations in society is reversible. Understanding the effects of inequality means that we suddenly have a policy handle on the wellbeing of whole societies. (Wilkinson & Picket 2009: 33)*

In advanced economies, increasing levels of affluence and the usually concomitant increasing inequality has resulted in reducing 'quality of life' measures. This paradox is not open to analysis by purely quantitative methods. Skidelsky's revisitation of Keynes considers possible responses. Keynes himself side-stepped this problem by suggesting quantitative measures were appropriate till such time as 'abundance reigned', when ethical or 'quality-of-life values could come to the fore' (Skidelsky 2009: 140).

For most economists, including Keynes, the sole purpose of industry and business was to create that abundance, such activity not being recognised as having any intrinsic merit. Consequently, for them industrial life had the effect of teaching society to value love of money above any measures of what has been described as 'love of goodness'. Manufacture was the way to achieve both money and love of money, but the possibility that it might provide opportunities for satisfying any higher level motivations is not accommodated, or even understood, within economic theory.

Within management theory, McGregor's human side of enterprise (McGregor 1960) has long been recognised as a potential source of individual and social fulfilment, not just for senior people within the enterprise but for people at all levels of organisation. Work can be fulfilling in the same way as art, sport or leisure and can provide opportunities for personal development which far exceed those available in other aspects of life. This potential value of working in a modern firm is entirely overlooked by all economists, and especially the dominant ideology with its dismal assessments and presumptions.

The Challenge to Ideology

Since the Second World War the freeing of international markets has stimulated economic growth. But with fewer substantial markets remaining to be opened up, the benefits from further deregulation and market freedom are declining. Moreover, the gains to be achieved from increasing regulation to ensure security and sustainability are likely to be substantial.

As with domestic markets, if one competitor establishes a competitive advantage over the rest, that first step would tend to lead towards monopoly. The only thing that would stop a monopolistic position being achieved would be some form of preventive external regulation or control. In international markets the free market process is apparent with the advance of China becoming increasingly dominant as the workshop of the world, replacing manufacturing operations in advanced economies. China's progress will result in it becoming a global manufacturing monopolist, unless inhibited by external regulation and control, either on an international basis or state by state.

It remains true that increasing regulation and control limits the size of markets. In particular, restricting a market to its domestic competitors, rather than opening it up to international competition, limits the division of labour and application of specialised capital, as Keynes acknowledged in the concluding notes of *The General Theory*. Writing at the time between two world wars, he recognised the possibility of international conflict arising from economic causes, 'the pressure of population and the competitive struggle for markets' (Keynes 1936: 381). That competitive struggle might be limited if 'nations can learn to provide themselves with full employment by their domestic policy' (Ibid: 382).

Thus, in traditional markets, even without having regard to resource depletion and pollution, there is a growing need to regulate international trade in order to maintain some degree of competition and so preserve domestic employment levels. The necessity to ensure economic activity is also sustainable, makes regulation and control of traditional markets increasingly necessary, to inhibit the polluter and assist the development of sustainable technology.

The case for regulation of speculative market activity is even more apparent. The original aim of trading in derivative products was to reduce the risk involved in frontline investment and so encourage additional investors to share the risk and returns. But, as has been amply demonstrated, there are limits to the extent of risk reduction that can be achieved. Moreover, the belief of advanced mathematicians that risk and uncertainty could be calculated away has been shown to be at best naïve, at worst deliberately corrupt.

Speculative trading remains risky and therefore lucrative. In the absence of regulation, that riskiness has in practice been underwritten by the taxpayer. Speculative trading, in the absence of any social value, is difficult to justify except on the basis of a crude neoclassical ideology. In the absence of prohibition, speculative trades require regulation to ensure, at the least, that traders are both risk takers and risk bearers. Its reduction, where no social value exists, would benefit the real economies it feeds off and reduce activity in those world financial centres which have become too big to be fully underwritten as well as too big to be allowed to collapse. Some regulation and control of markets will be essential to a sustainable future rather than maintaining the dominance of the neoclassical dogma.

The real source of economic progress and employment is the traditional firm. It is the firm that has produced the affluent society while depleting earth's resources, polluting and damaging the climate. And the firm is the means by which all these problems can be targeted as opportunities for the development of new technologies, systems and products. It provides employment, distributes income and provides opportunities for personal and social satisfactions, and helps shape working lives and the way people interact with their fellow human beings.

Firms, and human behaviour in them, have been studied over the past hundred years and understanding has consequently increased. Work in firms can be so organised that it will satisfy the intrinsic needs of people with benefit for all stakeholders and the long term prosperity of the firm itself.

The economic dogma does not address any very satisfactory personal objective beyond the pursuit of growth and self-interest. If continued growth is becoming unsustainable then the last justification for the self-interest, maximising economic man – that it benefits the economy as a whole through its achievement of growth – becomes irrelevant as well as untrue. Moreover, maximising self-interest, while it can never be satisfied at an individual level, will in the macro be self-defeating. Dedication to the pursuit of money may consume the individual while never providing satisfaction, but still earning the 'hatred and contempt' of their peers.

Now when relative abundance reigns in the developed world, a different, less dismal pursuit might seem more relevant. One such might be the reduction of inequality, as suggested by Wilkinson and Pickett. This is argued not from a moralistic perspective, but from the study of different social measures which suffer as a result of increasing inequality. Other alternatives are not difficult to propose which might appeal to the more public spirited or generous aspects of human nature.

Economic theory ignores any such human motivations, making the reductionist assumption that they are simply irrational, while political science might pigeonhole them as being from the left of the political divide and therefore leading to totalitarian collective socialism. Nevertheless, such human motivations persist and are amply demonstrated every time the world is subject to any human disaster.

The challenge to people is how the public spirit and generosity which is present in the majority, but corrupted by neoclassical dogma, can be made to prevail over the self-interest maximising behaviour of economic men, without the debate becoming left against right, socialism against capitalism, and the basic thrust being clouded with all the political baggage that typically accompanies such dichotomies.

Sustainability

The issues briefly referred to in this chapter coalesce around the idea of sustainability. The external costs of economic activity, currently being incurred but not paid for, are unsustainable. Rates of pollution, including greenhouse gas production, of resource depletion, especially food, oil and water, driven by the continuing pursuit of increasing affluence for an increasing global population, are all unsustainable. Moreover, so is the continually widening inequality which results from this manic pursuit of economic growth. So, in the end, is population growth itself. At some stage, as is becoming increasingly clear, ways round all these unsustainabilities will have to be found and implemented.

That realisation is no longer new. Children are taught it at primary school. Self-interest, maximising economic man and finite earth are increasingly understood to be on a collision course. The idea of sustainability is gathering momentum and may become a world changing 'megatrend' which radically alters practice and finally will also change the underlying theory as new realities are incorporated.

So far as practice is concerned, corporate investment in clean technology was, by 2008, approaching $9billion dollars a year, with G20 governments planning some $400 billion of their stimulus funds to be invested in clean technology and sustainability programs (Lubin & Esty 2010: 42–50). Growing awareness of the need for sustainability is accompanied by a continually increasing capability to monitor accurately how businesses perform in this area and to measure the external costs they incur and to pay for them.

The former asbestos companies provide an earlier example of this process and its outcome. The leading companies were aware of the dangers of asbestos. British factory regulations, regarding allowable asbestos dust levels, were based on research carried out by Turner & Newall Ltd, the leading British asbestos firm. Industry participants were the experts in all aspects of asbestos. Nevertheless, the industry did not exploit its expertise to ensure the safety of its various stakeholders, and responded only slowly to the increasing awareness of the health impacts. In some cases operations were carried on, regardless of consequences, for as long as they were allowed. In due course, the reputation of the major operators was destroyed and the cost of compensating the damage they had caused bankrupted the industry.

While asbestos had a particular virulence, the impact of industry as a whole on the earth's climate is a far more serious proposition with almost every industrial sector producing some externalities in which they are expert and will in due course be held responsible as monitoring becomes more accurate. Companies and their leaders are increasingly assessed on their longer term impact on the general wellbeing, so that:

> *Selling a simple cup of coffee, for example, already requires much more*
> *knowledge than how to brew and serve it. Where was the coffee grown,*
> *under what labour conditions, and with what pesticides? Is the cup*
> *made from recycled paper, and how many trees were cut down and*
> *how much water was used to manufacture it? Does the plastic lid leak*
> *toxins, and does it snap shut well enough to prevent burns from spills?*
> *(Kanter 2010: 42)*

On a different plane, it has been estimated that if food waste was eliminated in the United States it would pay for American automobiles' consumption of petroleum. Such startling statistics are continually being published and will eventually have practical effect.

The idea of sustainability will have real impact when it is seen to be a big influence on how firms develop, when employees who are the source of a firm's intellectual capital understand the business context and its future impacts. It is not so much about operating within constraints, but grasping the opportunities its imperatives present.

The broader perspective presented by concern for sustainability provides the opportunity for a reappraisal of the progress man has made over the past 250 years, with the vastly improved levels of affluence but the threat to earth's finite capacities. The dominant criteria of the industrial past, productivity, profit and shareholder value will need to be restrained by the more personal Theory Y type criteria which encourage the creativity and innovation which will be of greatest importance to a sustainable future.

Conclusions

It is a relatively recent realisation that we may be reaching the limits of growth and that therefore the thrust of orthodox economics has to be refocused on different targets. Maximising self-interest, a shabby and dismal target as well as being self-defeating, has led to this dead end. Maximisation itself can only lead to dead ends and impoverishment. An alternative of satisficing in the balanced interests of all stakeholders, including the environment, will be essential for the long term security of the planet.

Balancing the interests of all stakeholders is clearly inconsistent with the neoclassical dogma by which we are currently ruled. It is in part motivated by the realisation of our vulnerability to inequality, and how that vulnerability is magnified by the particular problems now confronting the world, and their highly inequitable distribution. The benefits from resolving those inequalities would be similarly magnified.

The key to balancing stakeholder interests, and to overcoming the worst excesses of inequality, would be the pursuit of sustainability for its own sake and for the sake of the planet. In this the whole human race shares an interest. Sustainability, rather than economic growth, must become the strategic aim of future businesses and of economies as a whole.

Philosophical concerns with the ultimate fulfilment of human purpose can be postponed for the foreseeable future. There is sufficient to be getting on with in terms of sustaining existence within the constraints of finite earth, and doing so with efficiency and fairness both within and between generations and nations.

Such a revised context, if it were achieved, would require systems of corporate governance to take account of the broader accountabilities and responsibilities of industrial management. The following chapters briefly describe systems of governance which are currently operational and suggest the critical characteristics of a sustainable governance framework.

References

Kanter, R.M., (2010), It's time to take full responsibility, *Harvard Business Review*, vol. 88, no. 10.

Keynes, J.M., (1931), *Collected Writings*, vol. ix, *Essays in Persuasion*, London: Macmillan.

Keynes, J.M., (1936), *The General Theory of Employment Interest and Money*, London: Macmillan.

Lubin, D.A. & Esty, D.C., (2010), The sustainability imperative, *Harvard Business Review*, vol. 88, no. 5, 42–50.

McGregor, D., (1960), *The Human Side of Enterprise*, New York: McGraw Hill.

Schumacher, E.F., (1973), *Small is Beautiful: A Study of Economics as if People Mattered*, London: Blond & Briggs.

Skidelsky, R., (2009), *Keynes: The Return of the Master*, London: Allen Lane.

Wells, S., (2010), *Pandora's Seed: The Unforeseen Cost of Civilisation*, London: Allen Lane.

Wilkinson, R. & Pickett, K., (2009), *The Spirit Level: Why More Equal Societies Almost Always Do Better*, London: Allen Lane.

PART III
Corporate Governance and Accountability

Few trends could so thoroughly undermine the very foundations of our free society than the acceptance by corporate officials of a social responsibility other than to make as much money for their stockholders as possible. (Friedman, 1962: 133)

A corporation is simply an artificial legal structure ... it's neither moral or immoral. It's simply what it is. But the people who are engaged in it ... they all have moral responsibilities. (Freidman 2003)

Part I indicated some of the errors, omissions and lunacy in neoclassical economic theory's explanation of a modern industrialised economy, its markets, firms and people. Despite its striking inadequacies in description and prediction, the neoclassical dogma is still dominant in the Anglo-American economies. Part II then briefly described some important aspects of the real economic context as we currently understand it. Industrial activity, extraction, manufacture and distribution, coerced by the bad theory referred to in Part I, has abused earth's finite capacities in the pursuit of economic growth and has not paid the cost of that abuse. The ultimate risk is that life on earth will be damaged and could even be brought to a premature end. While it is industrial activity that has achieved this jeopardy, it will be through industry that an alternative future might be accomplished.

Achieving that alternative will require industrial companies to adopt objectives and practices which are significantly different from those required by neoclassical dogma. Such a fundamental change would depend on the direction and control of industrial companies, that is, their governance.

Responsibility for corporate governance has been defined by company law, albeit inadequately, since joint stock companies first came into existence.

The legal status of companies and the duties and accountabilities of company directors, as well as the various limitations on their activity and discretion, have all been specified by law since the first British Companies Act of 1844. The example of that and subsequent Acts has been widely followed in the English speaking world and beyond. However, custom and practice often departs from the strict legal requirements, and these departures differ in different parts of the world.

The custom and practice of corporate governance in Britain, the United States, Japan, Germany, China and India are briefly reviewed in this Part. These six nations suggest a wide variety of approaches to governance, partly the differences being particular to the national identities but also, it appears, partly as a result of the individual nation's stage of economic development.

The idea of the product or industry life cycle is a commonly used tool in corporate analysis, but might be equally applicable to whole economies. The idealised life cycle curve depicts four distinct stages of development: start up, growth, maturity and decline. The early stages are slow with, typically in the case of product life cycles, many false starts. But once commitment to a particular approach reaches a critical mass, then growth takes off. During this growth phase innovation dominates, with new technologies applied to produce genuinely new products with more features and better performance, and participants in the industry focus all their development efforts on producing the latest and best technology. In due course, generally accepted standards of performance for the product emerge as the industry moves into the slower growth mature phase. During this critical transition to maturity there will be a radical reassessment of growth projections and fierce competition will force weaker competitors to close or withdraw.

During the ensuing, relatively stable mature phase, the emphasis of innovation tends to move from product to production process, where innovations are largely aimed at reducing costs and improving efficiency. For some industries the mature phase may last a long time: several decades, even centuries, or more. The mature phase comes to an end when either a completely new technology takes over or some other structural change eliminates the existing business. Again the reduction in expectations of future growth will be accompanied by increased price competition which forces the marginal businesses to be eliminated through either closure or amalgamation.

These transitional changes, from growth to maturity, and maturity to decline are notoriously difficult to predict. Extrapolating the existing state of affairs is much simpler and within the reach of most forecasting models. Even when the transitions occur they may still be denied as a 'blip', rather than a permanent adjustment, till long after the change has become firmly established.

While life cycle models were used primarily for the analysis of products and industries, its application to economies appears instructive. All the basic system characteristics appear to apply without problem. The jurisdictions that have been chosen in this Part to illustrate alternative approaches to corporate governance are readily applicable to different stages of the economy life cycle.

Britain, being the first industrialiser, has for long been in the stage of decline relative to other economies. In 1914 Britain owned 45 per cent of the world's foreign direct investment, but has been in decline ever since and now has less than 10 per cent. America's share of foreign direct investment peaked at 50 per cent in 1967 and is now less than half that. Today China, including Hong Kong and Macau, has a share of just 6 per cent, but is growing fast. American manufacturing productivity gains also started to decline during the 1960s, averaging 2.8 per cent per annum through the 1960s and 70s, well behind other manufacturing economies such as Germany with 5.4 per cent and Japan with 8.2 per cent. American R&D expenditures started to decline in the mid-1960s as management turned their attention from strategic investments on to tight short term, low risk quick payback projects (Hayes & Abernathy 1980).

Manufacturing in Britain has for decades been a declining proportion of GDP as successive governments have looked, in accord with neoclassical dogma, to the financial sector as their salvation. Successive governments have focused on satisfying the needs and wants of the City of London, rather than the real economy. The result has been that the financial sector has grown disproportionately large, has become 'too big to fail', and has become the dominant factor in government economic thinking. Thus, Britain has clearly become a post-industrial economy.

Though the United States remains the world's biggest economy and leading manufacturer, its shift of focus is clear. Its industrial decline relative to the industrial and industrialising economies is accompanied by its refocusing on finance. From Reagan on, successive administrations have been dominated more by the interests of Wall Street than General Motors. The infiltration by Goldman Sachs alumni in US government, the Federal Reserve and NGOs as well as international bodies such as the WTO and IMF, is widely documented and has drawn attention to the extent to which the real economy has been overtaken by the financial speculative sector. In some areas the decline in manufacture and distribution is absolute, with consequent long term impact on diverse employment. These are the characteristics of a post-industrial economy.

Post-industrial economies appear inevitably to experience an explosion in inequality, originating in the new-found dominance of the financial sector. This is a new experience, more pervasive and extreme than the inequalities perpetrated by the robber barons of the late nineteenth century. So far it has benefited from massive lobby investment, supporting the status quo. How stable it will prove to be remains to be seen.

Japan and Germany have the characteristics of those still with a focus on the real economy, manufacturing and distributing physical products, concerned to maintain their position in terms of industrial, rather than purely financial, criteria. China and India are still in the relatively early stages of their industrial development.

The company or firm is established as a legal entity in all significant jurisdictions, with the almost universal legal requirement that industrial companies must be governed for the common good as well as their immediate stakeholders. The firm is controlled by its board of directors whose freedom of action is not only limited by the law, but is heavily influenced by economic ideology as well as the custom and practice of their particular jurisdiction.

The company is, of course, not itself a moral entity. Actions taken on its behalf without moral constraint would result, for example, in avoidance of payment for as many of its real costs as possible, including the externalities referred to in the previous chapter. De George (1993) argued that the corporation could only be as moral as the people controlling it and they, like everyone else, have it in them to be saints or sinners and almost without exception are corruptible.

The practice of governance is thus shaped by national economic positioning, national history and culture, the prevailing ideology and the law plus the integrity and personal values of those controlling and directing the firm. Their interests might well go beyond those of the shareholder, to include concerns for employees, the community and the environment.

Issues of corporate social responsibility and business ethics cannot be legislated. Good practices may be followed by those who are so inclined, but rejected by those who are not. The integrity of company directors determines the impact of such initiatives, whether they are real or merely window-dressing. That integrity may frequently be compromised by the dictates of neoclassical ideology requiring all other stakeholder interests to be sacrificed for the gain of shareholders.

The following chapters discuss various approaches to governance, how they define and confront problems and the various solutions that have emerged in different jurisdictions with different cultures and histories, some of which are not yet so dominated by the neoclassical free market ideology. In a globalising world the direction of harmonisation appears so far to be generally towards the neoclassical solution, but consolidation on that norm is by no means inevitable. Different solutions may be more likely to provide the means to a more equitable and sustainable future.

References

De George, R.T., (1993), *Competing with Integrity in International Business*, New York: Oxford University Press.

Friedman, M., (1962), *Capitalism and Freedom*, Chicago: University of Chicago Press.

Friedman, M., (2003), Extracted from interview with M. Achbar, J. Abbott & J. Bakan *The Corporation*. (see www.thecorporation.com based on *The Corporation: The Pathological Pursuit of Profit and Power*, New York: Free Press and associated video film.)

Hayes, R.H. & Abernathy, W.J., (1980), Managing our way to economic decline, *Harvard Business Review*, (July-August) pp. 138–149.

6

Governance in Post-Industrial Economies

The industrial entrepreneur is the governance ideal, combining management responsibility with ownership, taking operational decisions and carrying the financial risk. The advent of big business separated shareholding from management control and drew attention to the question of corporate governance. It has been seen as particularly pertinent in the Anglo-American jurisdictions dominated by the neoclassical ideology with its focus on shareholder interests.

The dogma holds that it is shareholders who undertake the heroic role of risk taking with their own money. However, provision of finance is not restricted to shareholders. They provide permanent equity capital, but the banks typically provide working capital in the form of overdraft or longer term debt, and bonds or loan stock is issued with fixed and preferential returns attached. All these provide capital and incur some of the risk undertaken by the company.

Moreover, the directors and managers of the company also share in the riskiness of the enterprise. Though they may not put up their own money, they devote their working lives to it and, if the business fails, they too suffer loss, personal as well as financial. The welfare of other employees in the company is similarly at risk should the company fail. Moreover, these last, being on less secure employment terms, are at higher levels of risk than the managers and directors.

The risks incurred by stakeholders other than shareholders is most apparent in the post-industrial economies such as Britain and the United States, where, at least partly because of the dominance of neoclassical dogma, large-scale manufacturing is in decline, with a permanent loss of traditional employment. At the macro level this decline is partly compensated by the burgeoning financial-speculative sectors which however provide neither employment nor investment in the real economy.

The company also has important interactions with various other external bodies: customers, suppliers, national and local government, the tax authorities, possibly research institutions and, certainly, the local community and the physical environment. None of these interactions is risk-free, and most of them involve aspects of commitment beyond the solely financial, which is the only dimension that neoclassical theory accommodates.

Corporate governance is concerned with the direction, management and control of all these interactions and relationships, rather than simply the relations between the directors of the company and its shareholders.

Governance Defined

The British Cadbury Report on governance, published in 1992, provided an early definition, though it was acknowledged to be focusing solely on the financial aspects:

> *Corporate governance is the system by which companies are directed and controlled. Boards of directors are responsible for the governance of their companies. The shareholders' role in governance is to appoint the directors and the auditors and to satisfy themselves that an appropriate governance structure is in place. The responsibilities of the board include setting the company's strategic aims, providing the leadership to put them into effect, supervising the management of the business and reporting to shareholders on their stewardship.*

Cadbury identified four parties involved in governance: boards of directors, shareholders, auditors and management.

The neoclassical free market definition is rather different:

> *Corporate governance refers to ways of ensuring that corporate actions, agents and assets are directed at achieving the corporate objectives established by the corporation's shareholders. (Sternberg 2004: 14)*

That definition identifies just two parties: shareholders and 'corporate agents', and goes on to suggest the company objectives, which are presumably intended to mean something different from Cadbury's 'strategic aims', would be found in the company's 'Memorandum of Association or comparable constitutional document'. Elsewhere in the same text it is made clear that company objectives are assumed to be the maximising of shareholder value. However, in fact, constitutional documents rarely express objectives, merely the activities a firm could undertake. These were always widely defined so as not to limit directors' field of action. Since the Companies Act of 2006 there has been no such limit in Britain.

The duties of company directors specified in that Act are:

> *to promote the success of the company for the benefit of its members as a whole, and in doing so have regard to a) the likely consequences of any decision in the long term, b) the interests of the company's employees, c) the need to foster the company's business relationships with suppliers, customers and others, d) the impact of the company's operations on the community and the environment, e) the desirability of the company maintaining a reputation for high standards of business conduct, and f) the need to act fairly as between members of the company.*[1]

This legal specification involves a wider responsibility for governance. The requirement that directors must promote the success of the company is the key issue. It is for the benefit of all its members, that is, its shareholders, but paramount is the success of the company, and that would exclude its destruction for the benefit of its members. The secondary point, that directors have regard to the various other interests, does not require a refocusing of governance onto those other interests, merely that they must not be disregarded. This is a weak requirement which might be difficult to interpret in any particular situation. Some directors would already be minded to have that regard, while those who don't, would be enabled to disregard them with reasonable equanimity.

Other definitions of governance have proposed the prime focus should be on social responsibilities towards the community or the environment. Ted Levitt (1958), sometime editor of the *Harvard Business Review*, referred to these as making 'sweet music', and warned against management allowing itself to become distracted from the business of business.

---

1   British Companies Act 2006, Part 10, Chapter 2, paragraph 172.

While there has been some diversity of view as to the precise focus of corporate governance, there is agreement that it defines the roles different actors, always including the company directors, play in directing and controlling the company. Corporate law and neoclassical ideology have influenced, often in opposing directions, the shape and structure of corporate governance.

Governance and the Law

The primary purpose of corporate law, from 1844 onwards, is to establish the corporation as a separate legal entity, usually emphasised by its legal right to sue, and be sued, in its own name. It is brought into existence by the legal process of incorporation and can be terminated through the legal process of dissolution.

Incorporation requires the company's constitution to be formalised with details of its share capital, and broadly defining the range of the company's activities, and confirming its internal management arrangements such as the nature and frequency of general meetings at which shareholders are able to vote on specific issues.

Curiously, the voting at company general meetings has become progressively less democratic over time. In the days of the old, trading companies such as the East India Company, voting was on the basis of one member – one vote, no matter how many shares were held, with no proxy voting being permitted. In the United States democratic voting was said to be justified by the:

> American fear of unbridled power, as possessed by large landholders and dynastic wealth, as well as by government. (L.M. Friedman 1973: 168)

Such checks on the power of large shareholders were designed, as a 1766 Act of Parliament explained, to protect:

> the permanent welfare of companies' from being sacrificed to the partial and interested views of the few. (Maier 1993)

A German commentator in 1837 suggested the democratic American approach had a profound impact on the way the corporation was managed. That compared to what he referred to as the 'aristocratic' system of one share – one vote which favoured those with large holdings (Dunleavy 1998). Votes at general meetings were often taken on the basis of a show of hands, which was clearly democratic, and only if a formal poll was requested would larger shareholders gain greater influence and even that was usually limited to a graduated scale of votes per numbers of shares held.

Nevertheless, protections against the overweening power of the wealthy were gradually removed in America, and voting arrangements were tending by late nineteenth century towards one share – one vote, referred to as the plutocratic system, that is, relating to wealth rather than heredity.

In politics the movement was towards democracy, but in the corporate world the move was in the opposite direction. Between the 1840s and 1880s graduated voting scales (whereby the number of votes per share declined as the number of shares held increased, usually with a cap on the number of votes per shareholder) more or less disappeared in the United States while, at the same time, in political voting, the property qualification was being removed.

Britain moved more slowly to plutocratic voting. Voting by a show of hands at general meetings was still the norm in Britain well into the twentieth century unless a poll was requested by at least five members. The procedures for a formal poll, with or without proxy voting, were set down in the company's articles of association. By 1916 graduated voting had also more or less disappeared in Britain.

Investment banking in the United States, which had played a major role in rationalising ownership and organisation of the railway system, had, by the early twentieth century, innovated various different classes of shares, with ordinary or preferential rights, with or without voting rights. This facilitated control of companies by small groups of shareholders who might own no more than half of the voting shares (Hopt et al 1998). Control by small groups was further facilitated by the establishment of cumulative voting (votes per share times the number of directors to be elected). The intention of this system was to ensure minority representation on the board. The unforeseen consequence was to enable minority shareholders to gain control of the corporation. Thus, for all its economic leadership and exemplary political democracy, the United States harboured a corporate world which was largely undemocratic and vulnerable to fixing and minority control. From the mid-nineteenth century, voting practice in Britain generally followed that in the United States.

The legal status of employees, including managers, was defined by their contracts of employment, which often remained informal till the mid-twentieth century, and offered little security beyond what could be achieved through collectively bargained settlements. Employees had no representation at general meetings and no votes. Company directors fulfilled a dual role as employees and as agents of the company, the details of their duties and responsibilities being spelled out both in company law and more specifically in their contracts of service.

This is the position which agency theory challenged by denying the company its legal status. Jensen and Meckling's pretence that the company was a 'legal fiction', rather than a legal fact, was, and remains, the key component of the theory which then dictates that directors owe allegiance directly to shareholders with no other social responsibilities. The theory associated with the agency idea is founded on this simple falsehood. The company's true role as the principal in the principal-agent relationship with its directors is explicit in legal contracts of service and employment.

Nowhere is there a legal statute which confirms company directors as the agents of shareholders. A review of the legal position was conducted by Lan and Heracleous (2010) who quoted the one item of American case law, Dodge v Ford Motor Co. in the Supreme Court of Michigan in 1919. Ford had retained a cash dividend within the company for its future expansion and the consequent benefit of its employees. However, the judge held that the firm was not a quasi-charity, but a business, and must be managed for the benefit of shareholders, rather than any other interested parties. Lan and Heracleous (2010: 299) point out that:

> the courts have only cited this case once ... which indicates the weakness of both its precedent value and its influence on legal doctrine. Corporate law in most Anglo-American countries still confers ultimate power to directors, not shareholders ... Shareholders' rights over directors are remarkably limited in both theory and practice..

American case law is quite definitive that directors are not agents of the shareholders. Lan and Heracleous quote half a dozen key cases, the last being in 2007, which make this explicit. Directors are fiduciaries of the corporation, which is formally confirmed in the British Companies Act of 2006, requiring directors to act in good faith for the long term success of the company.

This issue is of primary importance. In particular circumstances it is decisive. If directors were the agents of shareholders they would be legally bound to put shareholder interests above all others. But American case law, as well as British statute, explicitly allows directors to favour other interests over shareholders. Lan and Heracleous refer to eight key cases confirming this right.

Company law in the United States is generally enacted in State legislation, rather than at federal level, except in exceptional circumstance such as those prompting the passage of the Sarbanes-Oxley Act in 2002. So far as the duties and responsibilities of company directors are concerned, State legislations are broadly compatible and identify the following prime duties:

> *To establish the company and ensure its continuity and to act in good faith in the best interests of the corporation and its shareholders, having regard to various other interests.*

> *Appoint a CEO and other executive directors to take responsibility for the company's administration and development.*

> *To monitor and report on the executive's performance regularly and to recommend continuation or termination of the executive's employment.*

> *Agree the company's broad policies and strategies.*

> *Agree the necessary funding arrangements to support the company's strategy.*

> *Report to the public for the financial and business performance of the company.*

A proposed amendment to state law in California required directors to have regard for the following rather broader responsibilities:

> *the effects that the corporation's actions may have in the short term or in the long term upon any of the following:*

> *The prospects for potential growth, development, productivity, and profitability of the corporation.*

> *The economy of the state and the nation.*

The corporation's employees, suppliers, customers, and creditors.

Community and societal considerations.

The environment.[2]

The alternative approach to justify shareholder primacy treats the company the same as any other item of private property, even as a 'slave', that is legally owned. However, company ownership is by no means a straightforward concept. The ownership rights attached to company shares are as confirmed on share certificates and in company constitutional documents. They are restricted to receipt of dividends and to specified voting rights at general meetings. Shareholders' liability for the company is limited to their initial investment when they purchased the share certificates. Their duties and responsibilities for the company were fully discharged on purchase. As shareholders, they owe no debt to the company, fiduciary or otherwise. The upside potential of their shares is unlimited and they may sell their shares at any time. They may also vote at general meetings entirely according to their own interest, having no responsibility for the survival and future success of the company.

Thus, they do not own the company in the usual sense of ownership, but they can get to control it through control of in excess of 50 per cent of the voting equity. That proportion of ownership grants control which is, in most practical circumstances, total and absolute, though with the privilege of limited liability. Under that circumstance, the company becomes in effect private property and its character as a legal entity in its own right ceases to be of much value. This discontinuity in ownership, with on the one hand the company being the principal in a great many critical relationships, to it becoming on the other hand a piece of private property that can be stripped and abused at will by its 'owners', occurs with the change in ownership of a very small number of shares.

In summary, the aspect of corporate governance which is covered by the law is dominated by the legalities of the relationship between the company and its shareholders. The legalities of the company's relationship with employees and other stakeholders are only briefly referred to in both American and British law. This results naturally from the fact that most such law is derived from considerations of private property and its protection. However, it provides only a limited explanation of corporate governance. The broader duties and

---

2   Assembly Bill 2944, to amend Section 309 of the California Corporations Code.

responsibilities of governance have been addressed, to some extent, in the British case by the establishment of codes of governance practice, which have attempted also to interpret the spirit of the law and to do so in ways which ensure accountability for corporate governance is both honest and transparent. Codes of practice are not legally binding, but compliance is generally required by the relevant stock exchange, or alternatively an explanation of non-compliance to be provided in the firm's annual report.

In the United States, though codes of practice have been adopted in many States, the emphasis is on compliance with the law which is more prescriptive than British legislation. However, in both jurisdictions there remains a gap between custom and practice and the formal requirements whether of law or codes of practice.

Codes of Practice

The motivation behind the development of the first code of practice, contained in the 1992 Cadbury Report, was related to the widespread abuse and fraud perpetrated by company executives during the 1980s. For example, the Guinness share trading fraud involved Ernest Saunders and other senior directors, including non-executives, trying to fix prices on the London Stock Exchange, using the good offices of American insider trader Ivan Boesky so as to reduce the cost of acquiring the Distillers Company. Other examples, referred to in the preface to Cadbury, were Maxwell and the Bank of Credit and Commerce International (BCCI) which collapsed amid revelations of extensive fraud and criminal activities involving drug dealing and money laundering.

Robert Maxwell, already once disgraced and identified by the Department of Trade and Industry inspectors as an unfit person to be a director of a British company, had revived his corporate career, but in the aftermath of his assumed suicide was found to have stolen millions of pounds from his companies and their pension funds.

The express aims of the Cadbury Code was to inhibit corporate criminality, restrain directors' pay and align directors' interests with those of their shareholders by emphasising principals of openness, integrity and accountability. It is not clear which was the more powerful motivation in drafting codes. However, while criminality and excessive directors' pay continued to expand with little restraint, codes have been more successful in persuading directors that it was their duty to focus on satisfying shareholder interests.

The Cadbury Report was narrowly focused on the Financial Aspects of Corporate Governance rather than any wider concerns. It was adopted by quoted companies on the basis of 'comply or explain', and it was rapidly followed by most advanced economies, so that there is now hardly a developed or developing nation without some explicit code of governance practice (Solomon 2007: 188).

On accountability the Cadbury report declared:

> The formal relationship between the shareholders and the board of directors is that the shareholders elect the directors, the directors report on their stewardship to the shareholders and the shareholders appoint the auditors to provide an external check on the directors' financial statements. Thus the shareholders as owners of the company elect the directors to run the business on their behalf and hold them accountable for its progress. The issue for corporate governance is how to strengthen the accountability of boards of directors to shareholders.

Thus, the agency relationship was foundational to the Cadbury code even though there was no explicit mention that 'to run the business on their behalf' meant maximising shareholder value. This is an example of how the neoclassical perspective has been adopted in preference to the law which requires directors to 'promote the success of the company'. The difference is crucial in the event of hostile takeover bids.

The details of the code itself covered arrangements for the board of directors, including the separation of the roles of chairman and chief executive, the independence of non-executive directors, limitations on the contracts of executive directors and disclosure of their pay, the establishment of a remuneration committee made up wholly or mainly of non-executive directors, arrangements for public reporting and audit and the establishment of an internal audit committee as well as relationships with shareholders.

The code largely reflected what was already widely accepted as good practice. Publicly quoted companies on the London Stock Exchange were required either to comply or to explain and justify their non-compliance. The London based Institute of Directors led objections to the code and many quoted companies opted for explanation rather than compliance, there being limited guidance as to what constituted a satisfactory explanation.

Since 1992 successive British enquiries and reports have resulted in various revisions to codes of practice, culminating in 2010 with the publication by the Financial Reporting Council (FRC) of the UK Corporate Governance Code which was developed in the light of experience during and after the 2007–8 credit crisis, which was accompanied by excessive remuneration for top managers and traders, as well as massively expensive taxpayer funded bailouts for the banking sector and 'quantitative easing' naively intended to revive the broader economy. Despite that severe learning experience, the code focused its main attention on tying the company ever tighter to its shareholders, advocating that a senior independent director should meet with major shareholders in order to gain 'a balanced understanding of the issues and concerns of major shareholders'.

The nature of shareholding has radically changed since the mid-1980s deregulation and computerisation of stack exchanges. It has become increasingly concentrated in the hands of fund managers who themselves exercise control largely without ownership. It has been estimated that institutional shareholders were responsible for less than 7 per cent of the total share value of quoted companies in Britain and the United States in 1960. By 2003 this figure had reached around 60 per cent and by 2010 was probably over 75 per cent. When shares were mainly owned by widely dispersed individualholders, who may or may not have had a long term interest in the companies in which they were invested, there was little opportunity for them to have a very active relationship with their investee companies. But that is no longer true and the stewardship role of those controlling the shareholdings has attracted increasing attention.

Of the three aims cited for the original Cadbury code, two were explicit – to inhibit corporate criminality and to address excessive boardroom pay – while one was unstated – to reinforce the neoclassical free market idea that corporate governance should focus exclusively on shareholder satisfaction. While the two explicit aims appear to have been spectacular failures, the unstated aim appears to have been achieved in that its focus has been so widely accepted. Later code amendments projected the idea of shareholder primacy above all other considerations.

With share ownership control concentrated in so relatively few hands, active share ownership is more feasible, and the 2010 FRC UK Stewardship Code provided guidance on good practice for 'firms who manage assets on behalf of institutional shareholders such as pension funds, insurance companies, investment trusts and other collective investment vehicles'.

The Stewardship Code focused on means of monitoring investee companies and to establishing 'clear guidelines on when and how they will escalate their activities as a method of protecting and enhancing shareholder value'. The aim is clearly to address 'the agency problem' of company directors not focusing exclusively on maximising shareholder value and the role institutional shareholders might play in solving the problem.

However, the real problem with this now dominant form of share ownership is that control of shares is held not by their ultimate owners, but by investment professionals and traders whose interests are in making quick money to achieve a high rating as traders, while the ultimate owners of shares, the members of pension funds and the like, may prefer stability of employment rather than, for example, a quick return from an opportunistic takeover. Stewardship codes ignore this aspect of control without ownership. They also ignore the fact that around 80 per cent of trades are now made through ultrafast automated and algorithmic trading systems with limited human involvement.

The neoclassical free market approach to governance highlighted the apparent anomaly that managements without owning companies nevertheless controlled them. However, the outcome that has so far been achieved is institutional control of shareholding without ownership. Neither of the 2010 UK codes of practice address the conflict of interest between traders controlling investment decisions and the ultimate owners of shares.

Though various codes of practice have been developed at State level in America, the emphasis has been more on the development of law as an answer to criminality. Junk bond and insider trader Milken, and loan and savings fraudster Keating topped the list of 1980s corporate criminals, while top executives at Enron, WorldCom and others have joined the list of incarcerated fraudsters. The response of the federal administration was to enact the Sarbanes-Oxley Act in 2002 which promised up to 20 years imprisonment for certain misdemeanours. While this approach appears in stark contrast with the 'comply or explain' requirement of codes of practice, the practical reality is probably less differentiated than might be expected. Compliance with the law is not simply a matter of box ticking and non-compliance is rarely straightforward to detect.

Moreover, both Sarbanes-Oxley and codes of practice are widely criticised by insiders for their imposition of additional bureaucratic overhead.

Governance Roles and Responsibilities

The real duties and responsibilities of governance extend to the company's relationships with a wide variety of internal and external stakeholders. Relations between the company and its employees, of which there are various distinctive categories, are clearly crucial to the company's survival and prosperity. So too, under particular circumstances, its relations with various external bodies might become critical to the company's survival at any time. These external stakeholders include as well as its shareholders, its customers, suppliers, bankers, other creditors, the local community, the physical environment, the tax authorities and various offices of government, as well as some possibly less direct relations with technology suppliers, research institutions, trade associations and the like. Any of these relationships could become critical to the company, and should necessarily be the concern of its governance.

DIRECTORS

While company law in both Britain and America recognises that company directors' primary duty is to the company having regard to the various stakeholder interests, in practice governance is influenced by neoclassical ideology to focus on the duties and responsibilities of company directors to the company's shareholders. The corruptive effect of this is seen when a company receives a takeover bid. Typically, the recipient company will experience a rise in its share price by something averaging around 40 per cent. To maximise shareholder value appears therefore to suggest directors have a duty to find and initiate their company being taken over. The alternative route to achieving that 40 per cent increase in value would be likely to take years and not be without risk.

Directors' legal duty requires them to focus as a board collective on the long term success of the company. But the conflict between this legal requirement and the dominant ideology confuses the proper roles of directors in governance. Directors might not pursue the neoclassical free market argument to its logical conclusion by regarding it as their duty to actively seek out takeover bids. Nevertheless, they are likely to be persuaded, as recipients of a takeover bid, to construe their duty as being to maximise the acquisition price. The result, not infrequently, is that the acquired company is then saddled with the debt raised for its acquisition and the acquiring company removes asset value from the acquired company.

Directors hold the pivotal role, executive directors responsible for company management with more or less absolute power inside the company, and non-executive directors with special responsibilities for reporting on the board's stewardship of the company. Non-executive directors, not being employees, provide two quite different inputs: the provision of special expertise not otherwise available to the company, and a monitoring role to ensure special interests, such as a large shareholder, are not overlooked.

One example of the monitoring role concerns executive remuneration. Successive codes of practice have required remuneration to be approved by a board committee led and dominated by non-executive, presumed to be independent, directors. The unintended consequence of this requirement is that a cartel of interrelated directorships has dominated remuneration committees. They have sought to ensure that no company falls behind in terms of remuneration and therefore unable to attract 'talent'. Far from ensuring directors do not pay themselves too much, the remuneration committee process has ensured that executive remuneration has advanced rapidly across the corporate sector.

The UK Corporate Governance Code requires the board to 'present a balanced and understandable assessment of the company's position and prospects', and to establish an audit committee of 'independent non-executive directors', at least one of whom should have 'recent and relevant financial experience'.

In the United States accountability practice is determined by law and was most recently strengthened by the Sarbanes-Oxley Act which was the federal response to the corrupt practices revealed by the Enron fraud, which among other things resulted in the demise of big five auditor Arthur Anderson.

Sarbanes-Oxley requires financial statements to be accurate, not to contain false information or omit material information, specifically including information on all material off-balance sheet liabilities, obligations or transactions. The act imposes penalties for transgression of fines and/or up to 20 years imprisonment.

SHAREHOLDERS

The role of shareholders in corporate governance is as laid down in a firm's constitutional documents. Generally, they are required to approve certain corporate decisions such as the appointment of directors, auditors and other senior posts in company general meetings. Also they have the right to raise issues and make proposals at company general meetings and to vote in general meetings. The nature of their ownership role has already been briefly discussed.

AUDITORS

In Britain professionally qualified auditors are appointed by the board and approved by shareholders. Their role is to certify the truth and fairness of financial statements issued by the board. The audit committee is responsible for monitoring the integrity of the company's financial statements, reviewing the company's internal financial controls and its internal audit function and recommends appointment and remuneration of external auditors. Additionally, it reviews the external auditors' independence and the effectiveness of the audit process and develops a policy regarding non-audit services supplied by the external auditors.

It is open to boards of directors to comply or explain, and in particular to comply with the supposed spirit of the code. But it is customary practice for the supposed 'independent' non-executive directors to be executive directors of other companies and their 'independence' to be a somewhat elusive characteristic. Moreover, the provision by auditors of non-audit consultancy, a multi-billion pound business, would clearly compromise the auditor's independence, but the code does not suggest companies should not use their auditors for non-audit consultancy, merely have a relevant policy to address such an obvious conflict of interest.

In the United States a parallel requirement is imposed by Sarbanes-Oxley which also increased the accountability of auditing firms to remain objective and independent of their clients.

MANAGEMENT

With governance practice, in both Britain and America, being focused exclusively on the relationship between directors and shareholders, management is in effect the operational wing of the executive directorate. The neoclassical ideology has destroyed good management practice, resulting in the bottom line and shareholder fixation characterised by Ghoshal as quoted in the preface to this text. Thus, management is focused on deal making, outsourcing, mergers and acquisitions, and is largely unrelated to the real business of employees, customers, technologies and suppliers.

This has impacted on the public sector also, where attempts have been made to force managers to provide value and choice where no market exists and where creating a replica of market condition generally fails to produce real competition and frequently results in massive bureaucratic overheads.

EMPLOYEES

Within the British and American jurisdictions, employees, other than directors, are recruited and retained under specific terms and have no explicit role in governance. They are nevertheless clearly crucial to the firm's success, more so today than ever as intellectual capital continues to grow in importance. The employees' role is to fulfil the terms of their employment contract. Beyond this, they have the right to withdraw co-operation and labour. Otherwise, they are no concern of Anglo-American corporate governance.

EXTERNAL STAKEHOLDERS

External stakeholders other than shareholders have no explicit role in governance. The company's responsibility to external stakeholders is simply to fulfil any contractual obligations and in general to operate within the law. External stakeholders have no responsibility to, or for, the company.

Conclusions

Company directors' legal responsibilities, in both the United States and Britain, are to ensure the long term success of the company and to have regard to the interests of all stakeholders, making sure the stewardship is exercised and reported truthfully and fairly. However, this legally defined approach has been increasingly dominated by custom and practice focused exclusively on shareholder interests.

A measure of how that ideology has increased its domination is illustrated by the American Business Roundtable: An Association of Chief Executive

Officers Committed to Improving Public Policy. Its 1990 Statement on Corporate Governance and American Competitiveness included the following:

> *Corporations are chartered to serve both their shareholders and society as a whole. ... a corporation's stakeholders beyond the shareholder ... are vital to the long term successful economic performance of the corporation ... The thrust of history and law strongly supports the broader view of the directors' responsibility to carefully weight the interests of all stakeholders as part of their responsibility to the corporation. (Khurana 2007: 320)*

By 1997 the Business Roundtable's position had changed somewhat as reflected in its revised Statement on Corporate Governance:

> *the paramount duty of management and boards of directors is to the corporation's stockholders ... The notion that the board must somehow balance the interests of stakeholders fundamentally misconstrues the role of directors. It is, moreover, an unworkable notion because it would leave the board with no criterion for resolving conflicts between interests of stockholders and of other stakeholders or among different groups of stakeholders. (Ibid: 321)*

The earlier commitment of the Business Roundtable became 'unworkable' as the neoclassical ideology tightened its grip in America. Balancing the interests of all stakeholders was something directors and managements across the globe had been working to for generations. But it simply did not accord with the dogma.

In Britain both the Confederation of British Industry (CBI) and the Institute of Directors (IoD) confirm their commitment to shareholder primacy, though perhaps with less conviction than the Business Roundtable. The IoD has expressed the view that the emphasis on maximising shareholder value has perhaps been taken too far.

The corporation as a social organisation with various different, potentially competing, actors working within it is now largely ignored as an aspect of ideologically driven governance both in Britain and the United States. It is open to conjecture whether this focus of Anglo-American governance is rooted in the post-industrial stage of economic development that both jurisdictions clearly exhibit. Or if the adoption of neoclassically determined governance has resulted in the exhibition of post-industrial symptoms.

Over the long term, companies are only likely to be successful if the various actors work in broad co-operation with each other. Shareholders, being external to that social organisation, can only make a peripheral contribution to the corporation's success. In other jurisdictions this external relationship appears to be recognised and addressed with some advantage, as discussed in the following chapters.

References

Dunleavy, C.A., (1998), Corporate governance in late 19th Century Europe and the United States: the case of shareholder voting rights, in Hopt, K., et al, (eds) (1998), *Comparitive Corporate Governance*, Oxford: Oxford University Press, p. 15.

Friedman, L.M., (1973), *A History of American Law*, New York: Simon & Schuster Touchstone.

Hopt, K.J., Kanda, H., Roe, M.J., Wymeersch, E. & Prigge, S., (1998), *Comparative Corporate Governance – the State of the Art and Emerging Research*, Oxford: Oxford University Press.

Khurana, R., (2007), *From Higher Aims to Hired Hands*, Princeton: Princeton University Press.

Lan, L.L. & Heracleous, L., (2010), Rethinking agency theory: the view from law, *Academy of Management Review*, vol. 35, no. 2, 294–314.

Levitt, T., (1958), The dangers of social responsibility, *Harvard Business Review*, September-October.

Maier, P., (1993), The revolutionary origins of the american corporation, *William and Mary Quarterly*, 3rd Ser., 51–84.

Solomon, J., (2007), *Corporate Governance and Accountability*, Chichester: John Wiley & Son.

Sternberg, E., (2004), *Corporate Governance: Accountability in the Marketplace*, The Institute of Economic Affairs.

7

Governance in Industrial Economies

The last few years have witnessed a marked upsurge of interest in the subject of corporate governance in both Britain and the USA. At least three related developments have contributed to this. First, there is widespread unease about the damaging long term results from which is now considered to be an excessive level of takeover activity during 1985–9, often financed by imprudent amounts of debt. Second, the pay levels of senior executive directors in general, and chairmen and chief executives in particular, has far too often risen to excessive levels when related to performance. Not infrequently it has been inversely related. Third, and most important of all, there has been a growing perception that British and US corporations, particularly in the manufacturing, high technology, and construction industries, are increasingly uncompetitive with most of their main rivals in Western Europe (as typified by Germany) and in the Far East and South East Asia (as typified by Japan). (Sykes 1994: 111–112)

Neoclassical free market ideas have shaped Anglo-American governance, which serves as a model against which other governance approaches are commonly assessed. Moreover, the harmonisation of international standards, for example, in corporate law and accounting practice, has tended to develop in the direction of the Anglo-American approach. It is dominant in the English language literature on corporate governance. It has served firms in speculative markets well, and appears to have enabled rapid development of the global economy. However, it also leads to the various externality problems outlined in Part II, as well as producing inevitably bursting speculative bubbles. Nevertheless, the direction of harmonisation seems clear, despite other governance possibilities being apparent.

Governance in both Japan and Germany has remained distinctive, both being thoughtful and perhaps indecisive in adopting neoclassical norms. Both Japan and Germany developed successful real economy sectors, notably in manufacturing, success which they were careful not to undermine. However, their financial sectors, especially in Germany, remained relatively underdeveloped by comparison with financial sectors in the post industrial economies. Approaches to corporate governance are receiving much attention and the future direction of any moves to international harmonisation is being carefully considered.

The post-Second World War recovery of both German and Japanese economies was driven by successful manufacturing industries. Now, the newly industrialising nations of China, India, Brazil and others are taking leading workshop roles in the world economy. In contrast, Britain and the United States are allowing their real economic strength to be reduced in order to defend their financial sectors, and an ideology.

The taxonomy of corporate governance systems is limited. Roe suggested a simple dichotomy: those that are shareholder centric and those that are focused on employees. He suggested that the difference between these two approaches was, to a great extent, determined by political considerations, with social democracies being oriented to employees, while non-social democracies, such as the United States and Britain, being oriented to shareholders (Roe 2003). The political correlation appears to have some validity, as may be apparent from consideration of approaches in totalitarian China and the world's largest democracy, India.

However, Roe's dichotomy appears over simple: other possibilities clearly exist. Governance might be oriented directly to the corporation and its success, measured as to its security and long term prosperity. This might provide a more balanced orientation than a focus on employees or shareholders, both of which are problematic and not necessarily correlated with company success. Other orientations are also possible, focusing on the interests of other stakeholders, or even the common good.

Solomon distinguishes approaches to governance as to whether they are insider oriented or outsider oriented. Both Germany and Japan are insider oriented, with firms owned largely by insider shareholders who also control management. The United States and Britain are outsider oriented, focused on satisfying outside shareholder interests:

It is the functioning of internal and external corporate governance that determines whether a company, or even a country, displays more of the negative or the positive aspects of the capitalist system. The level of inherent trust within the business sector and within society as a whole has been questioned in recent times, with a general acknowledgement by sociologists of a decline in social cohesion. Specifically, there has been a decline in society's confidence in institutions, such as corporations and institutional investment organisations. (Solomon 2007: 4)

This decline in 'society's confidence in institutions, such as corporations', might be addressed by a broader definition of corporate governance. Solomon suggests:

the system of checks and balances, both internal and external to companies, which ensures that companies discharge their accountability to all their stakeholders and act in a socially responsible way in all areas of their business activity. (Ibid: 13)

This broader orientation, often referred to as the stakeholder approach, is more closely aligned to the European model as expressed in the legal form of the European Company ('Societas Europaea' SE). This finally became law throughout the European Union (EU) in 2004, after three decades of discussion and negotiation. The aims of the legislation were expressed as follows:

... to create a 'European company' with its own legislative framework. This will allow companies incorporated in different Member States to merge or form a holding company or joint subsidiary, while avoiding the legal and practical constraints arising from the existence of fifteen different legal systems. This legislative framework also provides for the involvement of employees in European companies, giving due recognition to their place and role in the business. (Introductory paragraph of the Statute for a European Company)

Within the EU, and its now 27 different jurisdictions, the orientation is specifically towards company employees as well as shareholders. The SE is an enabling format, allowing either a single management board of directors, or a two-tier system comprising both an executive board and a supervisory board. The executive board is intended to focus on operational issues and is chaired by a CEO, while the supervisory board is responsible for appointing and removing members of the executive board for their remuneration and for their general supervision. The supervisory board is all non-executive and chaired by the company Chairman (male or female). The aim of the SE legislation was to ease the process of merger and acquisition between companies of different countries within the EU. By the end of 2007 there had been less than 70 SE registrations, and progress since then has been further reduced as a result of the financial crisis.

While there was previously no single European standard of governance practice, the concept of two-tier boards of directors had long been common, with executive directors on the management board and non-executives, including employee representatives, serving on the separate supervisory board. The extent of employee representation on the supervisory board has varied in different EU Member States, as have the voting rights attached to different classes of company shares. Nevertheless, it is clear that practice across Europe shares a broad orientation of governance responsibilities, in contrast to the simple shareholder centred approach.

The following sections consider the different governance systems in Japan and Germany, while the following chapter deals with China and India. The different approaches to governance are practised in industrial systems which, for various reasons, appear to be more effective for the real economy than the neoclassical shareholder primacy model. Moreover, each of the systems is evolving. Chinese and Indian governance systems are rapidly emerging as their industrial economies develop, while Japanese and German systems have resisted pressure to conform to neoclassical ideological norms. Harmonisation may continue in that direction or it could be reversed. Therefore, rather than take a snapshot of systems as they exist in 2012, the following discussions take a more evolutionary perspective, taking account of the persistence and development of national differences.

Corporate Governance in Japan

The Japanese system of governance is characterised as an 'insider system', protected by cross shareholdings which are stable over the long term, with investment financed largely from retained earnings and debt provided by main banks within a traditionally closed system of industrial keiretsu groupings and alliances (Solomon 2007).

While this summary has been broadly accepted in Western literature, it is not without challenge. Moreover, in apparent response to the prolonged 1990s recession, the separate identity of Japanese governance has been changing, albeit slowly and carefully, with the general direction of change being towards the neoclassical shareholder primacy model. Nevertheless, Japan has retained many of the distinctive features of its model of governance, and might be presumed to do so for some time to come.

The Western précis divides Japanese industrial development into two parts: pre- and post-Second World War. Japan emerged late as an industrial power, starting its industrial development almost a hundred years after publication of Smith's *Wealth of Nations*. Japan adopted German company law in the beginning, which in the late nineteenth century prescribed detailed capital requirements as well as upholding strong shareholder rights over corporate decisions. But whilst in German law there was provision for a supervisory board and some degree of co-determination with employee representation, in Japan there was no supervisory board. Instead there was a statutory audit board established to monitor and report on the company's compliance with the law, and to provide an internal audit of the company's financial statements, primarily for the benefit of shareholders and major creditors.

Japan's industrial development was accelerated by various government initiatives to support the development of private industry. From the late nineteenth century the distinctive Japanese firm began to emerge: the industrial conglomerate (zaibatsu). These controlled a large proportion of all Japanese capital assets, especially heavy industries such as iron and steel, shipbuilding and construction. They were family owned holding companies atop a pyramid of subsidiary companies, controlling majority shares in subsidiaries which owned majority shares in their subsidiaries and so on. There were also horizontal cross shareholdings which increased the impenetrability of the system and helped support the commitment to providing lifetime employment within the zaibatsu's network of companies. A lead bank was invariably included in the shareholdings of the zaibatsu founding families, which provided, or underwrote, the financial needs of member firms.

After the war in which zaibatsu members had, of course, played a leading role in armament production, the American occupation administration disbanded them, confiscating family owned shares, banning previous zaibatsu executives from office, making industrial holding companies illegal, preventing non-financial companies from holding shares in other companies and preventing financial companies from owning more than 5 per cent of another company's equity. The confiscated shares in member companies, representing around 40 per cent of all Japan's corporate assets, were later distributed to individual investors, employees, local residents and the wider population in an attempt to establish dispersed share ownership as in the United States. However, it didn't work. Gradually, the restrictions imposed by the American authorities were relaxed and by the early 1950s individuals had mostly sold their shares, mainly to companies, so that by the late 1950s most companies were in effect owned by other companies.

The reasons why dispersed ownership failed to work are debatable. At that time, Japan was still in a period of post-war reconstruction and many individuals may have had dire need of the cash they realised from selling their shares. Alternatively, it has been argued that widely dispersed ownership made Japanese firms vulnerable to hostile takeover, especially given the low price of securities on the Tokyo Stock Exchange (Yafeh 2000: 76). This was a situation which, given their zaibatsu history, was completely foreign to them. They therefore acquired their shares as a defensive mechanism and formed close relationships between themselves and their corporate partners, and in many cases, competitors.

Whatever the reason, the dispersed ownership intended by the American authorities survived less than a decade and by the mid-1950s the old zaibatsu type of organisation had re-emerged in the shape of less formal networks referred to as keiretsu, which provided natural partners for firms in their financing arrangements and in their supply chains and distribution systems. These linked shareholdings, both vertically as in the pre-war zaibatsu but also with horizontally interlocking cross shareholdings, were reduced during the early 1960s while industries were restructuring to organise around new technologies. However, they were reinforced again towards the end of that decade after Japan had joined the OECD and its corporate sector was again fearful of hostile takeovers by foreign firms.

Nervousness regarding the threat of hostile foreign takeovers appears to come in waves. There have been times when the Japanese defences appear to be lowering, but before the free market shareholder primacy model is adopted, some new crisis stops the process in its tracks and the traditional closures are reinvigorated. Free market ideology makes the case that the Japanese model is anti-competitive and should not work. But it does.

The Japanese way is one of custom and practice rather than formalised systems. It is bone deep in the Japanese culture and has proved impervious to military defeat, the imposition of foreign law and seduction by the opportunities for short term gain. This cultural stability is illustrated in the Japanese company's approach to people. The big company tradition, albeit in most cases implicit to contracts of employment, has been famously to provide lifetime employment and to remunerate on the basis of seniority, rather than market valuations.

Such comfortable and stable arrangements are anathema to the neoclassical free market ideology which assumes that, under such arrangements, employees would become 'shirkers' and 'free riders'. As with other aspects of Japanese corporate culture, from time to time lifetime employment has been under severe threat and is probably not sustainable, but the perception of responsibility remains and influences corporate actions.

Nippon Steel's handling of its surplus employment in the early 1980s demonstrates the difference between Japan's approach and that of companies operating under the neoclassical ideology. Saddled with 3,500 surplus employees, Nippon made various elaborate arrangements which enabled them to avoid any redundancies and so fulfill their implicit duty to provide lifetime employment. It was achieved by ceasing any new hires and by outplacing employees across Nippon's customers, suppliers and subcontractors. Mostly outplaced workers were doing lower level work than they had in Nippon and so were paid less by their new employers, the difference being made up by Nippon. Thus, employment was reduced without any serious breaches of trust between the company and employees (Kester 1993). In the 1990s Nippon had to repeat the reductions in employment on a much bigger scale, reducing steel numbers by 19,000, and to achieve this, planned various diversifications into new non-steel activities to provide employment for the redundant steel workers.

The changing global market, with the rapid rise of China, India and other developing economies, has made lifetime employment difficult to sustain. Consequently, over the past decade or so Japanese companies have reduced their permanent employees to whom the promise of lifetime employment still applies, and increased their use of low-cost part-timers, contract workers and temporary staff. These groups now account for over a third of Japan's labour force. Nevertheless, employees continue to be oriented to their employing company rather than external bodies such as national trade unions. Union membership is generally at plant or company level with the union oriented to achieving success for the company from which its members benefit. Industrial action is rare and broadly seen as being counterproductive to employee interests.

The distinctive characteristic of the keiretsu, despite the informality of their organisation, was the stability of their interlocking shareholdings which was supported by and included members of the banking sector which held equity for long periods and did not actively trade in most of the equity they held. These stable shareholdings, which included the banking system within its interlocked ownership, accounted for around two thirds of all quoted equity in the 1980s.

From a neoclassical shareholder primacy perspective, the system appeared to be based on shareholders being 'passive, friendly, insider, sympathetic to the incumbent management', and who refused to sell their shares 'particularly to hostile takeover bidders, or bidders trying to accumulate strategic parcels of shares' and who if they needed to sell their shares would 'give the firm an opportunity to arrange for some or all of the shares to be taken over by another stable shareholder' (Sheard 1991). This was clearly against neoclassical norms, restricting competition especially in the market for corporate control, and giving company management too much power. Moreover, to the extent that members of a keiretsu were constrained to operate within the network, for finance, supplies and sales, it might be expected that they would achieve less profitable arrangements than would be achievable on an open market. At least this was the neoclassical critique, couched in terms of Japanese practice restricting competition, trade and investment.

The results however indicate otherwise. Post-war Japan has been, and still is, successful, even allowing for the 1990s 'lost decade' following the bursting of the property bubble. Japanese firms 'grew rapidly', 'developed new products', 'revolutionised industries' and 'earned their investors spectacular returns' (Miwa & Ramseyer 2005). Elsewhere, it is argued that this success was achieved through a distinctive Japanese approach to industrial management which was initiated post-war by American quality specialists Deming and Juran. However, their work was undoubtedly facilitated by the stability of Japan's governance arrangements, both in regard to its shareholdings and its employees, which explains why they achieved greater impact in Japan than they did in the United States.

Nevertheless, the neoclassical assault on the Japanese approach has continued. Various codes of practice have been proposed. For example, the Japan Corporate Governance Forum argued in the preamble to a paper proposing revisions to governance principles in 2001 that ' good company maximises the profit of its shareholders by efficiently creating value'. The principles follow the orthodox neoclassical argument regarding private property ownership, failing to identify the curious and distinctive nature of a company with its limited liability ownership.

Similarly, the Asian Corporate Governance Association (ACGA), which is largely representing financial institutions, published a 2008 'white paper' on Japanese corporate governance in which it complained that the Japanese system was failing 'By protecting management from the discipline of the market, thus rendering the development of a healthy and efficient market in corporate control all but impossible'.[1]

In like vein, the Japan Corporate Governance Research Institute (JCGRI), a think tank described as comprising academics and business people, proposes governance principles which still in 2010 argue that it is the shareholders who bear the responsibility for a corporation's performance and have the responsibility of governance'.[2] Supporting that statement JCGRI argues that 'Shareholders are the owners of the firm, and ... bear risk from business activities'.

These examples illustrate some of the pressure that has been brought to bear on the Japanese corporate sector to conform to governance arrangements driven by the neoclassical ideology. Whether or not that will prevail is not yet clear. A 2008 article on Japanese governance pointed out that Japan's politicians and companies were still resisting 'activist shareholders and dealmakers'. They had 'renewed their cross shareholdings and built takeover defenses which protect them from outsiders' (*Economist* 2008).

The distinctive Japanese approach to corporate governance in relation to shareholders appears to have survived so far. The traditional relations with employees appears less secure though the spirit of mutual responsibilities between employees and the company seem likely to remain intact, embedded

---

1   See the ACGA web site at http://www.acga-asia.org/public/files/Japan%20WP_%20May2008.
     pdf
2   See JCGR web site at http://www.jcgr.org/eng/principles/index.html

in Japanese culture and history and not to be simply a matter of changing a law or introducing a new code of practice.

Corporate Governance in Germany

There is a popular caricature of the Anglo-German difference in approaches to corporate governance:

> When British managers describe their companies they do so in the language of financial analysis, with precise figures on the development of profits, return on investment, the price earnings ratio, and shareholder value. In Germany the situation is quite different: ... discussion tends to centre on products and turnover, market share, and the number of people on the payroll. Profits seem to be rather a subsidiary issue.
>
> ...
>
> In Britain, the main goal is the maximisation of shareholder value, whereas in Germany, directors pursue a number of goals which are longer term in nature including, inter-alia, the long-term success and viability of the company. It seems that the British system is dominated by the firm intention of shareholders to participate in their company's success as 'instantly' as possible. By contrast, it was found in the German corporate landscape a broader concern which weighs up the interests of all who are involved in the company's fortunes, ie shareholders and employees as well as customers, suppliers, and the relevant sections of the general public. It could be described as a consensus model. (Schneider-Lenné, 1994: 285)

This nicely expresses some fundamental aspects of the apparent difference. It might result from a different history or political culture or, of course, from acceptance of a different economic ideology. From early nineteenth century, free market ideas based on Adam Smith and his successors led the economic development of Germany as elsewhere. However, the legal requirement to acquire a state concession prior to formation of a stock corporation was not abolished till 1870, the high water mark of free market Germany (Baum 2005: 3–29).

Bismark's creation in the 1880s of the world's first welfare state established German polity on a more socially oriented basis. The first German confederation of unions dates to the late nineteenth century with the *Allgemeiner Deutscher Gewerkschaftsbund* (ADGB), predecessor of today's DGB (Confederation of German Trade Unions), being established in 1919 with 52 unions and more than 3 million members. The Nazis terminated all trade unions in 1933 and it was not re-formed till 1947 with 16 single trade unions representing membership from individual industries.

In the immediate aftermath of the Second World War Germany was disarmed, much of its industrial manufacturing capability destroyed or removed by the occupying powers and limits set on its industrial regeneration. Valuable intellectual property was confiscated and many of Germany's best scientists were persuaded to migrate to the US. Restrictions were progressively relaxed as the Cold War emerged, and autonomous West Germany was established in 1949, joining the European Coal and Steel Community (forerunner of the EU) in 1951 and NATO in 1954. Through the 1950s and 1960s West Germany achieved the '*Wirtschaftwunder*' (economic miracle) with spectacular rises in standards of living and economic growth.

Despite its history over the past century, reunified Germany's orientation is social democratic and that, at least in part, explains the German difference in corporate governance. That difference has been instrumental in causing different outcomes. While the free market expression has led to an expanding and successful, though less secure, financial sector in Britain, the German expression resulted in a less successful but more secure financial sector and a more successful and secure real economy.

The London stock market is one of the major financial centres in the world, while the Deutsche Börse in Frankfurt, similarly positioned regarding its engagement with the world 24 hour stock market and having vainly sought to acquire London in the early years of the new millennium, remains the 12th largest stock exchange:

> *Germany lacks good securities markets. Initial public offers until recently have been infrequent, securities trading is still shallow, and even large public firms typically have big blockholders that make the large firms resemble 'semi-private' companies. (Roe 2003: 71)*

In manufacturing, on the other hand, Germany lies 4th in the world after the United States, China and Japan, with Britain achieving less than half the manufacturing output of Germany. In 2009 Britain was 13th in the world in motor vehicle production, compared to Germany's 4th. Moreover, Britain's production was almost entirely not British owned, whereas Germany's producers were predominantly in German ownership. Even in raw material production, such as steel, Germany maintained 7th position in the world, compared to Britain's 17th. Britain has ceased to be a significant producer in industries such as machine tools, textiles, motor cycles and many others, where it was formerly a leading player. Moreover, British manufacturing continues to lose ground and especially British owned manufacture.

The differences go very deep into the nuts and bolts of corporate practice, even, for example, in accounting where international harmonisation has proceeded apace. The primary focus of British accounting practice is supposed to be to provide a transparent picture of the company's affairs for the benefit of the shareholder. In Germany, on the other hand, the focus has always been simply the protection of creditors. Accounting norms for the valuation of assets highlight this difference. British balance sheets include properties at their latest professional valuation, whereas German law has required property to be included in the balance sheet at the lower of cost or market price. This allows German companies to accumulate large hidden reserves which could be utilised as and when company management deem them to be really needed, rather than them being paid over to shareholders at the first opportunity. The German approach has enabled their companies to take a longer term perspective than is feasible under the neoclassical shareholder primacy system.

To enable such different systems to work clearly requires different legal and institutional arrangements. The German orientation could not prosper or even survive in the British or American context, nor could the British in the German context. The distinctive legal and institutional arrangements which enable the German orientation arise from two broad categories: the boardroom arrangements required by law and the sources of industrial finance. These two issues are not unrelated and themselves result in many deep-seated differences from free market governance.

A neoclassical interpretation of the relatively closed nature of corporate Germany is that it arises from the shortcomings of the German financial sector which prevented company founders from selling their family holdings for a fair price:

> *Family founders in Germany may have wished to cash out and diversify like their Anglo-Saxon counterparts, but if the buyers would not have paid 'full' price for the stock because the buyers would have had to deal either with a weak board or strong labour, then the founders may have retained the block and induced the next generation of the family to enter and run the firm. When they sold, they might have sold a block to new blockholders who could monitor the firm and its managers, and the evidence suggests this was so. Blocks persisted and the demand for better corporate law was low. (Ibid: 77)*

That hypothesis, expressed from a neoclassical perspective, is countered by the argument that the German financial sector is the result of the relatively closed nature of corporate Germany. The different cultural history, Germany's development of the welfare state and its social democratic foundations are all contributory factors. Whichever was cause and which effect, the two are inextricably intertwined and it would not be straightforward for Germany to adopt the neoclassical free market approach.

The critical difference, which serves to close or protect the corporate sector from external financial opportunism, is the two-tier board system which operates with employees represented on the supervisory board. Employee representation for large companies has been required by German law since the 1870 act which established the modern stock corporation, the AG (AktienGesellschaft), publicly quoted company. The smaller, limited liability company, the GmbH (Gesellschaft mit beschränkter Haftung), is not required to have a supervisory board unless its employees regularly number more than 500.

The two-tier system establishes a management board with responsibility for day to day running of the enterprise and the supervisory board with various legally defined responsibilities including the appointment of management board members. From the outset the supervisory board was strictly separated from the management board with no common membership allowed.

The supervisory board was established to protect the interests of various stakeholders including shareholders, employees and creditors, which were usually banks, as well as some stewardship of the public interest. Its members were chosen by those various constituents. Originally, employee representatives on the supervisory boards of major companies held a third of the board membership, but in 1976 this was increased to 50 per cent for companies with more than 2000 employees. By law the AG supervisory board now comprises 20 members, 10 of whom are elected by the shareholders, the other 10 being employee representatives. The supervisory board not only appoints the members of the management board and approves their remuneration and sometime dismissal, but must also approve major strategic decisions, notably including those involving mergers and acquisitions.

These arrangements might well frustrate the aims of shareholder primacy. For example, it has been claimed that when employee representation was increased to 50 per cent, there was a loss of shareholder value of between 10 and 20 per cent (Roe 2003: 32). The shareholder primacy argument was that agency costs rose since, unless managers were tightly monitored, they would tend to favour employees ahead of shareholder interests, for example, by paying higher wages or by pursuing strategies that they and employees, but not shareholders, preferred. Therefore, it was argued strenuously by the shareholder primacists that German co-determination undermined diffuse ownership.

For agency theorists the only justification for the supervisory board was that it would monitor company management and so inhibit 'shirking'. However, the appointment of supervisory board members has not been transparent. In practice, members may be appointed as a result of executive recommendations which may be expected to lead to inefficient monitoring and poor corporate governance. From this perspective the supervisory boards are seen as weak and inefficient. For some, this lack of 'strong' supervisory boards is seen as the cause of Germany's lack of 'good securities markets' (Roe 1998, 372).

From the neoclassical free market perspective, it appears to be widely accepted that supervisory boards are weak, but that the weakness is mitigated by German banks holding large blocks of shares – lead banks frequently holding more than a quarter of a company's issued shares – and so preventing what agency theorists refer to as 'the free rider problem of corporate control'. German managers do not seek to maximise shareholder value because:

> they are sheltered from capital market pressures by a dense network of cross holdings and under developed disclosure obligations. Therefore they perform less well in terms of total shareholder returns. (Wenger & Keserer 1998: 177)

However, German managers, while not seeking to maximise shareholder wealth, have performed substantially better than their British and American counterparts from a long term corporate perspective. The fact that shareholder primacy is not their aim has produced some curious claims for shareholder rights:

> *It is the shareholders who, after all, are the owners of their enterprise and they should, consequently, have strong rights, including rights to a fair dividend and a satisfactory performance of the share price.*
> *(Schneider-Lenné 1994: 299)*

Clearly, the shareholder may have such expectations and hopes, but no such rights, the essence of shareholding being that it is a risk investment.

The supervisory board is not intended to serve the sole purpose of limiting 'agency costs'. It is specifically excluded from playing any direct role in day to day management of the company. Its supervisory role is to ensure that the interests of employees and the public are served, as well as those of shareholders. On a day to day basis this role might not require a strong supervisory board. Indeed, strong supervision might well be counterproductive to company performance. However, under particular circumstances, for example in the face of a hostile takeover bid, representation and defence of the wider interests of employees and the public, as well as of the corporation itself, may be vital. That representation and defence is ensured simply by the existence of the supervisory board and its legally defined composition.

It is apparent from published accounts that German firms have traditionally been financed to a much greater degree by debt, as opposed to shareholder capital, than are British and American firms. The Bank of England estimated figures for 1981, showing that non-financial firms in Germany were financed roughly 80 per cent by debt and 20 per cent equity, whereas in Britain, firms were financed roughly 50–50 (Edwards & Fischer, 1994: 259). This apparently higher gearing has led to the possibly simplistic conclusion that the financing of German firms is bank based rather than market based. The problem with this analysis is that the data on which the comparisons are based is inconsistent. Accounting practices differ as already noted. Consequently, the underlying strength of German balance sheets may not be apparent. Whereas British balance sheets, though claiming to be transparent to the shareholder, may be deliberately 'engineered' so as to hide liabilities and consequently their underlying weakness may not be apparent.

Comparisons are thus highly problematic. However, it seems clear that the German focus achieves a substantially larger proportion of new investment from retained earnings and therefore benefits from relatively low costs to finance development. British and American firms necessarily focus on high dividend payments to facilitate raising equity capital, and so suffer relatively high financing costs.

Moreover, because of the differences in balance sheet presentation, it is likely that the external financing needs of German companies may well be less than they appear, while the financing needs of American and British companies may well be greater. This suggests a difference in the levels of risk actually entailed, with the higher risk evident in Anglo-American jurisdictions likely to result in a higher required rate of return for capital investment projects and consequent reduction in investment, as highlighted by Hayes and Garvin (1982). The consequence of that Anglo-American 'disinvestment spiral' has been inevitably failing competitiveness in international markets and consequent economic decline. The reverse process seems applicable to German non-financial firms which generate most of their finance for capital investment from retained earnings, which arrangements are commonly seen as having contributed importantly to German economic success.

German firms also differ from British in that banks providing debt finance also control large blocks of equity with substantial proxy votes supporting their own direct holdings. They consequently have strong representation on the supervisory board, frequently holding the company chairmanship. Representation on the supervisory board is held to improve the quality of company information available to the bank, so that loans are made available on more favourable terms. Thus, German companies and their banks have developed a close and long term relationship with companies using a single large bank (the 'house bank') which provides most of their loan needs and acts as lead bank should syndicated credits or other facilities be required.

The German system of financing investment involves a relatively intimate relationship between the company and its house bank, with the latter able to influence corporate governance as well as specific strategic decisions. However, bank involvement is not primarily concerned with close monitoring of management for the benefit of the market in corporate control, though it can provide early information on looming trouble and a mechanism for organising corrective action. The primary impact of the house bank relationship is protective rather than aggressive.

The German system, like the Japanese, appears to have successfully countered the short termism of the neoclassical free market focus on maximising shareholder wealth.

Conclusions

The corporate governance systems in both Japan and Germany serve to frustrate and inhibit hostile takeover activity, with considerable benefit both to the individual companies and the overall economy. Competitive positions, particularly in manufacturing and high technology industries, have been protected. This has allowed firms to make long term and possibly risky investments, free from the fear of losing their autonomy and the jobs of those who work with them.

The apparent downside to this industrial environment being relatively protected is that the financial sectors in those economies do not have the easy pickings available in the post-industrial economies which have been so committed to the neoclassical free market dogma. Consequently, the financial sectors in Japan and Germany lag behind Wall Street and the City of London. Anglo-American firms, operating under the neoclassical shareholder primacy ideology, have the short term, deal making orientation forced on them.

The agency justification for encouraging a market in corporate management ignores the real and human aspects of enterprise. Under that regime, acquired companies not only lose their autonomy and strategic control but are very often saddled with the debt which was incurred for their acquisition, and suffer the stripping out of disposable assets, inevitably losing competitive position against economies which reject the neoclassical approach. In this text the protection of industrial firms and consequent reduced development of the financial sector is recognised as a substantial benefit for the industrial economies, which is likely to be jealously guarded.

Hostile takeovers have been likened to nuclear deterrents. The possibility of their actual use should be sufficient to maintain corporate performance. However, their repeated application only results in industrial destruction. The more protective governance regimes in both Japan and Germany have so far saved them from becoming rustbelt wastelands.

References

Baum, H., (2005), Change of governance in historic perspective: the German experience, in Hopt et al. (eds), *Corporate Governance in Context: Corporations, States, and Markets in Europe*, Japan, and the US, Oxford: Oxford University Press, pp. 3–29.

Economist, The (2008), *Corporate Governance in Japan: Bring It On*, 29th May.

Edwards, J.S.S. & Fischer, K., (1994), An overview of the German financial system, in Dimsdale, N. & Prevezer, M. (eds) (1994), *Capital Markets and Corporate Governance*, Oxford: Clarendon Press, p. 259.

Kester, C., (1993), *Japanese Takeovers: The Global Contest for Corporate Control*, Washington DC: Beard Books.

Miwa, Y. & Ramseyer, J.M., (2005), Asking the wrong question: changes of governance in historical perspective. In K.J. Hopt et al. (eds), *Corporate Governance in Context: Corporations, States, and Markets in Europe, Japan and the US*, Oxford: Oxford University Press, pp. 73–84.

Roe, M., (1998), German co-determination and German securities markets, in K.J. Hopt et al. (eds), *Comparative Corporate Governance*, Oxford: Oxford University Press, p. 372.

Roe, M., (2003), *Political Determinants of Corporate Governance*, Oxford: Oxford University Press.

Schneider-Lenné, E.R., (1994), The role of German capital markets and the universal banks, supervisory boards and interlocking directorships, in Dimsdale, N. & Prevezer, M. (eds), (1994), *Capital Markets and Corporate Governance*, Oxford: Clarendon Press.

Sheard, P., (1991), The economics of interlocking shareholding in Japan, *Ricerche Economiche*, vol. XLV, 421–48.

Solomon, J., (2007), *Corporate Governance and Accountability*, Chichester: John Wiley & Son.

Sykes, A., (1994), Proposals for a reformed system of corporate governance to achieve internationally competitive long term performance, in Dimsdale, N. & Prevezer, M. (eds), *Capital Markets and Corporate Governance*, Oxford: Clarendon Press.

Wenger, E. & Kaserer, C., (1998), German banks and corporate governance: a critical view, in K.J. Hopt et al. (eds) *Comparative Corporate Governance: The State of the Art and Emerging Research*, Oxford: Oxford University Press.

Yafeh, Y., (2000), Corporate performance in Japan: past [erformance and future prospects, *Oxford Review of Economic Policy*, vol. 16, no. 2.

8

Governance in Industrialising Economies

The harmonisation of international standards suggests that governance practice will generally progress towards the neoclassical ideal type. So far, both Japan and Germany have taken care to avoid its worst excesses by providing their real economy firms some protection against hostile takeovers. Both those jurisdictions are relatively closed to the market in corporate managements and appear to be in denial so far as the agency problem is concerned.

Both Japan and Germany appear to give only limited credence to agency theory as applied to corporate governance. Shareholders are important, but not the wholly dominant power they have become in Britain and the United States. Moreover, their interests are well represented inside the corporation, whereas in Britain and America, shareholders are external to the corporation with little influence or engagement other than through the threat of hostile takeover, Japan and Germany both appear to accommodate the interests of all stakeholders by pursuing the best long term interests of the firm.

It might be anticipated that the neoclassical free market ideology would be appealing to firms in industrialising economies, giving them the maximum opportunity for growth and profit. The success in global markets enjoyed by both China and India might be expected to reinforce their commitment to the free market ideal, though in China's case commitment to the shareholder primacy might be limited except for firms still in public ownership.

The free market model appears to offer much to these rapidly growing, emerging economies with their labour costs so much lower than those in more advanced economies.

Both China and India have been able to exploit their starting strengths and develop others, so that they are no longer just low wage, low tech manufacturers. Their technological strengths have rapidly developed so that innovation and design are beginning to be homegrown, though oriented to the needs of global markets. The impacts on employment in the post-industrial economies is clear to see, with whole industries falling behind the best with mounting rates of apparently permanent unemployment.

However, despite their very different histories and cultures, China and India, like Japan and Germany, appear to have managed to insulate themselves from the worst excesses of the free market model. Their industries, unlike those in the post-industrial economies, appear secure from foreign and hostile takeover. Their financial sectors are underdeveloped, and it may well be that they will remain under some control as a result of the protections provided to their real economy firms. The following sections consider how governance in these industrialising economies has developed the way it has and how it might be expected to progress in the future, and what lessons might be learned for the generality of corporate governance practice.

Corporate Governance in China

From its inception in 1949 the People's Republic of China (PRC) followed the Soviet model of state ownership and centralised economic planning and control. However, totalitarian socialism was no more economically effective in China than it was in the Soviet bloc. The impossibility of co-ordinating production with social needs had resulted in shortages of goods in demand and overstocking of other goods; the system offered no incentive for the efficient performance of state owned enterprises (SOEs), and a mixture of incompetence and corruption led to the misallocation of finance, materials and labour resulting in a technological decline relative to the West.

Following Mao Tse-Tung's death the PRC sought to develop a new approach to its economy. Firms in China were either wholly state owned or rural or urban collective enterprises. From 1978, under Deng Xiaoping's leadership, a programme of experimentation with alternative, more market oriented models of corporate management, ownership and governance was pursued. This included the tentative opening of China to foreign owned enterprises. When the Soviet system collapsed the economic approach there was changed, often almost violently, into a market oriented, capitalist system. But in China the political system, dominated by the Communist Party of China (CPC), remained intact while the economic system was developed in a more considered and careful process, with the direction of change being consistently towards market orientation with increasing private ownership.

The earliest changes were to grant increased autonomy to SOE managements in Sichuan province, expanding their decision-making powers in the hope and expectation they would be able to relate their production capacities more closely to genuine needs than had central planners. This experiment was quickly extended to SOEs in Beijing, Shanghai and Taianjin. Further experiments involved the transfer of economic responsibility from central government to local (that is, provincial, city and county) government and to the SOEs themselves, whereby fixed levels of 'profits' were transferred from the SOE to the state. This developed into the Contract Responsibility System which required SOE managements to contract to return an agreed level of profit to the state. By 1987 around 95 per cent of SOEs had adopted this system, with mixed results.

One problem with the Contract Responsibility System was that though managements would contract for profits, the state, as ultimate owners, remained responsible for losses. This led to management becoming unduly oriented to achieving short term results to avoid the ire of state controllers. Moreover, as the system was essentially negotiated, depending on how the negotiations were concluded, some SOEs became overstretched in terms of profit requirement while others might find the contracted profits achievable with ease. This asymmetry, together with the inherent short termism built into the system, led to much dissatisfaction.

The government also experimented in separate shareholding, re-establishing the Shanghai Stock Exchange in 1990 – it had been initially established in 1920 – with no more than eight firms being publicly listed. The Shenzhen Stock Exchange was established in 1991. The quoted businesses were SOEs with only a small part of their equity being traded on the exchanges. The CPC/government exercised extreme caution in its approach to privatisation, a term which is rarely used in China.

By the mid-1990s the experiments in management autonomy had suggested the need to extend private ownership into the model of devolvement. This was achieved through a programme of privatising small SOEs and releasing city level SOEs from the responsibility of maintaining levels of employment beyond the strict needs of the enterprise. Small and medium sized SOEs were responsible for almost 60 per cent of China's total employment and the lay-offs from the city SOEs, as well as those resulting from privatisations, amounted to around ten million in 1996 and over eleven million in 1997. Redundant workers were offered compensation and assistance in finding new employment, but widespread social unrest was nevertheless anticipated. The effects of the lay-offs were partially mitigated by the job creating growth which the newly privatised firms were able to finance. Also, many of the privatised enterprises became stock co-operatives, in partial ownership of employees and managers (Cao, Qian & Weingast 1999). Moreover, unrest may also have been pacified by recollections of the events in Tiananmen Square some five or six years earlier and the subsequent clamp down.

The impetus for privatisation came from regional governments and only when it had been demonstrably successful in several areas for a number of years did the central government, in 1997, confirm its policy supporting the privatisation concept.

Other experiments involved the social security system, payment for and provision of retirement pensions and healthcare. Also the termination of staff housing schemes (houses formerly provided by SOEs for their staff were sold to staff members by deductions from their pay) were leading the Chinese economy further into the realms of private ownership. However, these experimental changes were driven, in the case of China, by the desire to establish practices that worked, preferably by small increments from the original socialist system, rather than, as in the case of Eastern Europe, to establish practice which conformed to an ideology.

The stock exchanges expanded rapidly. By 2000 there were 1088 firms listed with a total capitalisation of US$600 billion. By 2010 the Shanghai Exchange had become the sixth largest in the world with market capitalisation of US$2.4 trillion.

Prior to listing on the stock exchange, SOEs were directly managed by CPC/government appointees. They also dictated financial and accounting rules as well as planning the details of production and distribution. The general manager and his immediate subordinates were appointed by the CPC/government, as were three governing committees: a Party committee, an employee committee and a trade union committee. The intention was for the employee committee to monitor the general manager and his senior managers. However, in practice, it was the Party committee which controlled everything within the SOE.

To gain a stock exchange listing required the SOE to become a joint stock company, limited by shares. Listed companies were legally required to be controlled by a board of directors, monitored by a separate supervisory board and ultimately controlled by an annual shareholder meeting. Listed company boards of directors were required to include external or independent directors.

The supervisory board, unlike the German equivalent, lacked the power to appoint members of the management board. The Chinese supervisory board has been widely regarded as ineffective, if not dysfunctional. A 1999 study reported by the CFA Institute Centre for Financial Market Integrity (2007) found supervisory board members to be lacking in both the knowledge and professional expertise to fulfil their duties competently. One reason for this lack was their selection or recommendation by influential executive members of the board of directors, whose choice may have depended more on the anticipated friendliness of advice rather than its competence.

The supervisory board's actual role has varied according to situation and circumstances. One study identified it as playing any one of four roles: 'honoured guest', 'friendly advisor', 'censored watchdog' or 'independent watchdog' (Xiao, Dahya & Lin, 2004). The 'censored watchdog' role refers to the monitoring role of supervisory board members who might report verbally to a meeting of the board of directors, but would exclude such comment from any written report for shareholders. These different roles illustrate the varying degree to which Chinese companies implement their legally defined roles, always having to bear in mind the continuing dominant role of the Party.

The annual shareholder meeting is the means by which shareholders nominate and appoint members of the two boards. As governance systems develop so have the composition and roles of the two boards. It is required that the board of directors form three sub-committees (audit, nomination and remuneration), majority membership of which are required to be independent directors, the state of independence being defined by law.

The board of directors appoints the CEO and senior managers, calls shareholder meetings, implements policies agreed at shareholder meetings and is responsible for day to day management as well as being the vehicle for receiving independent director inputs. In an increasing number of companies independent directors already outnumber executive directors with a rising number not even being Chinese citizens. In the main, independent directors, who are not CPC/government appointees, are selected for their specialist expertise and experience, notably including knowledge of foreign systems, and are likely to be categorised as 'friendly advisors', though that does not necessarily imply that they have little power and influence on board decision-making. Progress in the direction of openness and market orientation is widely held to be improving the governance of Chinese companies.

The supervisory board is responsible for reviewing the company's financial performance and position, its compliance with all legal requirements, correcting any managerial actions deemed to be not in the interests of the company, calling extraordinary shareholder meetings as necessary and submitting an annual supervisory board report to the shareholder meeting, this report being incorporated in the company's published annual report.

The governance arrangements for listed companies are confused by the fact that for many SOEs even after gaining a stock market listing, the old arrangements continued with the Party committee, formally or informally, retaining a powerful role within the company, often its members being on the board of directors. In most cases, the Party secretary is the vice chairman of the board of directors with substantial power since the appointment of the management team, and including even the chairman, is decided by the Party committee.

According to some writers the Party committee members take all significant decisions, with the designated body merely rubber-stamping approval. This is most obviously the case for firms whose CEO is a former, or even a current, government bureaucrat. Not surprisingly, they are found to underperform firms whose CEOs are not politically connected, partly because they are 'more likely to appoint other bureaucrats to their board of directors rather than directors with relevant professional backgrounds' (Fan, Wong & Zhang 2007).

Chinese style privatisation was intentionally only partial, with the CPC/government retaining majority shareholdings in major enterprises and regional governments also retaining substantial shareholdings in smaller and medium sized enterprises. By 2010 three quarters of China's 100 biggest companies (by market capitalisation) were still controlled by their major shareholders which were almost entirely state owned. It is these CPC/government shareholders that nominate directors and senior managers and even independent directors.

Thus, the degree of real autonomy achieved by listed non-financial companies remains limited, while CPC/government control of banking and the financial sector is only now beginning to ease.

Mechanisms are in place which would permit the Chinese listed company to perform under a market oriented governance system, not unlike those already discussed. However, the gradualist Chinese approach means that while such arrangements are enabled, they are not fully implemented. Implementation is careful and based on experiential evidence. It is nevertheless progressive and generally in the direction of market orientation. Steps in that direction include the establishment of new accounting standards which are largely in line with International Financial Reporting Standards, and the requirement to report quarterly profit, balance sheet and cash flow data. These developments continue as the Chinese economy opens further to foreign participation. Nevertheless, in 2011 China's conversion to full-on free market capitalism is still very much work in progress with the CPC/government in total control.

Much of the English language literature reviewing China's corporate governance is written from the neoclassical free market perspective and one which is firmly focused on shareholder primacy. In this literature any orientation of 'corporate officials', other than to maximise shareholder wealth, is regarded as a weakness, or a sign that the Chinese system of governance is still undeveloped. However, the Chinese government, which is still the major shareholder in Chinese enterprise, is focused on the maintenance of urban employment levels and what the current leadership refers to as the 'harmonious society' regarding the non-financial and financial sectors as means to that end, rather than as means to the maximising of shareholder wealth. This was clearly apparent in the 2007–8 financial crisis when listed SOEs were required by the CPC/government to maintain staff employment without lay-offs, irrespective of any crisis in operations.

From the free market perspective progress is inhibited by the CPC/government's retention of so much of its traditional power and influence over the corporate sectors. In many Western accounts such government interference is seen as a late vestige from China's totalitarian commitment to central planning. The legitimacy of the 'harmonious society' is not acknowledged, other than simply as window-dressing by a non-democratic government which is prepared to repress its population by force if it deems it necessary. However, the government's stated aims of full employment with rising levels of social security and healthcare for the whole population would be difficult to argue as illegitimate. Such aims would certainly not be realised through the unregulated free market model.

China's economic success since Deng Xiao Ping's liberating intervention has not been achieved as a result of its grasp of free market ideology. That commitment is still uncertain. A major source of its initial economic strength was its massive and low cost labour force which enabled China to compete in international markets for relatively low technology, labour-intensive goods. The growth achieved in those markets supported extension into other more technological, less labour-intensive activity. A virtuous cycle was established with China's seemingly inexhaustible population as both a massive resource and itself a huge and developing market. While that population remains harmonious, the cycle would seem likely to be maintained.

The Chinese labour force is heavily dependent on migrant workers recruited from the rural hinterland and paid in a whole year around a twentieth of what an American equivalent would earn in a month. But pay is growing by around 17 per cent in 2010 (*Economist* 2010). Partly this may be because of the rising number of strikes resulting from exploitative pay and working conditions by producers of Western products for such as Apple, Nokia, Dell, Sony, Honda, Hyundai, Toyota and many others. The Chinese workforce appears to be realising its strength in what is now the second largest economy in the world.

Three decades of growth approaching 10 per cent per year has lifted hundreds of millions of Chinese out of poverty, but has seen rampant corruption in the privatised sector, a decline in health and education provision, horrific environmental degradation and an explosion in inequality between the rural poor and massively wealthy top 1 per cent (Milne 2010: 31). The CPC leadership's pursuit of the 'harmonious society' seeks to reduce inequality by improving the lot of the lower income groups, and in particular that of migrant workers, and by making healthcare and education freely available to all. However, the government has not so far risked disharmony by restraining any excess of the top 1 per cent earners. Perhaps the opportunity to restrain inequality through moderate means will be lost.

The dilemmas and opportunities facing China in 2012 make it difficult to predict whether its corporate governance system will continue its progress towards the Western free market model, or whether it will return to the crossroads to survey each direction, content to pause, Chinese style, while ever harmony lasts.

Corporate Governance in India

India's industrial and corporate history is shared with Britain. The Bombay Stock Exchange opened under the Raj in 1875. By 1900 there were four fully operational Indian exchanges, which by independence in 1947 listed over 800 companies. Indian corporate law was solidly based on the British model as it developed from the 1844 Joint Stock Companies Act, right up to the post-independence Indian Companies Act of 1956. With this common heritage, it might be expected that Indian corporate governance would have naturally followed the Anglo-American model. But that is not quite the case.

Prior to independence India was ruled for 90 years by the British government and prior to that by a combination of the British East India Co. and local hereditary rulers. By 1947 the governing bureaucracy was well established, but there was no democratic tradition. The greatest distinction of modern India is that, despite the many economic problems it inherited, its debilitating hierarchical culture and its huge ethnic and linguistic diversity, it has determinedly established its legitimacy as the world's largest democracy.

For around 40 years after independence, India flirted with full-on socialism. This period became widely known as the 'license-permit raj'. With Soviet support, successive Indian governments were highly interventionist, nationalising whole industries during the early years of independence. Later the banks were nationalised and government engaged in industrial planning and licensing so as to control those industries and firms which remained in private ownership. Mountainous tariff barriers were established to keep out foreign imports and imposing tight restrictions on foreign firms' operations in India as well as imposing strict direct controls on imports and exports.

The extent of bureaucratic control under the license-permit raj has been described as imposing:

> *Kafkaesque barriers in front of every business action or decision. Bajaj Auto was prohibited from making more scooters than its licence permitted; Bombay rickshaw drivers were required to own their own vehicles; the use of red or green ink – rather than blue – was limited to senior civil servants. Manufacturers found that closing a money-losing factory could require a decade's journey or longer through the bureaucratic maze. (Capelli et al 2010: 22)*

Moreover, the bureaucrats imposing the regulations were untrained and uneducated in industry and business and knew little about such operations. The result was economic stagnation, widespread corruption and bribery, and regression in terms of technology and innovation as firms were forced to focus their energies more on fixing things with government officials.

The corruption and criminality have not yet been eradicated from Indian culture. It continues to infect government, the civil service, the media and the political lobbying industry as well as the traditional corporate players in the real economy: these latter range from the infamous Satyam scandal, sometimes referred to as India's Enron, to the multitude of small operators like the builder that fails to observe building regulations and bribes his way out of being forced to comply, with fatal consequences. Overall, however, the opportunities for corrupt practice are being reduced by the removal of the 'Kafkaesque' regulation with its myriad opportunities for palm-greasing. Progress however is slow.

By the late 1980s India was beginning to experiment with ways of breaking out of this bureaucratic nightmare. The rapid success of the tiger economies of Taiwan, South Korea, Singapore and elsewhere was demonstrating the opportunity that India was missing. Additionally, China's economic growth was beginning to be noticed. Then with the fall of communism in Eastern Europe and the loss of the Soviet Union, India's main ally in both trade and ideology, India was forced to a reappraisal of its whole approach to political economy. The final straw came in 1991 with a severe balance of payments crisis resulting from the Gulf War which interrupted India's oil supplies. Under these various pressures, India embarked on its journey towards neoclassical free market capitalism, with an increasingly explicit, though not necessarily fervent, emphasis on shareholder primacy.

This direction of travel has required a decentralisation of the administrative power and its dispersion to various public and private groups and regions. The revised approach was initially set out in its 1991 Industrial Policy Statement which identified two primary initiatives of deregulation and privatisation. Both are still, in 2012, work in progress.

The Industrial Policy Statement specified the decision to reduce the industrial sectors reserved for public sector undertakings (PSUs) from 17 down to 8. This was later reduced to just 4: defence, atomic energy, certain specified minerals and the Indian railways. The 17 sectors formerly preserved for PSUs included everything from coal, iron and steel, air and rail transport, petroleum, chemicals, pharmaceuticals, electricity production and so on. These sectors, newly unreserved to PSUs, were also freed from the necessity to obtain a government licence to operate.

The initial round of privatisation, referred to as disinvestment in India, involved the disposal of some minority shareholdings so that the government retained control. Subsequently, more extensive disposals were recommended by a quasi-independent Disinvestment Commission which identified 'core' industries such as telecommunications, power, petroleum and so on in which the government should retain a controlling share of the former PSU's equity, and non-core industries where it was recommended the government dispose of up to 74 per cent of equity. These limitations on disposal were subsequently progressively relaxed, and from 2000 on, what were referred to as strategic sales involving the transfer of control, were allowed. The first of these, the sale of Modern Foods to Hindustan Lever (a multinational subsidiary), was achieved with little objection except some protest from employees' trade unions. A subsequent disposal of the Bharat Aluminium Company was greeted with more energetic objections and the unions took their challenge to the Indian Supreme Court. The Court dismissed their objections on the grounds that workers could not decide who the owners of their firm might be.

Strategic sales subsequently became more common with disposals either to existing Indian companies, mostly family controlled, or to Indian based subsidiaries of foreign owned multinationals. The effect of privatisation, it has been argued, has been to improve competitiveness and in many cases to raise product performance, quality and price to internationally competitive levels which have been key to India's economic resurgence. Cause and effect are not necessarily always clear and it has also been argued that it is not so much privatisation which has had these beneficial effects, as the opening of markets to international competitors which has forced Indian firms to raise their performance.

Deregulation has continued alongside privatisation, apparently en route to the fully fledged free market economy. Import tariffs which had been as high as 400 per cent in some sectors, were quickly reduced to an average of 25 per cent. There had been a total ban on importing consumer goods while importation of capital goods had been subject to costly and slowly implemented licensing arrangements, which process lent itself to much bribery and corruption. After the 1991 reforms, importation of capital goods was freed from the need for a government license and hugely reduced for consumer goods. By 2000 import restrictions on manufactured consumer goods and agricultural products were eliminated.

This new openness was matched by official encouragement of foreign firms to operate in India. Wholly foreign owned businesses were allowed for the first time in high technology sectors, so that with firms such as Sun, Microsoft and IBM, India became an active participant in new technology. At the same time Indian firms were newly allowed to open branches and employ people overseas.

After 40 years of stagnation, India's stock exchanges came to life with the Bombay Stock Exchange now listing around 5,000 companies and the National Stock Exchange over 1,200, both exchanges being among the busiest in the world, several times the number of trades on the London Exchange. These exchanges are growing at an increasing rate with 128 companies applying for new listing in 2010. In total there are now 11 operating stock exchanges in India. Also, Indian companies have become more aggressively acquisitive, especially in pharmaceuticals and computer services, as well as in more traditional industries such as textiles, steel and automotive.

Privatisation has continued, despite considerable misgivings by government coalition partners. For example, Coal India, the world's largest coal producer, became the largest ever initial public offering on the Indian Stock Exchange in late 2010. Only 10 per cent of its shares were on offer and realised US$3.4bn for the Indian government. The issue was oversubscribed 15 times by investors from all over the world. At the end of the first day's trading Coal India was valued at US$49bn. Such disposals, irrespective of their long term economic impact, will be difficult for the Indian government to refuse.

The Securities and Exchange Board of India (SEBI) was established in 1992 with its basic duty being defined as the protection of the interests of investors in securities and to promote the development of, and to regulate, the securities market, by any such measures as the Board thinks fit. Under its guidance, custom and practice in the financial sector has moved to harmonise with international standards as has India's accounting processes.

The development of this new balance between public and private sectors and reduction in regulatory control over the latter are widely seen as critical to the country's development as a modern democratic economy, generating massive economic gains. Since the balance of payment crisis in 1991, GDP growth has accelerated through over 6 per cent pa for the decade since 2000, and some predictions that India will eventually overtake China as the fastest growing big emerging economy.

India's success in maintaining its democratic form of government has encouraged it in adopting the neoclassical free market shareholder oriented model of corporate governance. Legislation establishing new governance rules has gathered pace, particularly since 2000.

Though India's corporate law was drawn from British legislation, it was overlaid in post-independence decades by the heavy, socialist motivated regulations detailing most aspects of corporate affairs. The 1956 Indian Companies Act was, like its British predecessor, not very comprehensive so far as rules of governance were concerned. It did not deal with the composition of boards of directors or any requirements for directors to be qualified, or for any of them to be independent of the company. Nor was there much more than minimal requirement as to financial and other disclosure and transparency, and little to do with the protection of investors. Under the law, companies which were not listed on a stock exchange were not required to publish interim financial results to shareholders. While successive amendments to the 1956 Act have filled in much of these voids, not much has been added which affects issues of governance regulation.

For listed companies, guidance on corporate governance has been the responsibility of the SEBI which publishes a Listing Agreement with which companies quoted on Indian Stock Exchanges are required to comply. Corporate governance issues were first specifically addressed by their inclusion in Section 49 of the Listing Agreement published in 2000. Since then, Clause 49 as it came to be known has itself received several amendments.

Initially, the SEBI guidelines specified requirements for the listed company's board of directors, its composition, the roles of CEO, chairman (gender neutral) and key committees. For example, if the CEO and chairman roles were combined, then 50 per cent of the board had to be independent, non-executive directors, whereas if the two roles were separated, then only a third of board members needed to be independents. The board's audit committee must have three independent and financially competent directors. Director's fees were to be publicly disclosed and a section on governance included in the annual report.

The 2004 version of Clause 49 defined the independence of directors more rigorously and strengthened the role of the audit committee, increased the accountability of CEOs and CFOs and further specified the requirement for appropriate internal controls to be confirmed. Without going into further detail it is clear the increasing requirements of Clause 49 are broadly compatible with the requirements of America's Sarbanes-Oxley Act and the British codes of governance and stewardship practice. While the specific details may differ, India's line of direction is clearly towards the free market shareholder primacy model.

Compliance is, however, as yet far from complete. For example, the reason for the emphasis on independent directors in free market governance systems is for their role in solving the agency problem by monitoring the behaviour and performance of executive directors and managers and invoking the market in corporate managements if behaviour or performance were to fall below shareholder expectations. In India compliance is achieved in terms of the board composition and the qualifications/expertise of independent directors. But their practical role is quite different from that required to solve any agency problem. Rather than monitoring and reporting, they aim to support, help and advise the executive directors by bringing their diverse expertise and experience for the benefit of the company. This fundamental difference has been succinctly described as the difference between a 'compliance board' and an 'entrepreneurial board' (Capelli et al 2010: 160). The former is concerned merely with monitoring performance and enforcing behaviour and legality, primarily on behalf of shareholders, while the latter is concerned more with contributing, as best they can, to the development of the business, rather than the interests of any particular stakeholder, least of all shareholders.

India's distinctive governance characteristic is the practical concern which most Indian boards have for all their stakeholders, shareholders being far from the top of the list. Employees are recruited, supported and developed at considerable expense, which for British and American shareholder primacy firms might be regarded as part of the agency problem, a waste of shareholder value. Most successful Indian firms are acutely aware of their social responsibilities. In a country where mass poverty is still dominant, both in the cities where companies have their offices as well as in the rural hinterlands, inequity and corporate responsibility for it are never far from the surface. Many examples of Indian corporate philanthropy are quoted in *The Indian Way*. But if Indian governance achieves convergence with the American model these broader concerns will necessarily be jettisoned for the benefit of investors.

So far Indian practice has been preserved because its ownership structure is quite different from that in the United States. Less than 20 per cent of publicly quoted Indian companies are truly independent firms with diverse share ownership and thus vulnerable to hostile attacks from corporate raiders intent on making quick killings. Around 60 per cent in 2010 were members of business groups, around 12 per cent were still under government control and a proportion of the remainder were subsidiaries of foreign companies. However, the position is fluid, and government holdings are likely to continue being divested, so a larger proportion are likely to become vulnerable to attack while ever the accepted ideology favours free trade shareholder primacy.

As with Germany, Japan and China the formal position regarding corporate governance is clear and largely expressed in terms which are more or less compatible with the American approach. Certainly, movement and change are in that direction. Actual practice however is quite another thing.

Conclusions

While both China and India are progressing from variations on the centrally planned socialist system towards market orientation, neither appears fully committed to compliance with the neoclassical model of deregulation, privatisation and shareholder primacy.

China's movements in that direction are careful and considered, frequently the result of careful experimentation before full implementation. The Party is clearly aware that the system it operates currently is successful and fundamental change might put that success at risk.

India's former system was implemented by a democratic government and its moves toward market orientation are less fundamental. As a consequence they may not require the same degree of caution as the Chinese, but its opening up of markets, getting rid of regulatory excess and reducing government involvement in ownership have also been effective in encouraging economic growth.

Neither China nor India seems likely to adopt the full-on neoclassical model while they are in the rapid growth phase of their development. In China's case it would be difficult to do so without also moving to acceptance of a fully democratic political system. India is developing corporate networks which offer protection for their real economy companies against opportunistic attack, while China provides even more complete protection through its continuing partial state ownership.

The Japanese and German systems, providing real economy firms some continuing protection from predatory financial sectors, seem more likely role models for both China and India than the Anglo-American post-industrial model.

References

Cao, Y., Qian,Y. & Weingast, B.R., (1999), From federalism. Chinese style to privatization, Chinese style, *Economics of Transition*, vol. 7, no. 1, 103–131.

Cappelli, P., Singh, H., Singh, J. & Useem, M., (2010), *The India Way*, Boston Mass: Harvard Business Press.

CFA Institute, Centre for Financial Market Integrity, (2007), *China Corporate Governance Survey*.

Economist, The (2010), *The Rising Power of the Chinese Worker*, 29th June.

Fan, J.P.H., Wong, T.J. & Zhang, T., (2007), Politically connected CEOs, corporate governance, and Post-IPO performance of China's newly partially privatized firms, *Journal of Financial Economics*, vol. 84, no. 2, 330–357.

Milne, S., (2010), The strikes are good for China – and for the World, *The Guardian*, 1st July, p. 31.

Xiao, J.Z., Dahya, J. & Lin, Z., (2004), A grounded theory exposition of the role of the supervisory board in China, *British Journal of Management*, vol. 15, no. 1, 39–55.

9

Corporate Accountability and Integrity

The brief outline of approaches to corporate governance in the previous three chapters suggests considerable variation, despite the pressures of globalisation and international harmonisation of standards and practices. Governance is prescribed by law in all jurisdictions but, especially in the United States and Britain, it is custom and practice to ignore the law. Codes of practice are voluntary and can generally be ignored with impunity, and frequently are. In most jurisdictions it appears quite permissible merely to offer lip service to both the law and to codes. Variations in practice also derive from national histories, cultures and political realities. The picture of governance realities, like most others, is messy.

The neoclassical free market model of governance has the great virtue of simplicity and clarity. But in identifying the shareholder as the principal for whose benefit the company exists, it has turned the economic system on its head.

In the beginning, shareholders were a critical means to industrialisation, but the purpose of industrialisation was never to provide a return to shareholders. The canals were built to provide transportation for the bulk products on which the new industries were dependent. They had to make sufficient money to maintain operations and pay their creditors, including shareholders, but making money for those shareholders was not their prime purpose. However, in the neoclassical version of governance, maximising shareholder wealth is held to be the driving purpose of industry and business.

That is the system which has been more or less fully implemented in the post-industrial economies. The industrial and industrialising economies benefit from their limited adoption of the neoclassical model. They support the freedom of traditional markets for products and services in which they successfully compete. But, crucially, they distinguish between firms in traditional markets and those in speculative financial markets, and take care to ensure their real economy firms are protected from the latter.

However, it is apparent from the literature on governance that there is increasing pressure for international harmonisation towards the neoclassical model. That is not solely because it has the great virtue of simplicity and clarity, nor is it because the literature on governance, like all other aspects of business management, is largely American and therefore predominantly neoclassical. The benefits are clear for industrial firms of free access to deregulated, globalised markets.

For industrial and industrialising economies, adoption of international standards is persuasive and immediately beneficial, and measurable in the resulting trade imbalances, so long as their existing protections against financial predation are not compromised.

In the post-industrial economies, industrial firms have been weakened by the new competition from industrialising economies, some even to extinction, so that considerable damage has been done to employment and to the economies as a whole. For firms which have successfully developed monopolistic positions there may still be some gain from deregulated markets, but the general benefit is frequently lost from the post-industrial economy as such firms take advantage of opportunities to relocate their tax base to reduce payments. Thus, the neoclassical model appears to be of substantially less benefit for the post-industrial economies which, paradoxically, are the prime promulgators of neoclassical dogma.

Where companies are protected from predatory financial sectors they have the advantage of being able to focus on real business objectives related to technologies and customers, and are enabled to accrue surpluses which give them the ability to invest for the long term, without having to pay all surplus resource immediately to shareholders. Whilst that is a great strength it means also that there is at least a risk that such firms become the unaccountable tyrannies referred to by Chomsky and others. In the absence of the neoclassical disciplines it is important that firm managements are made subject to adequate constraints and accountabilities, as outlined in the following sections.

Accountability to the Firm

Most accountabilities to the firm are the subject of written contracts, whether they are simple contracts of employment, supply contracts, purchase orders or invoices and the like. In broad terms these clarify the different liabilities and responsibilities of the various contract holders. Shareholders have no such accountability to the firm, or responsibility for it, all such having been fully discharged when share certificates were acquired.

Beyond these accountabilities, more or less specified by formal contract, the senior managers and directors within the firm have more complex accountabilities which are not usually specified in detail. A full time executive director is typically bound by his or her service agreement with the company, formally agreed by the board of directors, to devote themselves to the best interests of the company, those best interests being normally specified only in the most general terms. A typical director's service agreement,[1] framed in expensive legalese, might still have its primary clause reading, as it did 40 years ago, along the following lines:

> *EXCEPT as hereinafter provided (name of director) shall unless prevented by ill-health or accident throughout the term of this Agreement devote the whole of their time and attention during business hours (except during holidays) to the business and affairs of the Company and as may be required by the Board to the business and affairs of the subsidiary and associated companies of the Company and in all respects shall conform to and comply with any directions and regulations from time to time made by the Board and shall well and faithfully serve the Company and use their utmost endeavours to promote its interests. (Read 1971: 189)*

There is rarely any mention of shareholders in service agreements and no suggestion that shareholders are the principal in any relationship with the company or its directors. The company itself is recognised as the principal, suggesting that for corporate governance to be strictly legal it should be oriented to company primacy, rather than shareholder primacy.

Directors' duties to the company are affirmed as a generality in company law. The UK Companies Act of 2006 indicates a broad perspective which was

---

1   See service agreements at http://www.lawofcontract.co.uk/contracts/directors-service-agreement.php

referred to as 'enlightened shareholder value', a concept which is explained at some length but which has little statutory force. In addition, directors owe the company a duty to exercise their independent judgement, as well as reasonable care, skill and diligence, and to avoid all conflicts of interest and not to accept benefits from third parties and to declare any interest they may have in proposed transactions or arrangements.

These accountabilities to the firm are executable and transgression is punishable by fines and imprisonment. However, assessing whether a director has acted in the best interests of the business or not may be difficult. Both the business and, more particularly, its best interests, are open to interpretation. Consequently, there are few examples of directors being found guilty of acting against the best interests of the business, except when there is a direct conflict of interest. Usually such conflicts as are identified tend to be cases of straightforward criminality and fraud, of which there are a large and ever increasing number of examples.

Even in America the Sarbanes-Oxley Act, specifically framed in response to the Enron scandal, is rarely invoked except in cases of gross criminality. Minor transgressions and undivulged conflicts of interest are rarely pursued in law. Nor are the highly public reactions of company directors to hostile takeover bids. While the law requires them to act, in those circumstances as in all others, in the best interests of the company, it is customary for them to act in the best interests of the shareholders and of themselves, quite without any legal challenge. A recent example was the takeover of the long established and successful Cadbury by Kraft, in which Cadbury directors recommended the takeover and received multimillion pound payments from the acquirer. There was no legal challenge.

The main statutory responsibility of directors to the company is the preparation of its accounts and their annual report, the professional auditing of the accounts and their presentation to the company's general meeting and public filing with, in Britain, the Registrar of Companies. Lapses in fulfilling these responsibilities do have immediate consequences. It should be especially noted that these responsibilities are in fulfilment of directors' duties to the company, rather than to any other constituency such as shareholders. The annual report and accounts is the key vehicle for publication of the company's accountabilities to all its various stakeholders.

Company directors are thus contracted with the company to act on its behalf, as its agent, and to ensure it fulfils all its accountabilities, though non-compliance is unlikely to provoke any legal action.

Accountabilities of the Firm

The accountabilities of the firm that are legally specified in most jurisdictions include reference to employees, suppliers, customers, creditors, the community and the environment, as well as shareholders. But in practical detail most such legal accountabilities have proved difficult to enforce, being rather open to interpretation.

They are sometimes interpreted in a normative way, specifying how a company should be required to behave with regard to its various stakeholders. This is the perspective taken in the implementation of corporate social responsibility (CSR) programmes, and typically taught in business schools under the heading of business ethics, and sometimes promoted in codes of best practice. But these are more expressions of vulnerability and cannot be expected to have much practical effect.

Alternatively, corporate accountabilities to the various stakeholder categories could be interpreted as values free, calculated accountabilities, based on the legal requirement to put the interests of the company first and assuming that legal requirement had some potency. They might then, unlike moralistic accountabilities, lend themselves to being made practically executable. The following paragraphs consider the nature of such calculated accountabilities, contrasting them with the crude and simplistic notions embedded in the neoclassical model.

The basic company primacy concept suggests the following prior assumptions when defining accountabilities to stakeholders:

1. Waste avoidance assumption: the company would conduct relationships on the basis of avoiding waste, including any unproductive investment in stakeholder relationships. This assumption differs from profit maximisation in that it is measurable over the long term.

2.   Ongoing relationship assumption: the relationship of the company with all its stakeholders should be conducted on such a basis that they will be continued for the indefinite future, till such time as it is no longer in the company's interest. This assumption subsumes a foundation of 'let us do them no harm' with regard to its relations with all stakeholders.

3.   Calculated Theory Y assumptions: these are applied to all stakeholders, not just employees, and seek to develop co-operative strategies based on trust. But trust is not blind; Theory Y is calculated.

These three prior assumptions underpin the firm's accountabilities to all its stakeholders, as briefly outlined below.

THE ENVIRONMENT

A business does not interact with the environment in quite the same way as it does with other stakeholders. The environment itself is passive, available to be exploited so far as regulations and the law will permit. Accountability to the environment requires the identification of all those unaccounted costs and consumptions, the 'externalities', which the firm incurs but which are not recognised and charged.

The environment might be regarded as a proxy for the best interests of future generations and it is those with whom the business is really interacting when it impacts on the environment. A business that is in it for the long term needs to be aware of its impacts on future generations. It needs to conduct itself in a way which is not only regarded as generally acceptable by today's standards of awareness and understanding, but by the standards that will be applied by future generations. It therefore has responsibility for being expert on its particular environmental interactions and must take into account the knowledge that future generations will have of their environmental impacts, and for behaving in a way which future generations will find to have been acceptable. Otherwise, it will not survive those future generations.

Compliance with the law is the first requirement of the firm's environmental interactions. Measuring the externalities of its relationship and ensuring they are reported and compensated is a further requirement as increasingly active pressure groups seek more complete environmental protection. These are the notional accountabilities. Making them executable depends partly on external regulation, and partly on rejecting the neoclassical ideas which prescribe maximising the immediate wealth of shareholders as the orthodox wisdom on corporate governance. The essential characteristic of the revised ideology has to be that the business is at root seeking to survive and prosper in the long term.

It should not be overlooked that the environment also presents tremendous potential development opportunities created by the needs of sustainability in which firms currently imposing external costs on the environment should be expert.

THE COMMUNITY

Interactions with the local community might be similarly based around the calculation, reporting and compensating of externalities, with a similar requirement that firms be expert in their own interactions with the community.

Traditionally in Britain big firms played a more important role in the community than they do today. Many of the old Quaker companies, for example, built 'model villages' to accommodate their employees. Companies which dominated their locality not only built housing and shops but also provided schools and even in some cases churches. Companies laid on social events such as children's parties and Easter parades as well as providing sports and leisure and other social facilities. Companies supported their own football and cricket teams and their own brass bands while some even provided hospitals.

Few companies remain as mass employers and with few exceptions they no longer dominate their local communities. So their support for the community is more limited, rarely extending much beyond carefully targeted investment or sponsorship. However, any long term business will need, at least, to ensure that adverse effects of the business are minimised and compensated. Beyond this, the main responsibility of business management is to ensure survival and long term prosperity of the firm in order that it will continue to contribute to the local economy and employment.

TAX AUTHORITIES

While payment of taxes is what provides society with the means of providing education, health, social security and defence, the firm has no duty to provide other than the minimum tax payments allowable within the law. Any legal means of reducing tax payments should be pursued, as should any other form of waste. It is up to the tax authorities to ensure that firms are not enabled to avoid legitimate and intended tax payments.

CREDITORS

A firm's accountability to its creditors is simply calculated as fulfilling the payment terms as agreed. Creditors may be short term such as suppliers on credit, or longer term such as the firm's bank which may provide ongoing credit facilities, or even the holders of loan stock. Accountabilities to each category may differ with, typically, an especially close relationship with the firm's banker, which might be required to provide flexible facilities at short notice and would therefore need to understand fully the firm's position and possible financing needs. This relationship would aim to minimise the cost of credit facilities should they be required.

SHAREHOLDERS

The calculated accountability to shareholders in a company primacy environment suggests that a firm should be focused on its survival and long term prosperity, and to manage its share price on the stock market so as to avoid paying more in dividend than is necessary to maintain the share price at a level which ensures its continued autonomy. Paying more than that would just be wasteful. Surpluses should be retained as far as possible for long term investment and for ensuring security. Nevertheless, there are some particular accountabilities to shareholders. Shareholders are external to the company and do not have access to regular board meetings or to the various forms of internal communication and consultation that employees, for example, may benefit from. The main accountability to shareholders is to organise an annual meeting of the company to which shareholders are invited and apprised of the company's position and given the opportunity to exercise their constitutional rights to vote on specific issues. Shareholders also are provided with the company's annual report and accounts which are statements made public for any interested party and lodged with the relevant statutory body.

SUPPLIERS

The firm's accountability to its suppliers involves its payment on terms which are traditionally assumed to have been agreed according to their relative bargaining power. The individual transaction is seen as one which itself produces an economic surplus which will be divided between the two parties according to their bargaining strength. The buyer needs to be assured of the supplier's standing in terms of reliability and predictability of supply. Thus, it is a calculated relationship. However, the transaction becomes more complex when viewed as a continuing relationship over a strategic time frame. Businesses need to forge links with suppliers who can support long term as well as short term objectives. This might involve strategic relationships involving joint developments, exclusive supply deals and so on.

There is also an increasing pressure to ensure that a firm's suppliers perform in ways which are seen by its customers as ethical. Many firms are now committed to global sourcing guidelines which set out the terms on which suppliers would be engaged, committed to sourcing only from units which satisfy in terms of social and environmental criteria.

CUSTOMERS

Accountability to customers means interacting with them in ways which result in a long lasting and profitable relationship. Neoclassical theory is silent about customers. But yet the customer, in common parlance, is often claimed to be 'king'. Pleasing customers is not the ultimate aim of the business, but a means to long term prosperity. Therefore, the resources devoted to it are calculated. Having a passion for the customer, as is widely suggested, may lead to waste and to inhibiting the achievement of other objectives.

There is of course an extensive literature on a firm's accountability to its customers, which is wholly beyond the reach of neoclassical theory, but which is vital to enterprise management.

A firm's first contact with its customer is typically through its promotion. This is likely to set the tone of the whole relationship whatever form it takes. The aim of promotion may be to inform, to persuade or to alter the perceptions of its audience. Whatever the promotional activity and whatever its aims, it will create the customer's first impressions and establish initial expectations of trustworthiness and credibility. These expectations will be reinforced or reversed by the product or service itself and the subsequent customer relationship.

The most important accountability to the customer is through the product itself. The degree to which it satisfies customer expectations will be the most powerful and lasting communication. Products are loaded both physically and psychologically with many extras that may be important determinants of success. Marketing literature is replete with descriptions of the many and various components that comprise the modern conception of a product.

One widely held view sees the product as having several layers. The innermost layer is the core benefit or service which the product fulfills. An intermediate layer, the formal product, embodies such things as price, performance, reliability, design, specification and longevity. An outer or augmented product layer includes such things as warranty, service support and so on (Kotler 1984). The various attributes of a product, not necessarily related in any predictable fashion, could be categorised for convenience as physical, implied and psychological. What matters about this complex product is the customer's perceptions of its various attributes, any of which may be critical in adding up to a concept of value which is a combination of price and quality. Moreover, the concept of quality is not simply one dimensional, but complex. Its definition clearly depends on the type of product or service being delivered.

The product's characteristics are the components of value for which the firm is accountable to its customers.

Delivery and distribution channels can also play an important part in confirming the accountability that has been created by promotion and by the product itself. So also can the after sales relationship that a business has with its customers.

Accountability to customers is not just an ill-defined intention to make the customer king. It involves all of the customer transactions in a detailed calculation of how the greatest impact can be created for the least cost. If each aspect is effectively managed they will all serve to reinforce the customer's initial perceptions. If any particular aspect is not focused effectively on reinforcing the accountability, it will tend to undercut the intended image and customer perceptions and severely reduce the level of trust that the business is able to establish.

All customer transactions need to be conducted with trust building integrity, both regarding the product and its various attributes, and the personal interactions with customer representatives. Customer accountability is clearly not simply a matter of setting the quantity of product at the level which equates marginal cost with marginal revenue thereby maximising profit.

EMPLOYEES

Firms are involved in a variety of transactions with employees. They arise in the process of recruitment and selection, induction, health and safety, training and development, remuneration, working conditions, job content, supervision, management and motivation, discipline and grievances, holidays and working arrangements, achievement and recognition, promotion, equal opportunities and an endless list of factors which might conveniently be lumped together in the catch-all term culture – items which may crucially affect the working climate and behaviour of people at work.

Each of these interactions contributes to the firm's psychological contract with its employees, and they all interact. A flawed or dishonest transaction between the employer and employee in one area is inevitably going to influence the relationship as a whole and affect how transactions are undertaken in other areas. Having once been treated dishonestly, the party to the transaction, whether it is the employee or the employer, will be wary about any recurrence. The principle of trust which may have been painstakingly established will have been quickly destroyed or damaged and will take a great deal of concerted effort to rebuild.

From the very earliest days of industrialisation the firm's employees were its most important stakeholder. A century ago the relationship with employees was frequently conducted on the basis of a top-down, command and control relationship. Today, with the firm's prosperity depending more on people based intellectual capital, accountability to employees is necessarily based on Theory Y assumptions. It is nevertheless a calculated accountability rather than one based on an assumption of general goodwill.

An example of such a relationship was identified in studies of prisoners' dilemma tournaments. The prisoner's dilemma involves two individuals both accused of the same crime being kept separate from each other during interrogation. If they both plead guilty they each get one year imprisonment. If one prisoner pleads not guilty and turns evidence on the other he gets off and the other gets ten years. If they both plead not guilty and blame each other they both get five years. How should each plead? The best outcome for either individual is to blame the other, so long as the other prisoner pleads guilty. If they both adopt that strategy then they both get five years.

Axelrod studied prisoners' dilemma tournaments and noted that the tendency for players to co-operate (that is, both plead guilty) increased dramatically whenever a player was paired repeatedly with the same partner (Axelrod 1984). In this situation a strategy emerged with players co-operating on the first move, then following suit on all subsequent moves, that is, co-operate when your partner co-operates, cheat if they cheat, at least until the end of the game is in sight. This was referred to as a tit-for-tat strategy:

> Tit-for-tat embodies four principles that should be evident in any effective strategy: clarity, niceness, provocability, and forgivingness. Tit-for-tat is as clear and simple as you can get. It is nice in that it never initiates cheating. It is provocable, that is, it never lets cheating go unpunished. And it is forgiving, because it does not hold a grudge for too long and is willing to restore co-operation. (Dixit & Nalebuff 1994: 106–7)

Accountability to employees is best fulfilled by development of relationships conducted on a tit-for-tat strategy. This can be incorporated in formal contracts with, for example, provision for disciplinary procedures, formal warnings and so on, in the event of 'cheating'. The informal psychological contract could be similarly based. A relationship of trust would be developed over time, the reliability of which would depend on the integrity of both the firm and its stakeholders.

Corporate Integrity

A firm's relationships with all its stakeholders are at risk since the firm's continued existence is itself uncertain. Each of the stakeholder categories makes investments of one kind or another in the company's future. The consequences of a firm's failure impact on different stakeholders differently. For employees loss of employment may be a life changing experience, almost a matter of life and death. For suppliers a firm's demise may cause extreme difficulty and could result in reciprocal bankruptcy. Almost all stakeholders have a vested interest in the firm surviving and prospering long term. Only the shareholder's fund manager maintains a short term perspective, being unable to afford a long term commitment. For a fund manager or trader, investing in the firm's share as part of a portfolio, the firm's failure may result in the loss of a place or two on a fund managers' league table, a relative minor effect compared to the impact on other stakeholders.

The transactions with all stakeholders who share an interest in the firm's long term success would benefit from being conducted in accord with the tit-for-tat strategy so as to build trust, enabling the firm and its various stakeholders to collaborate to their mutual advantage.

Over time the mutually advantageous transactions which continue on this basis develop into lasting relationships based on mutual trust. The calculated nature of such relationships makes them more robust than if they were based on any extraneous value system or philosophy which might be espoused by individuals who, for the time being, hold leading positions in the firm.

The essence of maintaining such relationships is the need to maintain a consistency of integrity in all transactions across all relationships. Mistrust arising as a result of some shortfall in one area will affect the level of trust accorded transactions in other areas. Firms need therefore to behave as though they have internalised the principle of trust as a value affecting all their transactions and relationships with all stakeholders. To do this the firm, or its agents, need to be vigilant in all the areas where stakeholder transactions are active. Any actions by people acting on behalf of the firm which might adversely affect the credibility of the firm's trustworthiness would need to be 'punished' and be seen to be 'punished'.

If a company's interactions with its local community, for example, were seen to have adverse or pollutive (broadly defined) effects, this may well impact on the way other stakeholders perceive the business as a potential collaborator. This effect may then be multiplied if the firm makes any attempt to avoid compensation or to falsely deny the pollutive effects. Such denial, if recognised as such, would be perceived by potential collaborators as indicative of further untrustworthiness.

The firm must demonstrate the level of integrity which will make it generally acceptable as a partner and collaborator. Management's responsibility is to ensure the firm is perceived by all stakeholders with which it transacts, as trustworthy, keeping to agreements and fully meeting expectations.

The sole aim of this approach to integrity is to ensure a firm is perceived as trustworthy. Perceptions as to a potential partner's trustworthiness critically affect whether or not they will be invited to join in collaborations and alliances. While it is the firm's image that is perceived, if that image differs significantly from the reality, it is unlikely to be long lasting – in the end the 'truth will out'.

Integrity has therefore to be treated as an organisational characteristic which determines all the organisation's transactions. The constancy and consistency required to ensure that the firm's integrity is truly perceived by stakeholders are only likely to be achieved if it is absorbed deep in the organisation's culture of which over the long term it becomes an important part, internalised and acted on by all the firm's people.

With no integrity, communications will be perverted and secretive; individuals will be unable to make wholehearted commitment to the organisation. Barnard suggested, without integrity, it would be extremely difficult to complete the executive tasks of maintaining organisational communication, securing essential services from individuals and the formulation of purpose and objectives (Barnard 1938).

The neoclassical ideology destroys corporate integrity. Maximising shareholder value means the impoverishment of all else and prevents the development of any perception of trustworthiness among other stakeholders. It is the firm's integrity that makes its transactions with stakeholders predictable and trustworthy, and thus enables them to develop into long term relationships. The predictability of self-interest maximising relationships only ensures their transitory nature.

Conclusions

The accountabilities which have been discussed in this chapter are not as easy to adopt as the simplistic idea of maximising shareholder wealth. Clearly by accepting accountabilities to all stakeholders, nothing is maximised, and the most effective balance of accountabilities between stakeholders may be difficult to achieve.

Moreover, in jurisdictions dominated by the neoclassical orthodoxy it is difficult for firms to escape its clutches and focus on building their reputation for integrity. But some changes are happening. When Unilever Chief Executive

Paul Polman announced his company's dedication to sustainability he was greeted with some bottom line oriented cynicism. He responded:

> *Unilever has been around for 100-plus years. We want to be around for several hundred more years. So if you buy into this long-term value-creation model, which is equitable, which is shared, which is sustainable, then come and invest with us. If you don't buy into this ... don't put your money in our company. ... ... Consumers and retailers want this sort of initiative, and the planet needs it ... (it's) the right way to do business. (Skapinker 2010: 7)*

Even the British Institute of Directors, though granting primacy to the shareholder, accepts that it has been taken to excess, especially in circumstances where hostile takeover bids are mooted and the interests of all other stakeholders are ransomed for the short term gain of shareholders.

The pursuit of company interests, above all others, would be difficult to achieve in jurisdictions, such as Britain and the United States, where the neoclassical shareholder primacy model has become so dominant. But it would be beneficial. Company primacy would allow funds to be accrued, as already happens in the other jurisdictions considered here, for the firm's long term development and the benefit of all stakeholders.

References

Axelrod, A., (1984), *The Evolution of Co-operation*, London: Basic Books.

Barnard, C.I., (1938), *The Functions of the Executive*, Cambridge Mass: Harvard University Press.

Dixit, A. & Nalebuff, R., (1994), *Thinking Strategically: The Competitive Edge in Business, Politics and Everyday Life*, New York: W W Norton & Co.

Kotler, P., (1984), *Marketing Management: Analysis, Planning, Implementation and Control*, 5th edition, New York: Prentice Hall.

Read, A., (1971), *The Company Director: His Functions, Powers and Duties*, London: Jordan & Sons Ltd.

Skapinker, M., (2010), Corporate plans may be lost in translation, *Financial Times*, 22nd November, see at http://www.ft.com/cms/s/0/78cf6070-f66e-11df-846a-00144feab49a.html#axzz.

PART IV

Sustainability and Co-operation

> *The form of association, however, which if mankind continue to improve, must be expected in the end to predominate, is not that which can exist between a capitalist as chief, and workpeople without a voice in the management, but the association of the labourers themselves on terms of equality, collectively owning the capital with which they carry on their operations, and working under managers elected and removable by themselves. (J.S. Mill 1848: 773, quoted in Erdal 2011)*

Erasing neoclassical theory would make it possible to consider alternative futures based around the idea of sustainability, addressing the depletion of finite resources, environmental pollution and the gross inequality and unfairness between people and the positive possibilities of work in a modern industrial enterprise. Currently, the dictates of neoclassical economic theory prevent that pursuit.

The sustainability of all activity is approximately calculable, but the precise evaluation of such impacts is problematic because there is no effective way of valuing time. Orthodox discounting would render today's value of an impact in, say 50 years, as more or less insignificant at any apparently reasonable discount rate, but catastrophe in 50 years would still be catastrophic. It must only be a matter of time before sustainability will necessarily replace GDP growth as the overriding objective of economic activity. The 'degrowth movement' which first emerged in France over the past decade is one growing strand in the theory of this replacement (Fournier 2008). It is increasingly recognised that GDP growth does not equate with wellbeing and its returns, in terms of wellbeing, decline as GDP per capita increases. The pursuit of sustainability as the ultimate aim is only prevented by the continued dominance of neoclassical ideology. Adopting sustainability would therefore have to be driven by political initiative rather than economic dogma.

There have been alternative economic approaches which have sought to moderate economic theory and to apply its concepts to questions of public welfare and social balance. There has also been a challenge to economic orthodoxy to take account of the way real people really behave, rather than basing its description and prediction on mathematically necessitated assumptions. But these challenges to orthodox theory have had limited impact and it may be unlikely that any alternative approach would have any more effect, unless neoclassical theory was simply disregarded in its entirety.

Liberated from the restrictions of neoclassical ideology, governments, firms and individuals would be enabled to pursue their activities in rational legal ways, with the interests of all participants taken into consideration.

This final Part is concerned, first, with considering alternative theoretical parameters. Theory has been so decisive in shaping the practice of management and governance that an alternative framework may be an essential prerequisite of change. Secondly, more co-operative governance options are discussed which might facilitate the continued progress and sustainability of industrial firms. Finally, consideration is given to the necessary changes in the industrial and business context which might encourage and support a sustainable future.

References

Erdal, D., (2011), *Beyond the Corporation: Humanity Working*, London: Bodley Head.

Fournier, V., (2008), Escaping from the economy: the politics of degrowth, *International Journal of Sociology and Social Policy*, vol. 28, no. 11/12, 528–545.

Mill, J.S., (1848), *Principles of Political Economy*. (1973 edition available Clifton, New Jersey: Augustus M. Kelly.)

10

Towards a Sustainable Theory

From the perspective of corporate governance and management, the centrally planned socialist model does not provide a feasible alternative to neoclassical ideology. If it did, China would have made it work, but instead has made steady and careful progress towards a market oriented system. The subject matter of this chapter is therefore restricted to consideration of options within that market orientation.

In his account of the spiritual decline of American business schools, Khurana (2007) remarks one critical point of departure as the loss of pluralism in the teaching of economics. Prior to the re-adoption of the neoclassical orthodoxy in the early 1980s, alternative perspectives were taught in universities to succeeding generations of political, academic and business leaders. The primary distinction of neoclassical theory from alternative approaches is its reliance on unregulated markets to solve economic problems based on the idea that governments can only make matters worse. Alternative approaches had supported varying degrees of intervention to 'improve' the way markets work.

In practice, government interventions have played an important positive role in all successful economies, including the United States (Stiglitz 2010: 245). In East Asia, Japan, China itself and the tiger economies of South Korea, Taiwan, Singapore, Malaysia and others all have benefited from government interventions. This involvement has not been restricted to measures to protect infant industries, but include taxation and investment policies which have encouraged economic development both directly and through the provision of education and health, as well as the focusing of R&D investment. Moreover, economies with tighter regulation appear to fare better through financial crises than those committed to neoclassical dogma.

The argument for minimised government and deregulation as the source of economic success is hardly persuasive. The American government has regularly been persuaded to intervene in the economy to reverse the adverse effects of neoclassical orthodoxy. Nevertheless, the neoclassical view persists that government intervention in the economy leads not just to inefficiency but to both economic stagnation and to inflation.

Dissent among theoreticians has not been encouraged. Careers were most readily progressed by accepting the orthodox wisdom, rather than pursuing any challenging counter perspective. As the influence of economics became more pervasive, that singularity became increasingly decisive in shaping the real economy.

It is the orthodox wisdom which persuades firms to maximise shareholder wealth at risk of polluting the oceans and rivers, land and air, and wasting earth's finite resources. It is that orthodoxy which leads them to avoiding payment for any costs that can be avoided or externalised. It leads to the acceptance of inequalities and unfairness as unavoidable by-products of economic progress. It affects not only what firms do and how they do it, but how people inside firms are persuaded to behave in their pursuit of the bottom line.

That model has created a corporate culture of suspicion and mistrust as well as of greed. It justifies the grossest of inequities with the already wealthy encouraged to further excess, while a third of the world's population teeters on the brink of poverty and starvation.

In the face of such obvious injustice a moral case for change has been argued based on systems of values or convictions. But the impact of such argument has been limited. Good practice, based on an extraneous system of values or beliefs, will, in a democracy, always be voluntary, at most on a 'comply or explain' basis. And the practical effect of such voluntary codes is limited: those who live by the philosophy will practice accordingly irrespective; those who do not, will not.

Since the turn of the twentieth century there have been many dissenters. Within the ranks of generally conforming economic specialists there has always been a continuing critique, from such as those named on the opening page of this book. Some of them have clearly been renegades such as Thorstein Veblen who poured scorn and ridicule on those wealthy who made extrovert displays of their conspicuous consumption and waste.

In similar vein, J.K. Galbraith, having explained institutional truths as the lies that have to be internalised in order to progress in the relevant institutions, suggested:

> *The institutional truth of the financial world holds that association*
> *with money implies intelligence. And it holds broadly that the greater*
> *the amount of money, the greater the intelligence. (Galbraith 1989)*

He then, in 1989, proceeded to itemise the errors and stupidity of the mandarins heading up America's great financial houses. Veblen and Galbraith were popular economists, but their impact on the mainstream orthodoxy was minimal.

On the other hand, those who held to the neoclassical perspective such as Mises, Hayek, Friedman and colleagues, were heard within their own profession and their influence became dominant. It resulted in the dysfunctional distribution of income and wealth, with the wealthy having no more demands on their wealth than to invest it in order to increase it further, while the poor struggled to spend sufficient to keep the economy going, if not actually to survive. Moreover, the investments that the wealthy were drawn into making were increasingly oriented, for substantial and quick returns, towards financial products which had grown the speculative markets so rapidly, rather than the less immediately profitable projects of the real economy. It is this unregulated mainstream, and its increasingly unsustainable outcomes, which alternative approaches have sought to address.

But the mainstream never completely crowded out dissenting perspectives. More socially oriented, less prescriptive alternatives were pursued from time to time. In the main they used the same mathematical tools to focus on the interests of other stakeholders and the common good. Some rejected the neoclassical pretence of scientific objectivity and other approaches opposed specific elements of the neoclassical model. Yet other approaches have been explicitly based on a moral or ethical foundation.

The following sections consider some of these alternatives which might have different, more progressive outcomes. They are considered as far as possible on their merits without prior orientation to any particular ideology or set of values other than to the pragmatic perspective of what might work. Finally, some of the essential characteristics of a revised approach are suggested.

Welfare Economics

From its beginning, industrialisation created both great wealth and great poverty. Consequently, there has always been concern for achieving greater equity in the distribution of the economic benefits from industry. Despite being largely ignored by the economic mainstream, concern persists for social welfare and its distribution in a population. Welfare economics was concerned to address this issue by focusing on the welfare outcomes of policy decisions.

It is an explicitly normative, prescriptive study, as opposed to the avowedly descriptive, predictive nature of the neoclassical frame, which is sometimes referred to in this context as positive economics. Welfare economics is concerned with the economic wellbeing of individuals, households, cities, regions or whole countries with each category being the summation of welfares of individuals comprising the category.

Its foundation, and therefore its weakness, is in positive economics. It accepts the basic assumption of market efficiency, that resources will be allocated by the 'invisible hand' of market forces in such a way that full employment will be achieved and overall income maximised, or at least that no alternative allocation would result in a greater income for anyone with no one being worse off. Implicit in this model is the assumption that social welfare might also be maximised by that resource allocation and welfare economics seeks to achieve that maximisation through a variety of means which adjust resource allocations.

There are various theoretical approaches to the assessment of maximised welfare. The distribution of social welfare among citizens can theoretically be measured. The social welfare of all individuals could be assessed in terms of monetary value, making no distinction between the pound of a rich person or that of a pauper. These could then be added together to establish the social welfare of the whole society. Alternatively, welfare could be assessed making allowance for the fact that a pound is of less value to the rich than it is to the poor. This difference might be taken into account in assessing distributive efficiency which would be assumed to be maximised when welfare was distributed to those who would gain the greatest utility. The differently valued individual welfares could then be added to measure the social welfare of the whole society.

Clearly these ideas are theoretical. The possibility of measuring distributive efficiency is extremely limited, with little prospect of being practically implemented with any degree of real accuracy. Consequently, while the aim of welfare economics is laudable, its practical effects on policy in improving social welfare have been slight. It has developed as a branch of theoretical study, spawning an extensive literature, and with some methodological threads promising practical outcomes. For example, it has targeted the measurement of externalities by explicitly assessing the costs of actions including those incurred by, or inflicted on, public goods such as the atmosphere or climate.

Studies of the management of common pool resources such as pasture among rural African communities and village irrigation systems in Nepal (Ostrom 1990) may be indicative. Such an approach could, in principle, also be applicable to studying, for example, rainforest destruction or coal and oil shale extraction. As well as costs such as these, which are normally externalised, the approach could also be applicable to situations where consumption of a limited resource is not yet reflected in its market price because of the essentially short term emphasis of discounting techniques.

Input-output analysis makes explicit the assessment of such costs and benefits, including external costs not normally included in private profitability calculations. While the various methods available for assessing these costs and benefits remain more theoretical than practical, making the issues explicit was a significant step.

Welfare economics seeks to evaluate economic policies in terms of their effects on the wellbeing of the community. However, its assessments of social welfare and of the impacts of different resource allocations are necessarily expressed subject to so many unrealistic assumptions, as is the positive economics model on which it is based, that it offers little of practical value in measuring social wellbeing.

The more pragmatic approach resulting from the review of empirical studies presented by Wilkinson and Picket (2009) might be of more practical use. Their measures are real and policy recommendations derived from them would be clear, subject to agreement of an appropriate objective function for social welfare.

Social Balance

Social balance was the term used by Galbraith to express the desirable combination of private goods provided by the market with the public provision of necessary and desirable goods that the market would not or could not provide. Galbraith expressed it as the balance between private wealth and public squalor. The idea of balance contrasted with the simple market fundamentalist idea of minimising public provision.

Galbraith argued that classical economic theory had developed in a world of poverty whereas by the second half of the twentieth century it was being applied to a world of affluence. The rapid growth of automobile ownership was one sign of this continually increasing affluence, but their use required more and better publicly funded roads if increasing congestion and consequent waste of fuels and time were to be avoided.

Galbraith (1958) exampled the problem of social balance with the city of Los Angeles as it was in the late 1950s. The citizenry was by and large affluent with conspicuous, conspicuous consumption, but with no public provision of waste collection, people were forced to use home incinerators which rendered the air almost unbreathable in Los Angeles.

Clearly it would not be feasible to eliminate public provision of such goods as public roads. Nor did it prove desirable to avoid public provision of goods such as waste collection and disposal. If such items were privatised and made chargeable, some citizens might not afford the luxury of collection and disposal, or even home incineration, and so the environment would be damaged for all citizens. The problem of social balance is real enough; public provision of some goods is necessary and for others may be regarded as desirable.

Galbraith raised similar arguments for the public provision of education, health and social security. An educated population would be better fitted to work in a competitive post-industrial economy which would be ever more reliant on personal skills and expertise to develop technological innovation and intellectual capital. Rather that young members of the unemployed reserve army be educated to work in the new economy than to remain uneducated and a cost and liability on the state.

The most efficient social balance lay somewhere between no public provision and all provision being public. The fundamentalist argument that any small step in the direction of public provision would lead inexorably to full-on socialism was clearly nonsense. Galbraith quotes democratic socialist R.H. Tawney, drawing attention to the fact that high private incomes will not make the mass of people immune to disease and ignorance, whereas public provision for universal healthcare and education would produce a more enlightened, healthy and progressive society.

Just where public provision should stop and private begin was a question of political choice. Galbraith argued for increased spending on more and better public goods such as schools, parks and recreation facilities as well as hospitals and improved social housing. So much was subjective opinion, but the balance Galbraith would have drawn would have excluded private provision of goods for which there was no fundamental need or want, except that which was created artificially by aggressive and invasive marketing. His fear was not simply that such goods made no contribution to a better society, but that such artificially created demand would not be robust and its collapse might trigger or amplify recession.

That fear might well be valid, but it would be a problem that would be solved by the normal workings of market forces, albeit not without pain. The provision of more and better public goods, especially ones deemed desirable on purely subjective grounds, is less easy to justify unless they are explained in terms of benefiting the future development of the economy.

Galbraith does not, and could not, develop a mathematical model to explain and justify social balance. Nor does he completely reject the quantitative analysis of neoclassical economics. But he explicitly acknowledged that value of non-mathematical, qualitative expression in economic decision-making.

Behavioural Economics

Adam Smith suggested that human behaviour was motivated at the highest level by the desire to become proper objects of respect, 'deserving and obtaining this credit and rank among our equals' (Smith 1790: 213–4). Behaviour which includes elements of generosity and altruism is not simply to be denigrated as self-serving or irrational, as is the necessary neoclassical assumption. Behavioural economics seeks to get closer to the truth of what motivates human behaviour.

Behavioural economics argues that individuals' ability to maximize their utility is limited by their 'bounded rationality' rather than their intention to be satisfied with less (Simon 1956). Thus, satisficing was an alternative to maximisation as a descriptive and predictive variable, offered on the grounds that maximisation was neither descriptive nor accurately predictive. Similarly, melioration was also offered as an alternative behavioural proposition (Herrnstein 1988). Both offered the opportunity to escape the confines of mathematical modelling, but it would appear that rejection of the spurious quantitative witchcraft was a step too far for behavioural economics.

Cyert and March's behavioural theory of the firm developed a theory which reflected real behaviour more accurately than profit maximisation. Satisficing was certainly more realistic. Within the firm, satisficing was applied to the workings of coalitions such as the board of directors. Each coalition member required the fulfilment of some minimum performance level, all of which might be met through negotiation, rather than performance being maximised on one category but minimum levels on others not being achieved.

This version of satisficing more accurately reflected the perspective of Smith's artisans and entrepreneurs focused on making a living from their working occupations. They were prepared not to maximise profits, but to achieve a level which allowed them to provide a service to their customers and to pay their suppliers a sufficient price to justify their continuation in business. The satisficing concept is also consistent with firms building up some 'spare' resource as 'organisational slack' which might be held in reserve for future investment or emergency.

Behavioural theory applied to the firm provides some insights which confirm common sense but does not extend far into the psychology of human behaviour, which has been a fertile field for academic research. Studies of economic decision-making under conditions of uncertainty and how behaviour differed from the neo-classical prediction challenged the notion of economics as a 'science'. Ideas such as equity, generosity and altruism were built into models of decision-making and appeared under various circumstances to be significant influencers. Research also addressed the problem of decision-taking over extended time periods, where again irrationality was offered as a neoclassical explanation of decisions which did not fit with discounted values. Behaviourists were able to offer more psychologically informed explanations.

Behavioural economists have also used neoclassical methodology and assumptions to analyse a wide variety of human behaviours. Areas to have been studied include crime and punishment, marriage and fertility, government and democracy, health, religion and mass behaviour (Tommasi & Ierulli 1995), consumer choice and marketing, fertility and migration, entrepreneurship, psychology of hazards and stress, tax evasion and labour economics (Maital 1988). This breadth of subject matter suggests that the approach of behavioural economics, adapting the neoclassical model to the analysis of different behaviours, has been a fertile field for academic publication. However, the practical outcomes have been limited. For example, neoclassical methodology is used to study the practice of democracy, in particular the activities of lobbyists and pressure groups, as the means to getting representatives to do the bidding of constituents (Matsusaka 1995). The analysis appears to justify the activities of lobbyists largely on ideological grounds that lobbying limits the extent to which representatives would pursue their own personally held ideals. The problem of lobbying perverting the normal democratic process is not pursued, yet American companies, sometimes combining as an industry (for example, the pharmaceuticals industry), charge sufficient for their products to cover the tax allowable costs of lobbying the government in pursuit of their own interests. It was estimated that in 2009, for example, federal lobbyists and their clients spent more than $3.47 billion (Tomasky 2010).

This approach still accepts the assumption that human beings seek to maximise their own self-interest, even though their behaviour may not achieve maximisation. Market forces are assumed to allocate resources efficiently. And individuals' preferences are assumed to be fairly stable. While acknowledging all three of these assumptions are actually false, the approach nevertheless asserts they are sufficiently right to provide insights into human behaviour.

It has however been forcefully argued that any deviation from the neoclassical model, for example deviation from maximisation behaviour, would invalidate the model, just as any information asymmetry in an otherwise perfectly competitive market would severely damage competition. Moreover, if the model from which insights are drawn is invalid, then the insights themselves are likely to be worthless.

The New Economics

These various challenges to the neoclassical orthodoxy have been prompted by its long term dysfunctions and the short term crises to which it has given rise. Many of the changes and corrections presented by these alternative models are included in what has been labelled as The New Economics (TNE). This approach recognises the dysfunctional outcomes of the neoclassical mainstream and addresses them, one by one, and in so doing proposes what is referred to as a New Economic model.

Perhaps the most fundamental change is the rejection of gross domestic product as the key measure of an economy and its growth as the all-important target of economic management. Such a change would have basic and widespread implications. The justification for this is twofold. Firstly, it is the continuing chase for growth which causes the depletion of resources, pollution and climate change. Secondly, the achievement of growth does not appear to increase 'happiness'. These surely are powerful, if apparently simple, arguments. Rather than focus on growth, TNE's focus is on social and individual wellbeing. In this it appears to be sharing the objectives of the welfare economics model, though it is not clear whether TNE follows the welfare model in seeking to maximise wellbeing, in which case it would be drawn into the mathematical contortions that have frustrated the application of welfare economics.

TNE recognises the finite stock of the planet's resources and the damage being done by economic activity, particularly in terms of climate change. It also recognises inequalities of income and wealth as a major problem, also the growing importance of intellectual capital and the decline in importance of monetary capital in support of the real economy.

The wellbeing objective has to be identified in specific terms if it is to be made operational. Expressing it as a clear and simple target, as is maximising gross domestic product (GDP) growth, poses some difficulty. The objective of individual and social wellbeing is also constrained by the planet's limited capacities. The TNE model would therefore focus on achievement of specific measures of wellbeing for all, subject to mandatory achievement of environmental sustainability and fairness in the distribution of income, wealth and non-monetary benefits.

TNE treats the role of the financial sector as supportive of the real economy and the environment - in which treatment it is surely mistaken - and industry's role as constrained by the need to be sustainable in its treatment of the environment and local communities. The New Economics Foundation refers to a variety of proposals and initiatives under the TNE banner, including the localisation of enterprise, the regulation of banks and especially the promotion of localised and micro-banking and the limitation of speculative investment banking and trading, the taxing of pollution and subsidising of green investment and the equalising of economic development between regions. In addition, TNE advocates measures to end food speculation, to regulate off-shore tax havens, to regulate and supervise financial actors and products and to reforming exchange rates and global reserve systems. .

Finally, the New Economics Foundation recognises the world is increasingly interdependent, that the wealthy West 'over consumes' and 'over pollutes' to the disadvantage of poorer parts of the world. Moreover:

> *Rising levels of consumption have not delivered dramatically increased life satisfaction in wealthy countries. Getting off the consumer treadmill will be chance for liberation and the discovery of what really matters to us. And with consumption in the rich world reduced, there will be more space in the global commons for other people, who don't yet have enough, to meet their basic needs.*[1]

This is not a neat and simple package as is the neoclassical model. It has all the messiness of the real world. And it addresses the most pressing economic issues confronting the real world. But for it to succeed, the neoclassical ideology must first be displaced.

Escaping the Dogma

While the problems created by adherence to the neoclassical ideology are effectively identified by these alternative approaches, they do not provide a clear and simple alternative theory or model. The danger is therefore that the current dogma will survive all such challenges. It may not do so in its more recent, fundamentalist format, but the basic idea will survive. Utility maximising economic man and the profit maximising firm, operating within an

---

1   Extract from New Economics Foundation website http://www.neweconomics.org/projects/ interdependence

assumed to be efficient market, will be accepted as the solution to maximising economic growth which would remain as the ultimate goal.

The inequity of social welfare distribution would be regretted as necessary to the utilitarian result. Moreover, it might be suggested that care for the environment could be more readily financed by a successful economy, rather than by one which is struggling to survive.

Alternative approaches which are based on models which work according to neoclassical rules seem unlikely ever to have much effect. The injection of elements of moral conscience or altruism is simply incompatible with a maximising model and seems most unlikely to modify its operation to any significant extent.

Neoclassical economics models real things, whole economies, markets, firms and people in ways which bear little resemblance to the reality. In response to that common critique, Friedman argued that it mattered little whether an economic model was realistic, so long as it predicted accurately. But economics makes no more accurate predictions than it does descriptions. And when its predictions are really needed such as when a bubble is going to burst, or how best to repay quantitative easing, there is no coherent response, but a multiplicity of conflicting opinions. The neoclassical model contributes nothing to such dilemmas.

While neoclassical descriptions and predictions appear worthless, inaccurate and untestable, they are nevertheless still potent. It has become more a matter of faith and belief rather than coherent analysis. As such it has become difficult to modify. If alternatives such as The New Economics are to gain any traction, it would seem the neoclassical theory in its entirety would need to be replaced. Only when the neoclassical faith is destroyed will a more thoughtful, relevant and progressive alternative become practicable.

The application of mathematical procedures, in particular differential calculus, to model the economy appears to be a root problem. This required the definition of components of the economy to be represented in mathematical form and in particular to be assumed to pursue maxima or minima on a most commonly two-dimensional, or at most three-dimensional, map. Thus, two variables were used to describe economic components as complex as markets or firms. And their assumed economic purpose was expressed in the most simplistic and inadequate terms. This extreme reductionism has infected all areas of economic theory which adopt the mathematical approach.

Mathematical techniques and procedures may have been attractive at the end of the nineteenth century as a way of investing the study of economics with what appeared to be some scientific rigour. As a wholly theoretical study, unconnected with the management of a real economy, or the regulation of real markets or the management of real firms, this may have been a step forward. Certainly it opened up whole new fields for academic publication which are still actively pursued today.

Nor has the application of mathematics to more mundane practical problems been any more encouraging as to its relevance to social phenomena. The apparently simple task, relative to modelling economies, markets and firms, of calculating the risk and uncertainty of bundles of securities, has so far proved beyond the most sophisticated mathematical brains. Long Term Capital Management went bust on the back of the Black and Scholes formula, while the US sub-prime bust is widely attributed to David Li's Gaussian copula function. These failures matter less in themselves, but suggest the role for sophisticated mathematicians in economic theory, Nobel laureates or not, should surely be limited.

If mathematical modelling were banished to the ivory tower, much of applied economics would have to be rethought. Microeconomics would have been largely displaced. The assumption of artificial objectives for the firm, such as shareholder wealth maximisation, would no longer have any foundation in the real world, merely as part of the theoretic study which might fulfil the purpose of training for the academic mind. A similar purpose might be found for various threads such as agency theory, transaction cost economics, the theory of markets in corporate managements and any constructs dealing with markets, firms and people on the basis of mathematical representations.

Without the mathematical pretence there would be no necessity to assume maximisation and therefore no need for impoverishment of all else to be pursued. This would return the notion of economic man to its pre-neoclassical form, self-interested, but in the long term. Utility maximising economic man is the value judgement on which the whole of orthodox economics has been based. It is understood not to be a realistic model of human behaviour, notions of fairness and justice, for example, being prevalent in all groups. However, human beings are, with only a few heroic exceptions, corruptible, and the emphasis on monetary incentives successfully 'crowds out' other motivations, or corrupts. As neoclassical thinking intends it to do.

Acceptance of long term self-interest as the basis of economic man would enable the entrepreneur to pursue a balanced concern for the best interests of his or her own business future and, necessarily, for the future of customers, suppliers and creditors as well as employees. Also, within the social frame the classical version of economic man would allow a more rounded set of concerns and motivations, which might include aspects of altruism or kindness, without them being denigrated as self-serving, deviant or irrational. The stranglehold of neoclassical Friedmanite thinking on social culture might then be relaxed.

Displacing neoclassical theory in its totality would enable several basic errors to be avoided. Making markets the focus of economic analysis, rather than the firm, was an important error and one that Adam Smith did not make. He focused on the process of manufacture and the division of labour in his pin factory which he recognised as the source of economic strength. The failure of economic theory to comprehend and model the firm in any meaningful way, led to the focus on opening up and deregulating markets in order to achieve increasing division of labour, as Smith suggested. It also led to completely side-stepping the business of managing an enterprise and therefore ignoring all the ill effects of its adoption of agency theory.

Microeconomic theory also completely overlooks the simple and often remarked fact that competitive markets tend, unless regulated, to become monopolistic. The ideological belief in deregulation permitted competition to be destroyed and markets to be fixed and abused by dominant competitors and in the medium to long term for competition itself to become unsustainable.

Another important error that might simply be avoided if neoclassical theory was displaced is its conflation of real and speculative markets. That led to its failure to distinguish between the traditional economic roles (extraction, manufacture and distribution and associated services) on the one hand, with their benefits in terms of employment and income distribution, and on the other, the high risk–high return speculative activities of financial sector firms which serve no useful social purpose. Continued failure to distinguish between real and speculative markets leads inevitably to the financial exploitation of firms in the real economy, and the continued growth of firms in the financial sector, the latter's risks being underwritten by the real economy and its taxpayers.

A final error which would be avoided if neoclassical theory were displaced is the assumption of ownership primacy. There is limited rationale for this in the case of economic organisation, despite the fact that Anglo-Saxon law has been largely developed to protect private property. The neoclassical assumption quite ignores the ambiguity of ownership with limited liability as well as the levels of risk at which stakeholders, other than shareholders, are involved with the firm. Moreover, as argued by the New Economic model, monetary capital is of declining importance while people based assets, such as intellectual capital, are of increasing importance to the success of the contemporary firm. There is no justification for shareholders being granted primacy over all other stakeholders, especially employees.

Other errors, omissions and simple falsehoods buried within the neoclassical model have been previously highlighted. Together they suggest a block of theory, which is utterly misguided, but which nevertheless has a profound and malign impact on practice. But, more than that, it is a block of theory which is simply redundant.

Classical theory served the early days of industrialisation, but if the neoclassical amendment had never been invented, no one, bar the odd banker, hedge fund trader or ivory tower academic would have been any the worse off, and a great number would have been better served. Firms would have been better managed had they never been influenced by the idea of profit maximisation, much less shareholder value maximisation. That is demonstrable in the brief survey of governance in Germany and Japan where firms have been protected somewhat from such catastrophic ideas.

The important element in displacing this malign theory would be for university departments and business schools to cease teaching the mathematics of neoclassical theory so that future generations of 'madmen in authority' might not be so immersed in such corrosive beliefs.

Erasing the neoclassical ideology would also liberate government in its role of economic management to make use of national accounting data, including the composition and components of GDP. This information has been collected, with more or less accuracy, since the Great Depression of the 1930s when the need for reasonably accurate information as the basis for appropriate government interventions first became apparent.

Most analysis of GDP completely ignores the crucial difference between acrtivity in the real economy and that in the socially useless financial-speculative sector. It is a distinction that could readily be made. The basic components of recorded GDP are consumption, investment, government expenditure and investment, imports and exports. Data on these is collected on an industry by industry basis and by regions, and includes information on unemployment rates, household savings and consumption, inflation, long term interest rates, purchasing power parity exchange rates, house price movements, household wealth and indebtedness and various other statistics so that governments have a reasonably clear picture of the recent past performance as the basis for economic decision. Data is aggregated to provide national statistics. All OECD members collect information on a comparable basis and comparative data is published regularly.

Erasure of neoclassical ideology would liberate government to use the tools of national accounting without its judgement being perverted by false dogma.

Sustainability Economics

Neoclassical theory focuses at a macro level on maximising GDP growth and at a micro level on maximising shareholder wealth. It is incoherent as to how these two are related, other than through blind belief in ideology. GDP growth eases the task of government in a democratic world, solving short term economic problems on a broad front. The importance of shareholder wealth is entirely theoretical and falsely based. Both concepts pale to insignificance compared to the overriding need for the achievement of sustainability.

Sustainability is not a theory based on sophisticated mathematics, but an empirically observed necessity which will depend on actions and behaviours. Many of these issues have been identified in alternative approaches to economic theory already discussed. Others are more particular to the management of enterprise and have been identified in preceding chapters of this text. They are the components of sustainability which have an important economic impact and which are of particular significance to corporate governance and management.

The first and overriding concept implicit in sustainability is recognition of the interdependence of all people, bound together by the simple facts of the earth's fragile climate and finite supply of critical resources such as water, oil and food, and its limited capacities which are becoming ever more stretched as population continues to grow.

The external costs of pollution and consumption of finite resources are understood, are generally measurable and have been identified as the responsibility of the unit that incurs them. As with all such regulatory issues affecting the planet, global agreement would be important, though difficult to implement and police. If relevant markets remain unregulated, the post-industrial economies seem likely to progress more quickly to absolute decline with increasing levels of unemployment becoming permanent, particularly affecting unskilled and semi-skilled jobs. Current levels of inequality of wealth and income, particularly in post-industrial economies whose populations have become accustomed to general affluence, seem likely to prove unsustainable and to cause unprecedented social unrest. Moreover, levels of inequality between rich and poor nations, amplified by changes in climate, are also widely predicted to cause social aggravation.

To be sustainable, firms must acknowledge the balance of interests between stakeholders. The prime responsibility of company directors is for the survival and long term prosperity of their company, which will not be achieved by the maximisation of the interests of one stakeholder group and the impoverishment of the rest.

These various components of sustainability are made more urgent by two apparently accelerating trends. First, with China, India and others developing their economic strength at such a rapid rate, earth's resources will be exhausted and its climate damaged even quicker than predicted.

Second the explosion in inequality, both within and between nations, is accelerating. Plato suggested the richest should earn no more than four times the poorest. Drucker opted for a ratio of 20 to 1. The current ratio of big company CEOs' earnings to those on the minimum wage is between 400 and 500 and rising.

If these trends are allowed to continue the general suffering, inflicted either by the plant or by fellow man, is likely to be extreme.

This brief review of some aspects of sustainability indicates something of the necessary changes that might be facilitated by the wholesale rejection of neoclassical ideology. It is based on the recognition that, despite all appearances to the contrary, the human race is all in this together. The necessity to co-operate is not grounded on moral rightness or justice. It is not a question of values, but long term survival.

References

Galbraith, J.K., (1958), *The Affluent Society*, London: Hamish Hamilton.

Galbraith, J.K., (1989), *In Pursuit of the Simple Truth*, Commencement address to the women graduates of Smith College, Massachusetts, 28th July.

Hermstein, R., (1988), *A Behavioural Alternative to Utility Maximisation*, in Maital, S (ed.) Applied Behavioural Economics, Brighton: Wheatsheaf Books.

Khurana, R., (2007), *From Higher Aims to Hired Hands*, Princeton: Princeton University Press.

Maital, S. (ed.), (1988), *Applied Behavioural Economics*, Brighton: Wheatsheaf Books.

Matsusaka, J.G., (1995), The economic approach to democracy, in M. Tommasi & K. Ierulli (eds), (1995), *The New Economics of Human Behaviour*, Cambridge: Cambridge University Press.

Ostrom, E., (1990), *Governing the Commons: The Evolution of Institutions for Collective Action*, Cambridge: Cambridge University Press.

Simon, H.A., (1956), Rational choice and the structure of the environment, *Psychological Review*, vol. 63, no. 2, 129–138.

Smith, A., (1790), *The Theory of Moral Sentiments*, though first published in 1759, the edition referred is from 1790, as reproduced in the Dover Philosophical Classics Series, New York: Dover Publications.

Stiglitz, J., (2010), *Freefall: Free Markets and the Sinking of the Global Economy*, London: Penguin.

Tommasi, M. & Ierulli, K. (eds), *The New Economics of Human Behavior*, Cambridge: Cambridge University Press.

Tomasky, M., (2010), The money fighting health care reform, *The New York Review of Books*, vol. LVII, no. 6.

Wilkinson, R. & Pickett, K., (2009), *The Spirit Level: Why More Equal Societies Almost Always Do Better*, London: Allen Lane.

11

Degrees of Co-operation

The later conceptions of the firm derived from neoclassical theory evolved from concerns over the separation of corporate control from ownership, first highlighted by Berle and Means (1932). Questions arose regarding the legitimacy of corporate management. In large companies management generally had no ownership. Nor were they subject to any democratic selection or approval, but were appointed on whatever grounds seemed apt to the appointers and continued in office either till they resigned voluntarily, retired or committed some unforgivable misdemeanour. Shareholders who had the power to veto top level appointments or reappointments were generally passive and rarely countermanded any board decision. Questions of the legitimacy and accountability of management were rarely raised, but would not have been unreasonable.

Furthermore, corporate management has a tendency either to attract individuals who are already corrupt, or to corrupt them after appointment. Companies that have had criminal charges against them include Goldman Sachs, Exon, GE, Chevron, Mitsubishi, IBM, Kodak, Pfizer, Sears – actually, the list is endless. A comprehensive list of the greedy, the thugs and villains who got to the top of the corporate world would include such as Robert Maxwell, Bernard Madoff, Bernie Ebbers of Worldcom, Barclays' Bob Diamond, Enron's Jeffrey Skilling, Fred Goodwin of RBS, Ernest Saunders of Guinness and so on … the list would be longer than this book. Despite the real accountabilities of firms that would be operative in the absence of the neoclassical ideology, as identified in the previous chapter, the current reality is different and questions of executive legitimacy and accountability would seem highly pertinent.

The Unaccountable Tyranny

The possibility that company directors could run their firms as personal fiefdoms gave the agency theory some surface justification despite its false foundation. The theory suggested that accountability be reinforced by the appointment of external, independent, non-executive directors to monitor executive performance and behaviour, in particular ensuring it served the financial interests of shareholders. That was the theory. The approach predictably failed, firstly because shareholders remained largely uninterested in the internal workings of the firms in which they were invested, and secondly because the external, independent directors were deliberately chosen from the same corporate pool as the executive directors and were agreeable to being passive and generally supportive, rather than, as the Chinese describe them, 'independent watchdogs'.

The disinterest of shareholders investing through intermediaries is only increased by ultrafast automated trading systems which make ownership a temporary, often fleeting, status. For the vast majority of shareholders interest in the individual company is unlikely. The idea of shareholder loyalty to investee companies is a vestige from a different era.

The agency theory need to ensure that executive directors pursued the interests of shareholders led to share bonus schemes which converted executives into shareholders of immense wealth, ensuring their convergence of interest. The moral hazard this involved, with executives gaining from risky projects if they succeeded and not losing if they failed, was a small part of the story, mini versions of the moral hazard of the whole investment banking sector. Executives were seduced into actions from which they benefited personally, their gains far exceeding any perks, or benefits from 'shirking', of which agency theorists were so suspicious. More importantly, it also led to the engineering of 'hostile' takeovers transacted at share prices high enough to trigger bonus issues. Such takeovers would invariably be against both the best interests of the company and those of shareholders who were invested for the long term, if there were any.

Executive directors might well have a prior commitment to the long term success of their company, but that motivation could be readily 'crowded out' by monetary incentives. Executives are no different from other human beings in being generally corruptible by extreme amounts of money. Such was the explicit purpose of most share bonus schemes.

Thus, the agency approach to making corporate executives accountable for their management of the corporation not infrequently led to those executives setting up their company to lose its autonomy, have its assets sold off and employees reduced. The legitimacy and accountability of enterprise management under such a custom and practice clearly remain extremely valid concerns.

In interviews for *The Corporation* (Achbar, Abbott & Bakan 2005), Chomsky referred to the publicly quoted firm, 'the dominant institution of our time', as an 'unaccountable tyranny', while Hare described it as having all the characteristics of a psychopath:

> *Callous unconcern for the feelings of others, incapacity to maintain enduring relationships, reckless disregard for the safety of others, deceitfulness: repeated lying and conning others for profit, incapacity to experience guilt, and failure to conform to social norms with respect to lawful behaviours.*

These characteristics and the greed, corruption and criminality previously referred to, approximate to the popular conception of big business. Moreover, it is wholly compatible with the command and control style of management described by Ghoshal, the familiar picture of the corporate tyrant, asserting the sole accountability as to the shareholder personified in himself and ignoring the legally based accountabilities discussed previously. In practice, that accountability complies only with neoclassical dogma, liberation from which would enable consideration of other stakeholders than shareholders and other accountabilities than maximising value.

Opposing theories of management, providing the basis for more enlightened and effective approaches, have been in place and taught for more than half a century. The fact that they have been effectively crowded out by neoclassical dogma suggests the need for something more robust than a revised ideology. Other stakeholders than shareholders need some legally based franchise within the firm providing some real power and influence in specific situations or related to specific decisions.

Enfranchising Employees

The diversity of employee groups in industrial firms appears to exceed by far their community of interest. On the face of it, unskilled shop floor workers, time served technicians and technical specialists, highly qualified R&D scientists and transient MBA certified adminstrators appear to have little in common. They have very different external affiliations to trade unions, professional institutes and associations. The only clear common interest is the fact they devote their working lives to, and earn their living from, the company. They share a common interest in its survival and long term prosperity.

That basic commonality of interest is not however very apparent in the history of industrial relations, especially in Britain. Through most of the nineteenth century working people were exploited and abused. This led to some legislation, albeit generally too little, too late, being passed in Britain to protect the worker from exploitative employers. It also resulted in the formation of politically motivated worker collectives, trade unions and political parties aimed at defending working people from exploitation and advancing their social development. The struggle between employers and workers, identified by the latter as being class based, was the dominant fact of twentieth century industrial relations in Britain, as was the left-right dichotomy in the political field.

Conflict ideology drove trade unionism to industrial action which destroyed many companies and not a few whole industries in Britain. In 1971 the Upper Clyde Shipbuilders (UCS) workforce, led by Marxist and then member of the British Communist Party, Jimmy Reid, responded to the threatened closure of their plant with a work-in, completing orders then in progress. The orthodox union response under such circumstances would have been all out strike, which time and again was demonstrated to be wholly counterproductive to the workers' interests. Reid argued that the workers:

> knew more about the viability of their trade and their business than the managers, financiers and, not to be forgotten, the Treasury officials too, who all insisted there was no alternative but to bow to the markets and padlock the shipyard gates. (Kettle 2010)

The workforce clearly does have valuable inputs of knowledge and expertise about the business which is different from those of management, and sometimes that difference might be critical. Reid was unique in forcing the workers' inputs to be taken into account. In the UCS case it was the government which was being driven by ideology (neoclassical) and Reid, who was acting on the merits of the individual case. He was proved right since, four decades on, two of the three ex-UCS yards were still building ships.

Six years later, the government offered some elements of industrial democracy. A committee of enquiry was set up in 1975. It was, in part, an attempt to harmonise worker participation in company management throughout the European Community. But more importantly it was part of the Labour government's social contract attempt to resolve the then explosive industrial relations which eventually ended in the 1979 'winter of discontent' and the accession of the Thatcher government.

The resulting Bullock Report of 1977 recommended that companies employing 2000 or more should have employee representatives on the board of directors. The proposal was that the number of directors representing employees should equal the number representing shareholder interests. A third group of co-opted directors must not exceed the number of employee or shareholder directors. Representation was to be on the existing British unitary board system, with no two-tier boards. Employee directors were to be chosen solely through trade union machinery, with only unionised employees influencing the choice of employee directors, exclusively through a Joint Representation Committee representing the unions in the company, and not directly by employees.

The report met with a mixed response. A view expressed from the employers' perspective included the following:

> The more people are able to influence decisions which closely affect their work the more effective will that involvement be; the more effective the involvement the greater the commitment to the company's objectives which, in the final analysis, will be concerned with generating wealth or services for the community as a whole. (City Company Law Committee 1977 'A Reply to Bullock')

So much was positive, but direct participation was nevertheless rejected, as it was by the three industrialists on the committee, members of the Confederation of British Industry (CBI), who issued a minority report recommending employee directors should serve on the supervisory board of a two-tier system rather than on a unitary board, and also rejecting the unions' tight control on employee representation. Trade unions were seen as already too powerful and too irresponsibly militant. The minority report proclaimed shareholders as the 'owners' of companies who should retain the ultimate authority and control in General Meeting.

The Bullock orientation to the unions as the sole legitimate representative of employee interests was a characteristic of that time when union-led closed shops were a common feature and the use of industrial action was general and indefinite strikes were not necessarily used as the last resort. A more plant based orientation to employees, as adopted by the workers at UCS under Reid's leadership, might have been more effective and relevant to individual circumstances.

For the unions, the Bullock recommendations also presented difficulties. They had been traditionally opposed to taking any responsibility for company management, with their representatives accountable solely to union members on whose behalf they conducted 'free collective bargaining'. Anything which might compromise or weaken the collective bargaining strength of the unions was viewed with suspicion. In the end it was the unions themselves which rejected the proposals for industrial democracy in Britain. Bullock was consigned to history.

The pressure to harmonise corporate governance throughout the EU, which was one ostensible reason for the Bullock enquiry, eventually resulted in agreement among all members to accept the concept of a European Company (SE). This facility has been available in Britain since 2004. As indicated in chapter 7, the main thrust of regulations regarding the establishment and governance of SEs is permissive rather than obligatory. For example, an SE may operate under either a one-tier or two-tier system of administration, as laid down in the firm's own constitutional documents. The representative arrangements are unspecified by law, but must be stated in the company's statutes. Thus, any European firms, including British, could establish a two-tier board structure and could allot half the supervisory board places to employee representatives as is German practice. They could also adopt the European allocation of responsibilities to the two tiers, with the supervisory board having responsibility for the adequacy of internal control systems and external reporting.

Adoption of the two-tier board structure would enable various other aspects of accountability also to be adopted. Other stakeholder representatives could be appointed to the supervisory board such as a customer representative or an independent director to represent the interests of the environment. The roles of CEO and company chairman could be separated, as the UK code of practice requires, with the company chairperson being appointed by, and from among, the supervisory board and the CEO chairing the executive board, being appointed by the supervisory board.

Practice in EU member states differs regarding worker involvement in corporate management. These differing traditions were a major cause of the delay in adopting the SE format. The process for establishing an SE requires employees and management to agree the form and extent of employee representation before the creation of the SE is finalised. By January 2011 over 700 SEs had been formed in continental Europe where the differences between existing national governance arrangements and SE governance are limited. So far there have been no significant registrations of SEs in Britain.

Without adopting the European Company format, minor legal innovations might be achieved. For example, requiring employee representation on remuneration committees has been widely recommended and would be a relatively small step away from neoclassical orthodoxy. Similarly, the suspension of voting rights on shares that have been owned for less than six months was one of the departing Labour government's lists of election commitments in 2010. Such a change might have had a moderating effect. Similarly, the granting of voting rights to employees, without share ownership, on certain strategic matters such as mergers and acquisitions, which are particularly likely to affect their employment.

Industrial democracy as envisaged by Bullock, or any variation on the SE format, would have the immediate effect of overruling the Friedmanite dictum that management had no other social responsibility than maximising shareholder value. At the same it time it would provide some limited protection of firms against hostile takeover. But enfranchising employees has frequently been taken further, even to eliminating the role of external shareholders entirely. This is clearly in total denial of the neoclassical dogma, if not of capitalism itself. Nevertheless, firms which are run without outside shareholders appear to have been robust and less vulnerable to financial shocks than firms with outside and publicly quoted shareholdings.

The basic concept is one of co-operation between stakeholders, particularly the internal stakeholders. It is not only a practical way of doing things, but is based on a philosophy which is the direct opposite of neoclassical ideology. It has a long history stretching back to the earliest days of industrialisation.

Co-operation

Co-operation has always worked. It is in our genes as it is in most species, for example, bees, ants, apes and many others (Ridley 1996). Man's success as a hunter-gatherer depended on the co-operation within groups dividing their labour for the benefit of the group as a whole. The success of co-operation depended on two human character traits: the capability to make rational calculations and an instinct for reciprocity, to repay kindness with kindness and to punish deception (Seabright 2004).

Adam Smith's division of labour, which he argued was the engine of economic growth, was many times more complex than hunter-gathering, and today's specialisation is many times more complex and sophisticated than Smith's pin workshop. We now divide our labour not just within production processes, but in all areas of life, notably in the development of academic theory, and also between nations. The importance of co-operation has expanded as a consequence.Co-operation may be in the genes, but it is also learned behaviour as demonstrated by Axelrod's work on game theory tournaments and his development of the tit-for-tat strategy of co-operation. Co-operative behaviour was based on mutual trust which is developed progressively through repeated experience. In organisational terms, the necessity for hierarchical control can be reduced by rationally justified, trust based lateral controls (Jönsson 1996). In increasingly knowledge based industries, hierarchical organisation becomes less appropriate and effective.

The earliest formation of co-operative and mutual firms was generally in response to the unfair and exploitative behaviour of the mill owners/employers. For example, Robert Owen's company shop at New Lanark, selling good quality produce for cash at cost price to company employees, at a time when many mill owners were paying their people in company tokens that could only be exchanged at the company shop where stuff was sold at exploitative prices. Owen's initiative evolved over time, leading to the formation of the retail co-operatives and to the widespread adoption of the mutual idea relating to insurance and banking activity.

From the beginning, co-operative firms were based on the motivation to be fair to the many, rather than to maximise the wealth of the few. Their success derives from that coincidence of motivations: to do what works and to be fair. Selling at cost price, rather than making a profit for external shareholders, was developed by customer co-operatives which traded at a profit but returned the surplus as a dividend for customers. In all other respects, they were intended to be run as professionally managed competitive businesses. Similarly, employee co-operatives were intended to be run on normal commercial grounds, but with the surpluses earned being returned to the employees. In both customer and employee co-operatives the surpluses that were distributed were calculated after retaining sufficient funds within the business for future investment and to ensure its security.

Co-operative business is not simply a matter of being idealistic or utopian, but of calculating what works and adopting that strategy.

Both in Britain and the United States, a high proportion of non-banking firms in the financial sector, building societies and so-called friendly societies were originally organised as mutuals, having no shareholders and accruing profits, a substantial portion of which were repaid to members who were their customers, mainly borrowers.

With the deregulation which accompanied stock market computerisation, mutual societies in the UK were enabled to extend their activities into banking. Several large mutuals, with massive reserves which had been accrued over many decades, began to compete with traditional banks who had limited reserves beyond what the Bank of England stipulated in its role as lender of last resort. The existence of those reserves, protected by the building societies' mutual status, attracted much attention. Concerted campaigns were mounted to persuade members to convert into public limited liability companies. The justification given for such conversion was theoretical and largely neoclassically based. The real motivation was obvious: to get hold of the accumulated reserves which had been accumulated over generations of membership. In the process, the reserves were dispersed partly as a one-off payment, or bribe, to the final generation of members, and partly paid out to the financial specialists overseeing the conversion from mutual to public company. An estimated 70 per cent of former mutual building societies demutualised during the 1990s, invariably with the active support of managers and directors who stood to gain personally from the process (Birchall & Simmons 2004: 490).

Nevertheless, the three main categories of co-operatives, customer or consumer co-operatives, employee or worker co-owned co-operatives and mutual societies, still operate widely in banking, agriculture, retail and various manufacture and service areas all over the world. David Erdal provides interesting accounts of many substantial employee owned co-operatives in Europe and the United States, including the Mondragón federation, the John Lewis partnership, Guiseppi Bucci, Ernst Abbe and Lewis Kelso and other instructive examples supported by the Baxi Partnership established by Philip Baxendale (Erdal 2011).

Lopes-Espinoza and colleagues identified 47,000 co-operatives in the five countries they studied (Germany, France, UK, Spain and Portugal) (López-Espinosa, Maddocks & Polo-Garrido 2009: 274–306). The vast majority of co-operatives they surveyed were fairly small companies with an average of less than 300 employees. However, successful large scale co-operatives demonstrate the possibilities. The UK Co-operative Group employs more than 87,000, the Spanish Basque Mondragón federation employs over 85,000 while the UK based John Lewis Partnership has 69,000.

Less than 2 per cent of co-operative firms across the globe are customer owned, the UK Co-operative Group being by far the largest example with 2.5m members and a turnover of £10bn in food retailing, pharmacy, banking and insurance, funerals, travel, farming, legal services and motor dealerships. The group's history goes back to the 1844 Rochdale Pioneers and before that to Robert Owen himself. This is a distinctive backdrop which would be impossible to replicate, providing both a philosophical foundation and a practical example.

The Co-operative Group is what it is today because of that history. In the aftermath of deregulation, when so many mutual societies were being stripped and taken over, the Co-operative Wholesale Society (CWS), the distribution arm of the group confederacy of Co-operative Retail Societies, was itself threatened with a hostile takeover, the intention being to acquire the accrued reserves of the CWS and associated co-operatives. In this case the membership rejected the approach, preferring, on presumably idealogical if not idealistic grounds, to remain as a consumer co-operative. Since then, partly no doubt motivated by the nearness of the bid's success, the societies have rationalised their organisation as The Co-operative Group. Its continued success depends more on its effectiveness as a twenty-first century business which is seen to be mindful of the need for sustainability and sensitive to the excesses indulged by the neoclassical world. These long term considerations, which are so often compromised by the short term neoclassical focus, are part and parcel of co-operation and the co-operative movement.

A successful co-operative is not vulnerable to being sold to a competitor merely for the benefit of shareholders or so that its directors might receive a one-off payment for agreeing the deal, as was the case with chocolate firm Cadbury in 2010. Nor would they be vulnerable to crude share raids with the aim of stripping assets, 'releasing' people and saddling what remained with massive debt, as were Debenhams (Erdal 2011) and Boots the Chemist. These are considerable advantages for co-operatives. But the benefits go much deeper than that, especially for employee owned co-operatives.

The internal benefit is in terms of the interpersonal culture of fairness and integrity which engenders a spirit of commitment among all stakeholders:

> the commitment of people as human beings to their company and to future generations. They want to keep the company strong for their own sakes and they want to pass it on strong to the next generation. They are the people with the privilege of making themselves wealthier than their employee equivalents in similar companies. They want to give the same good fortune to those who come after them. They have human aspirations which include elements of conscience and of generosity: they are much more than the money grubbing automata of economist's models. (Erdal 2011)

Internal commitment and protection from external predators enable firms to invest for the long term, take the necessary risks to produce innovative products and processes as well as ways of managing for the benefit of all.

Co-operatives and Co-ownership

The distinctive characteristics which generally apply to co-operative organisation are:

- Ownership by members who may invest any amount.

- Directors are elected from among members.

- Members each have one vote at general meetings.

- Members are reimbursed according to their economic participation in the co-operative activity – purchases in the case of customer co-operatives, or pay in the case of employee co-operatives.

- Shares are usually redeemable at par value (that is, they do not accrue additional value).

The legal form of co-operatives varies from country to country. In Britain they are incorporated with limited liability either as industrial and provident societies or as private companies. The Financial Services Authority (FSA), which is the British registering authority, describes an industrial and provident society as:

> *an organisation conducting an industry, business or trade, either as a co-operative or for the benefit of the community, and is registered under the Industrial and Provident Societies Act 1965.*[1]

In addition to normal membership shares, co-operatives may issue other forms of financial security in order to attract funding. Some of these have been identified as privileged member shares, non-user member shares and tradeable co-operative shares (López-Espinosa, Maddocks & Polo-Garrido 2009). In general, these are intended to provide a sufficient return to induce investment, but carry no right to any residual surpluses and usually have no voting rights. Though they are identified as shares they clearly do not embody the attributes of ownership, a fact which causes some confusion over the distinction between debt and equity which is critical for the assessment of shareholder value, but less so in the world of co-operatives.

The interest in co-operatives and especially co-ownership has no doubt been stimulated by the failure of neoclassical ideology to prevent the 2007–8 financial crisis. That interest appears to have been greatest where the crisis has been most felt, notably the post-industrial economies. Interest in developing worker co-operatives in the United States, for example, has been highly active,[2] with articulate advocates such as the North American Students of Co-operation, founded in 1968, which proclaims a mission to organise and educate affordable group equity co-ops and their members for the purpose of promoting a

---

1 See FSA website at http://www.fsa.gov.uk/pages/doing/small_firms/msr/societies/index.shtml
2 See websites such as http://www.usworker.coop/front

community oriented co-operative movement.[3] Furthermore, the development of American co-operatives has been assisted by tax benefits encouraging the sale of founder owned businesses to employees under the Employee Stock Ownership Plan system.

An example of the larger, more established employee co-operatives, the British retailer, the John Lewis Partnership, has sales of £7.4 billion, owns 28 department stores, 4 John Lewis at home shops, 241 Waitrose supermarkets, an online and catalogue business, a production unit and an agricultural unit. Its employees, referred to as partners, are co-owners of the business and, as the John Lewis website says, 'they share in the benefits and profits of a business that puts them first'.[4]

Granting primacy to employees over outside shareholders provides a significant benefit for the employee co-operative, confirming all the best aspects of progressive management, as the John Lewis Partnership is not shy of doing, presenting its seven principles up front. These proclaim its ultimate purpose as 'the happiness of all its members, through their worthwhile and satisfying employment in a successful business'. They aim to make 'sufficient profit from its trading operations to sustain its commercial vitality, to finance its continued development and to distribute a share of those profits each year to its members'. Also, working relationships are expressed as being 'based on mutual respect and courtesy, with as much equality between its members as differences of responsibility permit. The Partnership aims to recognise their individual contributions and reward them fairly'. The principles also proclaim the commitment to honesty, integrity and courtesy in its relationships with external stakeholders: customers, suppliers and local communities. So much might sound like the sort of motherhood window-dressing so many firms indulge in, except that it is backed up with action:

> Up and down the country, the 69,000 people who work for the nation's favourite retailer are gathered, impatient. At head office in London's Victoria, in 28 John Lewis department stores from Southampton to Aberdeen, 223 Waitrose supermarkets from Plymouth to Norwich, the ritual's the same: a specially chosen staff member ('partner' in JL-speak) opens an envelope and reads out a number.

3 See http://www.nasco.coop/
4 Extracts from the John Lewis website: http://www.johnlewispartnership.co.uk/Display. aspx?&MasterId=768e29e8-41aa-4716-bce2-df302fa1c3d8&NavigationId=543

The number will be a percentage. ... It's the percentage of their salary that each John Lewis employee, from executive chairman to checkout operative, takes home as this year's bonus. ... A good one it is. ... In the depths of what everyone keeps telling us is the deepest financial and economic crisis since the second world war, John Lewis has plainly not done badly (operating profit up 20%) ... (Henley 2010: 5)

The Partnership is real. The benefits are tangible. The bonus is proof.

Empirical research on employee co-operatives and co-ownership is patchy, largely case studies and anecdotal analyses which lack a coherent framework against which different forms of co-ownership could be assessed. For some firms, control may be retained by the originating owners with employees participating in a minority of company shares. Alternatively, employees may own 100 per cent of the company's equity. Shares may be held in trust for the employees as a whole, or they may be allocated to individuals with specific arrangements made for their return when the individuals leave the company's employment. If held individually, shares may be owned by all employees, or by certain categories and sometimes a small group of senior individuals. However, unless shares are owned for the benefit of all employees, much of the benefit of co-operation and co-ownership, as outlined below, will be lost.

An employee co-operative, as identified here, is one where the employees own and control the firm, or the mechanisms for that are in place and ownership and control will be achieved in due course. Even so, the benefits of co-ownership are not necessarily achieved. Equity ownership is only part, though a vital part, of the employee co-operative story. Employees should also have the right to intervene in management, to attend and participate in general meetings and approve such things as the appointment of directors. To fulfil that role effectively, employees would also have to have the right to information about the company's position and progress. The rights to equity ownership, management influence and corporate information are the essential characteristics of an employee co-operative.

W.L. Gore and Associates, maker of Gore-Tex fabric plus thousands of advanced technology products for electronics, fabrics, industrial and medical markets, is another example firm which enjoys both benefits. It is a private company co-owned by the Gore family and the employees. Based in Newark, Delaware, it has sales revenue of around $2.5 billion and employs more than 8,500 people in nearly 50 facilities worldwide:

*There are no titles or conventional lines of command at Gore, where the
only way of becoming a leader is to attract followers – if a project can't
attract people to work on it, then it doesn't get done. (Caulkin 2009: 6)*

In 2009 Gore was ranked 30 in *Fast Company* magazine's 'Fast 50' list of the
world's most innovative companies. In 2010, Gore was listed by *Fortune*
magazine as 'One of the 100 Best Companies to Work For' in the United States
for the 13th consecutive year. For several years its overseas units have had
similar recognition in Germany, France and Italy, while its British plants in
Livingston and Dundee have headed the *Sunday Times* 'Best Companies to
Work For' list for four years in a row.

Another model of co-ownership is exemplified by the Scott Bader chemical
company which commenced operations in 1940 and now employs over 600
people worldwide with operations in ten countries. The company's founder
passed the company's shares to Scott Bader Commonwealth, a company
limited by guarantee and a registered charity which holds the shares on behalf
of its members, the employees, who elect directors of the charity as well as
the operating company. Scott Bader governance is overseen by a members'
assembly that represents the interests of all employees worldwide, with local
councils at each major plant to work with management on local issues.

This self-governing co-ownership structure provides Scott Bader with
protection from hostile takeover, enabling them to take a long term view of
the company's development, and engages employees in a more meaningful
relationship with the firm than a purely monetary contract. The decision to
opt for charitable status for the holding company has further significant
implications, described by company literature as follows:

*We as individuals, and we as Scott Bader will have a positive impact
wherever Scott Bader operates in the World. We will continue the
tradition of helping those less fortunate than ourselves by sharing our
business success through money, time and effort. We will be recognised
as a thriving international Trustee Ownership Enterprise, an exemplar
to others.[5]*

There are endless examples of co-operative and co-ownership success, in
various formats. They work. It is not a means of rescuing failing firms, as
was demonstrated by the several politically motivated reprieves granted in

---

5   Extract from Scott Bader website http://www.scottbader.com/global-corporate.aspx

1970s Britain under trade union leadership. But it is a highly effective way of developing and managing successful firms protected from hostile takeover and enabled to conduct their affairs co-operatively, with regard for all stakeholders and for the long term.

The benefits from co-ownership pervade the corporate culture of co-owned firms. The way they do things and the way people behave is vastly different from the way things are done and the way people behave in firms which exist to extract value for external shareholders. Work should not merely be a means to survival, but a source of satisfaction and personal development over a working life. That much should be achievable in the affluent society.

The reason co-operatives only account for a small proportion of total employment is widely held to be the perceived difficulty of financing such a business without money from the sale of shares on the open market. The point has been made often enough that the best way to finance a co-operative is to start a hundred years ago. But that perception ignores the reality.

Financing Co-ownership

Dow investigated why co-operatives were not more prevalent, comparing the two diametrically opposed forms of organisation which he referred to as Capital Managed Firms (KMFs) and Labour Managed Firms (LMFs). His emphasis on management rather than ownership was because of his recognition of the principle that people, a substantial part of what a firm is and needs to be, cannot be owned. Dow disproved the economic argument that LMFs' employee co-operatives were not as efficient or intrinsically profitable as orthodox shareholder-centric firms (Dow 2003). Co-operatives, having broader objectives than orthodox firms, would be unlikely to focus exclusively on maximising profit and thus may well not generate as big a net surplus for distribution. However, that would not explain their relative rarity. Co-operatives actually achieved better labour productivity which appeared to result from better working conditions (broadly defined) and a more trustworthy organisational setting with fewer lay-offs and plant closures, which in turn led to less absenteeism and aggressive industrial action.

The main practical barrier to the formation of employee co-operatives appeared to be their financing, without access to the orthodox issue of ordinary shares. Employees might be expected to have limited supplies of uncommitted funds at their disposal, but Erdal gives several examples where successful co-owned firms were partly financed by employees: €14,000 from each employee when they become members of the Mondragón federation, $16,000 from 50 employees to acquire the Maumee Authority Stamping plant after its closure by Ford, £8000 each from redundant miners to acquire Tower Colliery and save it from closure (Erdal 2011). The possibility of employees making direct investments is probably greater than might be assumed.

The other possible source of finance is debt. This might also be expected to be problematic, with employees generally having little collateral to put up as security against the debt other than the firm's assets, which if specialised would have limited value in the event of winding up. Furthermore, debt financing would involve some moral hazard with the employees standing to gain from high risk, high return projects, but lenders losing from unprofitable projects which might lead to bankruptcy. These various issues would all tend, in theory at least, to reduce the availability and increase the cost of debt finance.

A possible outcome, which is sometimes argued without empirical evidence, is that employee co-operatives would be established with less capital than their orthodox competitors, and would consequently operate with less advanced technology. This appears to be contradicted by Dow's evidence that employee co-operatives are more efficient than firms with external shareholders.

Whether financing employee co-operatives is a substantial problem remains uncertain. There has been limited serious empirical research, the issue often being clouded by ideological bias. Firms financed by orthodox means actually raise relatively little of their capital through the issue of shares. Established firms serving traditional markets make limited use of capital from shareholders. Typically, 80–90 per cent of shareholders' equity has, for such firms, been accrued through the retention of profit rather than being received for the issue of shares. The financing problem appears not to be substantial for established firms, but may be more significant earlier in a firm's development.

Dow identified means by which a publicly quoted company might convert itself into an employee co-operative. One approach was to establish an employee trust financed at least in part by payroll deductions which could purchase the company's shares on the open market. This could enable a quoted company to be converted to an employee co-operative by setting up a trust which acquires company shares on behalf of individual employees paid for in part by payroll deductions, company contributions to the trust being tax-deductible. The plan is that the proportion of shares owned by the trust would in due course be sufficient to achieve effective control of the company. The aim then would be to acquire the remaining shares by some form of debt financed buyout.

Clearly there would be practical issues arising, with such an arrangement, from the prolonged transition period, during which employees might leave the company and new employees join, as well as questions of board representation during the conversion period and the democratic process of agreeing the nuts and bolts of conversion procedures. However, none of these issues is insoluble. Moreover, it would not be necessary for the employee co-operative to be wholly employee owned. Employee control would be sufficient to provide external protection and the development of an employee centric internal culture.

In America employee ownership is facilitated through the Employee Stock Ownership Plan (ESOP). About 11,000 companies now have these plans in the United States, covering over 13 million employees.[6] ESOPs are frequently used to provide a market for the shares of departing owners of successful closely held companies, as well as to motivate and reward employees and to take advantage of some taxation benefits. Under the ESOPs scheme, shares held in the trust are allocated to individual employees who, when they leave the company, sell them back at 'fair market value'.

In an American study of employee ownership mainly resulting from the ESOP arrangements, it was noted that firms needed to be managed through an effectively designed and implemented 'employee ownership system' (Pierce, Rubenfeld & Morgani 1991). Knowledge, information, power and rewards were critical components of such a system and it was noted that employees' engagement with these rights needed to be carefully nurtured if the benefits of co-ownership were to be realised, and that training was essential to equip employees for the rights and responsibilities of ownership.

The idealism of departing owners is the starting point for many employee co-operatives, including the John Lewis Partnership which commenced its conversion to employee ownership in 1929 and completed it in 1950 when the trust set up to hold the company's share owned them all and holds them in perpetuity on behalf of the employees.

---

6   See the National Centre for Employee Ownership website at http://www.nceo.org/main/ article.php/id/8/

Another example employee buyout was Baxi, the leading British domestic boiler manufacturer, which its owners passed over to its employees:

> When he (Philip Baxendale) retired in 1983, he and his cousin transferred 90% of the company's value to a trust for its employees: it was valued at £50m and they sold it to the trust for £5m. ... over the next sixteen years, latterly through positive involvement of the employees, they made their factory the most productive in Europe. Then, in just 15 months, a hubristic and self-serving chief executive, together with a new big name City chairman and what turned out to be a cynical, fee chasing merchant bank, wrecked the company, through engineering a huge acquisition, many times bigger than Baxi itself. (Erdal 2008: 133–4)

Out of the wreckage, and that bitter learning experience, Philip Baxendale deployed the £20m still in trust to set up the Baxi Partnership[7] to advise and assist medium sized strong businesses to become employee owned. David Erdal gives an account of one such successful conversion, Loch Fyne Oysters which employs around 120 people, describing the financing arrangements facilitated by the Baxi Partnership in practical detail.

The two alternative routes to employee ownership are for the shares to be held in trust for employees as is common practice in Britain, or for the shares to be passed in the end to the individual employees, as is customary in America and required under the ESOP system. This latter approach also results from following the procedure of acquiring company shares through payroll deductions.

Complications arise with individual employees owning shares directly, firstly deciding a qualifying period for the acquisition of shares when they join the company, and more particularly, deciding the process of disengagement and share valuation when individuals either retire or leave the company. In Britain the shares are generally accorded a nominal value which does not change over time, as for example with shares in the Co-operative Group. Under the American ESOP scheme, shares are given an estimated market value at which the company is contracted to buy back from the retiring or departing employee. This legal commitment by the firm to buy back its shares can result in the firm being put under financial pressure. There have been instances where

---

7   See the Baxi Partnership website for detail: http://www.baxipartnership.co.uk/

this has led to employee owned firms being forced back to the stock market to raise the necessary finance.

The problem of financing employee owned co-operatives may be more apparent than real. And the benefits are substantial. The forces opposing co-ownership are substantial while ever the neoclassical orthodoxy drives government and business. In the absence of that dogma, the substantial benefits of co-ownership could be more readily recognised and governments couldtake simple steps to encourage its further adoption.

Conclusions

The version of the corporation which results from the application of the neoclassical economic model which focuses on the bottom line of profit and shareholder value maximisation is a dismal misconstruction of what the corporation set out to be, and could be again. It has led not just to the unsustainable excesses identified in Part II and elsewhere, but also to the greed and criminality which has increasingly infected our business culture over the past three decades.

As industries have matured and their markets become more concentrated with a few dominant firms becoming increasingly monopolistic, the accountability of those leading firms becomes more important. The tendency to fix, corner and abuse markets with their monopolistic power has been demonstrated time and again. Nevertheless, the still dominant neoclassical free market, shareholder primacy dogma, still drives government and increases the power of the monopolistic leader and reduces their accountability.

Co-operative formulations of the firm make business leaders accountable to stakeholders, and produce a more sustainable and more equitable outcome as well as being potentially more economically efficient. The employee co-operative model is based on all employees sharing responsibility for the corporate activity as well as its benefits. It renders external collectives such as trade unions unnecessary for the protection of the individual employee's interests and their major weapon, the firm damaging strike, redundant.

The arguments are ages old. Adam Smith's assertion of the butcher, baker and brewer's self-interest was no more than his expression of their natural desire to make a decent living from their trade. It was not an expression of their intent to maximise the immediate gain from the individual transaction – that was the neoclassical invention. John Stewart Mill (1871) argued for shared ownership and responsibility:

> So long as this idea remained in a state of theory, in the writings of Owen or of Louis Blanc, it may have appeared, to the common modes of judgment, incapable of being realised, and not likely to be tried unless by seizing on the existing capital, and confiscating for the benefit of the labourers; which is even now imagined by many persons, and pretended by more, both in England and on the Continent, to be the meaning and purpose of Socialism. But there is a capacity of exertion and self-denial in the masses of mankind, which is never known but on the rare occasions on which it is appealed to in the name of some great idea or elevated sentiment.

The history of co-operative and co-owned enterprise vindicates both Smith and Mill. Sustainability surely meets the criteria as a 'great idea or elevated sentiment'. A first step to its achievement would be the liberation of people, firms, markets and whole economies from neoclassical repression.

References

Achbar, M., Abbott, J. & Bakan, J., (2005), *The Corporation.* (see www.thecorporation.com) Based on *The Corporation: The Pathological Pursuit of Profit and Power*, New York: Free Press.

Berle, A.A. & Means, G.C., (1932), *The Modern Corporation and Private Property*, New York: Macmillan.

Birchall, J. & Simmons, R., (2004), The involvement of members in the governance of large-scale co-operative and mutual businesses: a formative evaluation of the co-operative group, *Review of Social Economy*, vol. LX, no. 4, 490.

Caulkin, S., (2009), Individuality can banish the downturn blues, *The Observer, Business & Media*, p. 6, 24th May, 2009.

Dow, G.K., (2003), *Governing the Firm: Workers Control in Theory and Practice*, Cambridge: Cambridge University Press.

Erdal, D., (2008), *Local Heroes: How Loch Fyne Oysters Embraced Employee Ownership and Business Success*, London: Penguin Viking.

Erdal, D., (2011), *Beyond the Corporation: Humanity Working*, London: Bodley Head.

Henley, J., (2010), Inside the wonderful world of John Lewis, *The Guardian, G2*, 16th March.

Jõnsson, S., (1996), Decoupling hierarchy and accountability: an examination of trust and reputation, in R. Munro & J. Mouritsen (eds), *Accountability: Power, Ethos & the Technologies of Managing*, Thomson Business Press.

Kettle, M., (2010), The late, great Jimmy Reid left a legacy for our times, *The Guardian*, 12.8.2010.

López-Espinosa, G., Maddocks, J. & Polo-Garrido, F., (2009), Equity-liabilities distinction: the case for co-operatives, *Journal of International Financial Management & Accounting*, vol. 20, no. 3, 274–306.

Mill, J.S., (1871), *Principles of Political Economy*, first published 1848, the quotation is from the 7th edition of 1871, Book IV, Chapter 7, Section 6, p. 266.

Pierce, J.L., Rubenfeld, S.A., & Morgani, S., (1991), Employee ownership: a conceptual model of process and effects, *Academy of Management Review*, vol. 16, no. 1, 121–144.

Ridley, M., (1996), *The Origins of Virtue*, Harmondsworth: Viking.

Seabright, P., (2004), *The Company of Strangers: A Natural History of Economic Life*, Princeton: Princeton University Press.

12

Enabling Co-operation and Co-ownership

This book started saluting the many great and good dissenters, renegades and revolutionaries who rejected economic orthodoxy. Most of them were partial in their rejection, focusing on some particular of the classical or neoclassical *oeuvre* which they recognised as limited in its description of reality as well as lacking in its power to predict. Together they rejected more or less the entirety of the theory inasmuch as it related to markets, firms and people. Today new generations have experienced the latter day excesses of that same theoretical core and its unfortunate outcomes and are not just fearful that the worst is yet to come but convinced of it.

Ad Broere, Ha-Joon Chang, George Cooper, David Ellerman, Bruno Frey, the late Sumantra Ghoshal, the late Tony Judt, Rakesh Khurana, John Lanchester, Jeff Madrick, John Quiggin, Paul Seabright, Robert Skidelski, Joseph Stiglitz, Spencer Wells and so on: the comprehensive list of serious contemporary critics of neoclassical excess would be very long, even excluding those ahead of their time, non-contemporaries such as Ernst Schumacher, Hyman Minsky and an equally long list of dissenters.

The message which is formed by these distinguished critics is, surely, that after 130 years of dogged perseverance by its devotees the neoclassical experiment has been seen to have failed. Theoreticians must go back to the drawing board and come up with a model that works, or try something completely different.

Removal of neoclassical analysis, and its spurious imperatives, from the governance and management of industry, business and government hardly leaves a void. There is plenty of guidance which is on a firmer foundation than neoclassical theory.

The aim of this final chapter is to identify changes that would be desirable, freed from neoclassical coercion, if governance and management are to escape the bottom line.

Change in Traditional Markets

The idea of the market encapsulates the means by which complex products are manufactured. It includes the acquisition of materials and components from the best and cheapest sources, the manufacture and assembly of products which can be profitably priced at a level which induces customers to purchase and the distribution and delivery of products to customers by various effective means. The traditional market works well so long as there is competition. Overproductions and underproductions are corrected by the market forcing adjustments in prices and production capacities, as well as innovations in the products themselves.

However, markets fail in terms of neoclassical efficiency. They do not automatically result in full employment and the allocation of resources which maximises economic growth and social welfare.

Central planning of extraction, production and distribution proved impossible to make work. It resulted in massive overproductions and underproductions. Moreover, without competition technological innovation was reduced, and a dysfunctional bureaucracy was created, with irresistible opportunities for corruption presented all down the planning hierarchy.

The processes of extraction, manufacture and distribution are more effectively controlled by market forces. They are the most efficient means of co-ordinating highly complex systems, and the best means so far identified for equating supply and demand through the price mechanism.

Competition is the key to market effectiveness. But in competitive markets, eventually, one competitor will gain competitive advantage and develop monopolistic strengths which will further increase their market position, against the common good. In unregulated markets this inevitable process of monopolistic market abuse and fixing is allowed to go unchecked and unpunished. Thus, a primary change in relation to the market is the requirement to be robust in the protection of competition, and to restrict the development of monopolistic positions and to eliminate anti-competitive practices among leading competitors.

The neoclassical ideology against market regulation is clearly destructive. Trade between post-industrial America and industrialising China, for example, has been allowed to become so far out of balance that unemployment in America, currently approaching 10 per cent, has no permissible effective solution. China, on the other hand, is itself being disrupted by so rapidly becoming the workshop of the world, while its food production capability is threatened. Trade regulation seems essential if evolutionary progress is to be maintained.

The dogma blocks regulation. International agencies such as the IMF and World Bank have previously insisted that assistance to Third World countries be dependent on them rejecting market regulation. Yet that approach is known to work to the poor countries' disadvantage without creating any general gain (Chang 2010: 62–73).

The benefits of international free trade are achieved differently in different situations. The best result is therefore dependent on the merits of individual cases rather than blind adherence to dogma. A coherent case for some elements of protectionism can be made, as has been done, from time to time for example, by the United States invoking the need to protect threatened industries such as steel. Carefully planned and agreed limitations on international trade might be beneficial to individual countries as well as to the global economy.

The protection of competition must be the prime purpose in regulating traditional markets. In both America and Britain regulations that exist have been interpreted more recently in sympathy with neoclassical ideas. For example, the tenor of decisions by the Office of Fair Trading in the UK has been to allow the establishment of dominant market positions which would previously have been prevented. It has been widely suggested a new rigorous defence of competitive markets must be raised, and the break-up of monopolistic positions given consideration wherever they have been established. Any acceptance of monopoly markets would need to be based on thorough analysis and democratic agreement.

In addition, the imperatives of sustainability, which have been widely studied and are now at least partly understood, require the intervention of governments to overrule the normal short term measures of economic return.

External costs involving the consumption of scarce resources and pollution, particularly production of greenhouse gases, need to be assessed and charged. Activities which aid and develop sustainability should be assessed and supported. Similarly, the impact of a firm's activities on its local community needs to be assessed and charged or reimbursed.

Consideration of these issues has often focused on the difficulties of accurate assessment and the costly bureaucracy that would be required to reflect that assessment in a tax and subsidy system. Alternatively, it has been suggested crude measures of positive or negative impacts would suffice with supplements or discounts made to rates of General Sales Tax, Value Added or Corporation Taxes. The practical difficulties are not insuperable. Sustainability requires the playing field to be sloped in its favour so that the polluter pays, rather than the general population, and that sustainability is subsidised.

Some discussions of these broad principles have taken place in relation to international trade, though any agreement appears to be a long way off. National adjustments, tariffs and subsidies would be made on imports according to the producing country's sustainability profile. Countries with high per capita greenhouse gas production could be required to pay an additional duty which might be contributed to green technology development and poor country green development.

Such changes would be best discussed, agreed and implemented on a global basis, but the improbability of that in the foreseeable future does not invalidate the desirability of progress where possible at a supranational or even national level.

Change in the Public Sector

The neoclassical objection to government involvement in the economy was amplified by Friedman's unsupported populist assertion that it costs twice as much for the public sector to do anything as it does the private. It has, as it was intended to do, raised public cynicism of anything done by the public sector. It has been an effective spur to privatisation and a barrier to public ownership, irrespective of the individual circumstances of any particular case.

In some situations the case for public ownership could be persuasive. Natural monopolies such as gas or water, where the characteristics of a competitive market can only be replicated inadequately and at considerable expense, might well be better organised on a public ownership basis.

For different reasons, healthcare and education would also appear to be appropriate fields for public provision. In those cases it may be possible for private organisations to provide excellent services, whether schools or hospitals, but it is completely unresolved whether private organisations would be able to provide the comprehensive universal cover as effectively as the public provision and make a profit. The consequence is that where public and private provision competes the private providers carefully select the areas they enter, avoiding those where they would inevitably make a financial loss. The result is a rise in cost of public sector provision.

Individual units can always be successful on a private basis, but universal coverage is a different problem. Carefully selected private mail delivery could be highly profitable, but not if the same urban service had to be provided to the Outer Hebrides.

The privatisation of British Rail services has highlighted some of the problems of private industry taking over public provision. The real effects are unclear. In the case of British Rail, the dogma led to lack of investment in the years prior to privatisation and several failed attempts to create competitive conditions after privatisation. Subsequently, private geographically defined monopolies of rolling stock running on publicly owned and maintained routes have been accepted. Comparison of the privately owned service with its continuation in public ownership is not possible, but the gain from privatisation is far from obvious, other than a windfall for the government of the day. Comparison of rail services in Britain and mainland Europe where services are publicly owned hardly makes a convincing case for privatisation.

In general, the public sector has been entrapped in the bottom line fixation just as has the private. The ideologically driven attempt to create pseudo markets with bureaucratically defined 'performance indicators' has resulted in what has been referred to as the 'target culture', which has famously drawn resource away from core tasks in order to perform against readily measurable targets which have to be measured, discussed, reported and subsequently converted into published league tables.

In some areas of public sector provision there is a profound cultural difference which has been summarised in questions such as 'would you like a profit maximising brain surgeon to open your head, or a dedicated professional specialist?'

The neoclassical argument that public sector is bad, private good, is extremely simplistic and clearly no basis for policy decision. Governmental fear of nationalisation in itself has no logical justification other than dogma. Freedom from dogma would permit each situation to be assessed on its own merits.

Change in Financial Markets

Neoclassical ideology drove deregulation in the financial sector. Critically, the barrier between speculative investment and support for the real economy was eliminated with the result that speculative investment came to dominate the whole sector, much to the disadvantage of the real economy.

The financial sector's investment wing seeks out anything it can invest in from which it can make a profit and the quicker the better. Thus, anything whose price can be predicted to be higher tomorrow than it is today attracts their investment, for at least a day. And for longer if prolonged speculations can be created.

The normal trading in company shares hardly excites great interest. But if an expectation of a deal can be created, then a quick profit might be made. So if there is rumour of such a deal, for example of a hostile takeover, or if one can be created so that a victim company is said to be 'in play', then speculative investment will be attracted.

The normal trade in commodities is not particularly exciting, but if expectations of price increases can be raised, then traders will invest and prices will rise. Resources which are being unsustainably depleted and whose prices are consequently fragile are particularly vulnerable to such abuse. Over the past four decades oil has been regularly subject to that treatment, firstly by the monopolistic power of the OPEC producers and then by the market fixing power of the financial sector. For example, crude oil prices were driven up to almost $150 a barrel in the summer of 2008 before collapsing to $33. Price collapses provide opportunities for successful trades so long as the timing is about right, using nothing more sophisticated than variations on the old fashioned put option. The oil price inflation cycle commenced again in 2010.

By April 2011, the price had recovered back to around $125 a barrel and might be expected at some stage to amplify the previous bubble. Such volatility has nothing to do with intrinsic supply and demand for oil, though logical analysis can help the speculation, as for example the interruption to Lybian supplies superimposed on an increasingly fragile long term supply position.

Other scarce resources, even including food, are already vulnerable to such speculative attack, endangering the lives of the millions of Third World populations who survive near the breadline.

Even gold and silver, the traditional hedge against the unreliability of other investments, notably money, is subject to speculative investment on a previously unknown scale, threatening their role as reliable stores of value.

Currently, speculation in carbon trading credits is unreasonably profitable and subject to large scale speculation, as, for example, the Alternative Markets website indicates:

> *Welcome to Alternative Markets – Dedicated to providing established green sippable alternative investments. Guaranteed investment opportunities with ROI ranging from 60% to 398%.*
>
> *Purchasing carbon credits to offset harmful emissions is a popular carbon reducing option. Investors can invest in companies that provide credits for carbon emissions, through forestry plantations for example, which are then sold on.[1]*

'Sippable' refers to the fact that investments are approved for inclusion in tax advantageous self-invested personal pensions (SIPPs). The reference to forestry plantations, ambiguous though it is, provides a surface rationale for the investment 'products', which though lacking in other specifics are claimed to produce a return of up to 398 per cent. Traders who stuck with investing in the real economy earning around 15 per cent, would be threatened with relegation from their league table for rejecting such opportunities.

The financial sector has become adept at creating wholly artificial, not simply derivative, 'products'. Their only characteristic of any importance is that tomorrow's price might be expected to be higher than today's. Any other characteristics of such 'products' are obscure, and mostly made deliberately

---

1   Alternative Markets website http://www.alternativemarkets.co.uk/carbon_trading.php

opaque so that it is not possible to make any assessment of their fundamental value. In case attempts should be made to assess fundamentals, the 'products' are often stirred up together and sold off as mixtures given obscure names which might lead outside investors to imagine that they really have been cleverly created to combine maximised profit with minimised risk.

The net result of the sector's investment machinations is that while prices continue to rise, big surpluses are accrued to the smartest and quickest dealers who, it is said from within the sector, demand to be heavily incentivised. Not only, they claim, is this achieved at no cost to the real economy, but some taxes, albeit at a low marginal rate, are in fact paid. However, the inevitable reaction when the bubble bursts does involve serious cost to the real economy. The 2007–8 crisis involved trillions of dollars and pounds being input to the banking systems in the United States and Britain to keep them in operation. After which the bubble inflating process was able to begin afresh.

Such generosity on the part of governments is prompted by their adherence to the neoclassical ideology. In Britain the former Labour government clearly feared being accused of what was referred to as 'the N word' – nationalisation – no matter how much money had to be spent on keeping individual institutions afloat. Neoclassical compliance was mandatory also in the United States where despite Lehman Brothers being allowed to collapse, the rest of the sector was bailed out. A prime beneficiary was Goldman Sachs whose alumni, despite the bank's criminal record, continue to dominate banking and financial institutions in America and elsewhere, as well as playing an important governmental role supporting the financial sector's exploitation of the real economy.

These are the results of the neoclassical maximising, free market ideology. If a banker is permitted to choose, as they are under neoclassical deregulation, between investing in a successful widget manufacturer earning something around 10–15 per cent, or a worthy sounding carbon credit security earning up to 398 per cent, there is little doubt which they have to choose.

If a bank's balance sheet has been destroyed when a bubble burst and the government gives them the money to stay in business, the banker will have certain priorities. The government will want the bank to support real industry so as to maintain employment levels and get the economy going again. However, the bank will be keen to rebuild its balance sheet, so it can return to business as a fully commercial operation as soon as possible. But the bank will have the opportunity to invest in such things as the high earning carbon credit security. The decision-makers in both government and banks will agree it is not for the government to take commercial banking decisions. The bank will find it all but impossible to support the widget maker, and will no doubt decide the quickest way to rebuild its balance sheet would be to invest in the carbon credit security, employing the brightest and best fully incentivised traders to manage the process.

The adoption of financial incentives as remuneration for financial sector insiders is a direct application of neoclassical ideology. Previously, incentive payments had been thought appropriate as compensation for shop floor work which might not be intrinsically rewarding, or to assist in the control of workers who were beyond the reach of management, such as the travelling salesman. The effectiveness of even those systems was challenged as far back as Brown (1962). Financial incentives 'crowd out' intrinsic motivations. The result is that those so incentivised fulfil the neoclassical prediction and in the absence of monetary incentive, will 'shirk' (to use agency terminology) as expected.

In the financial sector monetary incentives are structured in such a way that they also achieve the individual's identity with shareholders and consequently can be assumed to pursue the maximisation of their value.

The crowding out by monetary incentive is likely to be effective with the vast majority of corruptible human beings, clearly including even economists themselves, who stand to benefit from their covert connection with the financial sector (Economist 2011).

Without external assistance in the form of regulation, which they are ideologically bound to oppose, bankers are trapped in this vicious cycle of speculative investment presided over by the international system of incentive bonus payments. There is nothing they can do to change custom and practice without regulation. The financial sector will therefor continue to grow when the bubbles are inflating, without benefit to the real economy. And they will encumber the real economy with massive cost when the bubbles burst.

The regulatory controls which might help banks and the financial sector to bring themselves under control are obvious. In the main they were previously enacted following the 1930s experience, and have been widely advocated. In the main they amount to undoing some of the deregulatory initiatives undertaken over the past three decades:

1. Separating the roles of traditional banking and investment banking. To be effective the roles would have to be completely separate so that the two activities have no connection.

2. The central bank would act as lender of last resort only to those registered traditional banks which fulfil various requirements regarding liquidity and capital ratios. The central bank would have no such role or responsibility for the separate investment banking sector and would ensure that it was seen and understood to have no such responsibility. The feasibility of this would necessarily depend on having separated the two roles. Without that separation the central bank will continue as lender of last resort to speculative banking.

3. Reducing the scale of the investment banking role. It has been suggested some frictions would have to be introduced into the process, such as the Tobin transaction tax. This would add to the cost of each speculative transaction, reducing the viability of ultrafast, slice and dice, automated trading systems. The transaction tax would also impact on the non-investment bank players in these markets, such as hedge funds, private equity funds and so on.

4. It has been proposed to reduce the size of individual institutions so that none could be regarded as 'too big to fail'.

5. A national investment bank has been suggested to provide Keynesian stimuli to a recessionary economy, focusing on long term investment in national priorities such as public infrastructure, sustainability and the promotion of exports.

6. A progressive tax levy has been suggested on financial sector bonuses specifically to contribute to easing the deficits caused by quantitative easing, which has not yet and probably never will, be repaid. This progressive rate would have to go substantially higher than levels presently conceived, if it were to have any disincentive effect on speculative trading.

7. It has also been proposed that dealing in opaque financial products where the specifically defined fundamental value is not apparent

or stated, or is stated falsely, be made illegal, as it is for sellers of traditional products such as food.

8. It has been suggested the status of limited liability partnerships should be ended so that partners are once again made fully liable for the activities of their partnership, or convert to limited liability incorporated company status liable to paying corporate taxes.

9. It has been widely proposed that action must be taken on an international basis to limit the extent of tax haven activity. The British role in the development and preservation of tax havens is curious. Of the 35 OECD recognised tax havens, 10 are British colonial territories or dependencies, and of the other 25, 14 were formerly British. The City of London is the center of this tax avoidance and evasion industry. It has been suggested previously that it would be advisable to reduce the attractions of tax haven registration by levying a tax premium on the domestic activities of all firms so registered.

All of these changes have been fairly widely discussed in both the United States and Britain, some going before Congress and the House of Commons. They are simple to define but might appear difficult to implement unilaterally. If any one nation were to act alone, it is argued, there would be a mass exodus from that country, with a significant loss of tax income. Certainly it would be preferable if such changes were agreed internationally. However, a start would be made if the Anglo-American world were to lead such initiatives, rather than rejecting them on ideological grounds.

Progress would have the added benefit of reducing the sector's capture of bright young graduates who might be encouraged to contribute more usefully in the real economy. Though difficult, without international agreement a first step would be the wholesale rejection of neoclassical ideology.

Change in the Firm

It is curious that the post-industrial economies whose traditional roles in manufacturing and distribution have been most threatened by the industrialising economies, have been the most enthusiastic supporters of neoclassical ideology. For them, escaping the bottom line and the falsely based focus on maximising shareholder wealth would be the most profound benefit. If such escape were achieved, most desirable changes in industrial governance and management would follow almost automatically. Reorientation to focus on the long term best interests of the firm and all its stakeholders, as required by law, would change the nature of management and of work itself. The unaccountable tyranny of the ultra-macho, self-seeking business leader would rapidly become history.

Some initial steps have been considered which could provide firms with some protection against hostile and opportunistic takeover. The aim would be to reduce the shareholders' ultimate sanction over mergers and acquisitions. Legislation has been proposed which would postpone the acquisition of voting rights till share ownership had exceeded six months, or even a full year. This would frustrate most opportunistic share raids.

The reintroduction of different classes of equity is already allowable, with different rights attaching. Issuing securities which are in effect part debt and part equity could have similar results. Alternatively, employees could be granted the right to vote at general meetings, either on all issues or on specific items affecting them such as proposed mergers and acquisitions, their franchise extending to the equivalent of an identified proportion of issued equity.

All these options would serve to limit or dilute the voting power of shareholders. They would be relatively minor adjustments to practice, in most cases not requiring any legislative change. Making them mandatory has been widely discussed but governments have never made any such commitments. The reason why such steps have never been taken must be largely due to the dominance of the neoclassical dogma espousing financial sector: the markets and the bankers wouldn't like it.

More progressive steps also available without legislation would be the adoption of co-operative forms of governance, as discussed in the previous chapter. These would limit the power of outside shareholders and their appointed fund managers whose primary interest is speculative. They could be excluded from involvement in significant corporate decisions affecting the company's survival and long term prosperity.

The primary motivations for such co-operative forms of governance are twofold. Firstly, responsibility for the firm to be shared by all those who are contracted directly with it, who depend on it for their living and might gain personally through their experience and the opportunities for learning and development that the firm might provide. Secondly, to exclude the speculative interest of those controlling shareholder votes who are external to the firm with little real interest in its survival or future. To achieve these aims with certainty would require only a controlling interest in the firm. Ownership of all the firm's equity by the employees, or the body holding shares on their behalf, would not be essential.

Co-operation and co-ownership could not be established effectively through legal enforcement. The option is already open, as is the option of the European Company with a two-tier board with employee representation on the supervisory board. In Britain, as in America, the shareholders' position is still regarded as sacrosanct, in accord with neoclassical ideology. Any change of constitution giving increased power to employees would require approval by company members in general meeting, and would be unlikely to gain approval unless it was the prior decision by a dominant shareholder or shareholder group.

Developing a culture of shared responsibility could not be effectively imposed on a firm from outside. It would be primarily a concern of the company's management. However, legislation could require companies to make certain arrangements which would have some cultural impact. For example, a requirement to have employee representation, if not a majority, on the remuneration committee agreeing top management pay and bonuses, is one possibility that has been discussed widely.

The role of trade unions in such processes has also been given broad consideration, especially in Britain. The UK unions rejected the Bullock Report's 1977 offer of participation, preferring to retain their independence so as not to be compromised in their approach to 'free collective bargaining'. That combative approach no longer dominates the industrial scene, and it may be trade unions might find a more co-operative in-plant role. The idea of industrial democracy has largely been focused on employees as internal stakeholders, with all external stakeholders excluded. The interests of the firm and its internal stakeholders would be paramount. The active role of external trade unions might therefore be expected to decline as a more democratic culture developed inside firms.

As with other initiatives without international agreement on the way forward, progress would be more difficult, but not impossible. Firms might seek to leave jurisdictions, enacting elements of industrial democracy by law, and arrangements would have to be negotiated with foreign owned firms. The success of moves to industrial democracy might be critically dependent on the degree to which neoclassical dogma ceased to be the universal orthodoxy.

It has been proposed that the playing field could be sloped in favour of co-operation and democracy by providing firms so constituted with some significant tax incentive.

Within management theory, the human side of enterprise has long been recognised as a potential source of individual and social fulfilment, not just for senior people within the enterprise but for people at all levels of the organisation. Work can be fulfilling in the same way as art, sport or leisure, and can provide opportunities for personal development which exceed those available in other aspects of life. This potential value of working in a modern firm is entirely overlooked by the dominant ideology with its dismal assessments and presumptions.

However, mere recognition that changes might be advantageous for companies, for the economy and for the common good would be insufficient to achieve that change. Recognition of the damage done by neoclassical theory seems not to be sufficient to liberate us from its grip. Even the examples of how other jurisdictions protect their real economy from the parasitic embrace of shareholder primacy may not be enough to achieve change. Even understanding the unsustainability of economies being driven in that direction does not guarantee a change of direction in time to avoid disaster. But the combination of all these factors may be sufficient to speed the rejection of the dogma by the critical bodies that Keynes characterised as the 'madmen in authority'.

Change for People

Escaping neoclassical dogma, and the bottom line fixation it prescribes, would enable change within firms so as to realise the co-operative, human side to replace the nightmare approach eloquently summarised by Ghoshal. That is the most fundamental in-company change of all referenced in the previous two chapters.

The other aspect of change in people, enabled by the displacement of neoclassical ideology, goes beyond governance and management and relates to the inequality between people both within economies and between. The obvious solution is to tax inequality progressively and redistribute from the rich to the poor as advocated by Adam Smith. But the neoclassical arguments against this are strident, as though it strikes at the heart of its belief.

The dogma holds that all taxation is bad and any interference by government to redistribute wealth is worse, interfering with the basic freedom of individuals and far exceeding the remit of democratic government. It hods that inequality is the necessary ingredient to a liberal economy since it is the rich who don't spend all their money and are thus able to fund future investment on which the whole economy depends. Moreover, it is inequality which motivates social mobility and gives the economy its dynamic. The theories and arguments called in to support this fundamental belief are many, various and in most cases false.

The argument that progressive taxation damages the economy is not borne out by the facts. Between the Second World War and the 1980s, under Keynesian influenced governments, taxation got to be increasingly progressive in both the United States and Britain, with marginal rates in UK rising to around 98 per cent for the richest taxpayers. After 1980 marginal rates started to fall. Prior to the Second World War, GDP growth rates were averaging no more than 1.5 per cent per annum. During those three decades, 1950s–1970s, GDP growth was between 2 and 3 per cent in the US and between 4 and 5 per cent in Britain (Chang 2010: 142). Since then growth fell back to previous levels. Such statistics do not prove causation, but certainly do indicate that progressive taxation is not disastrous to economic growth and appears to contribute to it positively.

Keynes suggested the reason why taxing the poor less, especially in times of recession, was that the poor necessarily spent a much higher proportion of their income on consumption than did the rich. This could provide a substantial impetus to the economy. The counter-argument offered by neoclassical theory is that the rich invest their money, and therefore taxing them less would enable them to increase their investment, from which the economy as a whole, including job creation, would in due course benefit. But the truth today is that the rich will not invest their money in widget manufacturers for a 10–15 per cent return, but delegate investment to professionals who invest it in opaque junk securities such as the carbon trading bonds referred to previously. The rich may or may not like it, but their funds are being funnelled into speculative bubbles which will inevitably burst, rather than investments in the real economy.

Thus, not only is the neoclassical dogma demonstrably wrong, reducing tax on the rich does not benefit the economy but it actually does huge harm by funding speculative booms. Reducing taxes on the poor would stimulate the economy by immediately increasing the level of consumption.

As with previous changes, this change requires international agreement to be fully effective. But in this case, if a significant proportion of the traders and bankers on Wall Street and in the City of London were to move their operations to more accommodating jurisdictions, it might have a less damaging effect than if they stayed for another boom and bust before leaving.

Conclusion

The analysis in this chapter and the possible action points to enable co-operation and co-ownership have been raised many times elsewhere. Some of them have been formally considered by governments. Some have even been planned for implementation. None of them is unique. Even the wholesale rejection of the neoclassical theory is barely distinctive, it being discussed and commended in whole or in part in a thousand other texts at least. But so far the neoclassical mainstream has held firm. Even those whose interests it is most against have been persuaded to accept its 'truth'.

A primary reason for this is the cynicism with which politicians and big businesses are regarded. What seems not to be acknowledged is that politicians and business leaders are motivated largely by the neoclassical ideology in which they firmly believe. Without it, their words and actions would be different. The political–financial–industrial complex is still driven by Friedman and colleagues and it is their simplistic untruths which motivate the speculation, corruption and abuse which cause the cynicism.

Britain and the United States have both, in turn, passed their industrial prime. Britain appears to be approaching absolute decline while the United States appears to be in the stage of relative decline. Their moral leadership has also been severely damaged. So perhaps it matters less than previously to the world how the post-industrial economies behave.

However, the advanced nations must recognise that the whole of earth's population is at some hazard from their industrial activity and consumptions, in which first Britain and then America led the way. It will not be simple to achieve the change necessary for a sustainable future. Rejecting neoclassical theory in its entirety would be a necessary first step. Keynes may have underestimated the potential dangers of vested interests: he did not see the vast sums being sunk in politically motivated lobbying which subvert democracy and convince people of the ideology which is so much against their own interests.

If that change was achieved, then the road to co-operation would be clear, and escaping from the bottom line culture would make a major contribution to a more sustainable future.

People are, by and large, naturally generous and empathetic, but corruptible. The dominance of neoclassical economic theory has had that corrupting effect, teaching people that being selfish and greedy is necessary for a healthy economy, while being generous and kind is not just irrational but damaging to the economy and the general good. It is the corrosive and false economic theory which must first be buried.

References

Brown, W., (1962), *Piecework Abandoned*, London: Heinemann.

Chang, Ha-Joon, (2010), *23 Things They Don't Tell You About Capitalism*, London: Allen Lane.

Economist, The (2011), *Economics Focus Editorial: Dismal Ethics*, 6th January.

Bibliography

Achbar, M., Abbott, J. & Bakan, J., (2005), *The Corporation* (see www. thecorporation.com). Based on *The Corporation: The Pathological Pursuit of Profit and Power*, New York: Free Press.

Alchian, A.A. & Demsetz, H., (1972), Production, information costs, and economic organisation, *American Economic Review*, vol. 62, 778.

Axelrod, A., (1984), *The Evolution of Co-operation*, London: Basic Books.

Barnard, C.I., (1938), *The Functions of the Executive*, Cambridge Mass: Harvard University Press.

Baum, H., (2005), Change of governance in historic perspective: the German experience, in Hopt et al. (eds), *Corporate Governance in Context: Corporations, States, and Markets in Europe*, Japan, and the US, Oxford: Oxford University Press, pp. 3–29.

Baumol, W.J., (1958), On the Theory of Oligopoly, *Economica*, vol. 25, no. 99, 31–43.

Beatty, J., (1998), *The World According to Drucker*, Orion Publishing Group.

Berle, A.A. & Means, G.C., (1932), *The Modern Corporation and Private Property*, New York: Macmillan.

Birchall, J. & Simmons, R., (2004), The involvement of members in the governance of large-scale co-operative and mutual businesses: a formative evaluation of the co-operative group, *Review of Social Economy*, vol. LX, no. 4, 490.

Bork, R.H., (1993), *The Antitrust Paradox* (second edition), New York: Free Press.

Bower, M., (1966), *The Will to Manage*, New York: McGraw-Hill.

Brown, W., (1962), *Piecework Abandoned*, London: Heinemann.

Cao, Y., Qian, Y. & Weingast, B.R., (1999), From federalism. Chinese style to privatization, Chinese style, *Economics of Transition*, vol. 7, no. 1, 103–131.

Cappelli, P., Singh, H., Singh, J. & Useem, M., (2010), *The India Way*, Boston Mass: Harvard Business Press.

Caulkin, S., (2009), Individuality can banish the downturn blues, *The Observer, Business & Media*, p. 6, 24th May, 2009.

CFA Institute, Centre for Financial Market Integrity, (2007), *China Corporate Governance Survey*.

Chandler, A., (1977), *The Visible Hand: The Managerial Revolution in American Business*, Cambridge Mass: Belknap Press of Harvard University.

Chang, Ha-Joon, (2010), *23 Things They Don't Tell You About Capitalism*, London: Allen Lane.

Chomsky, N., (2004), in The Corporation video based on J. Bakan (2004), *The Corporation: The Pathological Pursuit of Profit and Power*, New York: Free Press.

Coase, R., (1937), The nature of the firm, *Economica*, vol. 16, no. 4, 386–405.

Cyert, R.M. & March, J.G., (1992), *A Behavioral Theory of the Firm*, Oxford: Blackwell.

De George, R.T., (1993), *Competing with Integrity in International Business*, New York: Oxford University Press.

Dimsdale, N. & Prevezer, M. (eds), (1994), *Capital Markets and Corporate Governance*, Oxford: Clarendon Press.

Dixit, A. & Nalebuff, R., (1994), *Thinking Strategically: The Competitive Edge in Business, Politics and Everyday Life*, New York: W W Norton & Co.

Dow, G.K., (2003), *Governing the Firm: Workers Control in Theory and Practice*, Cambridge: Cambridge University Press.

Drucker, P.F., (1950), *The New Society*, New York: Harper & Bros.

Drucker, P.F., (1993), *The Post-Capitalist Society*, Oxford: Butterworth-Heinemann.

Dunleavy, C.A., (1998), Corporate governance in late 19th Century Europe and the United States: the case of shareholder voting rights, in Hopt, K., et al, (eds) (1998), *Comparitive Corporate Governance*, Oxford: Oxford University Press, p. 15.

Economist, The (2008), *Corporate Governance in Japan: Bring it on*, 29th May.

Economist, The (2010), *The Rising Power of the Chinese Worker*, 29th June.

Economist, The (2011), *Economics Focus Editorial: Dismal Ethics*, 6th January.

Edwards, J.S.S. & Fischer, K., (1994), An overview of the German financial system, in Dimsdale, N. & Prevezer, M. (eds) (1994), *Capital Markets and Corporate Governance*, Oxford: Clarendon Press, p. 259.

Ellerman, D., (2006), *Helping People to Help Themselves*, Ann Arbour: University of Michigan Press.

Erdal, D., (2008), *Local Heroes: How Loch Fyne Oysters Embraced Employee Ownership and Business Success*, London: Penguin Viking.

Erdal, D., (2011), *Beyond the Corporation: Humanity Working*, London: Bodley Head.

Fan, J.P.H, Wong, T.J. & Zhang, T., (2007), Politically connected CEOs, corporate governance, and post-IPO performance of China's newly partially privatized firms, *Journal of Financial Economics*, vol. 84, no. 2, 330–357.

Fournier, V., (2008), Escaping from the economy: the politics of degrowth, *International Journal of Sociology and Social Policy*, vol. 28, no. 11/12, 528–545.

Frey, B.S., (1997), *Not Just for the Money: An Economic Theory of Personal Motivation*, Cheltenham: Edward Elgar Publishing.

Friedman, L.M., (1973), *A History of American Law*, New York: Simon & Schuster Touchstone.

Friedman, M., (1962), *Capitalism and Freedom*, Chicago: University of Chicago Press, (page numbering is as per the 2002 40th anniversary edition).

Friedman, M., (2003), Extracted from interview for *The Corporation: The Pathological Pursuit of Profit and Power*, New York: Free Press.

Galbraith, J.K., (1958), *The Affluent Society*, London: Hamish Hamilton.

Galbraith, J.K., (1989), *In Pursuit of the Simple Truth*, Commencement address to the women graduates of Smith College, Massachusetts, 28th July.

Ghoshal, S., (2006), Bad management theories are destroying good management practices, *Academy of Management Learning and Education*, vol. 4, no. 1, 85.

Giddens, A., (1999), Interview by Nyta Mann for BBC News Online, 19th March. (See http://news.bbc.co.uk/1/hi/uk_politics/298465.stm)

Gregory, K.L., (1983), Native view paradigms: Multiple cultures and culture conflicts in organisations, *Administrative Science Quarterly*, September, vol. 28, 75–85.

Hare, R., (2003), Extracted from interview for *The Corporation: The Pathological Pursuit of Profit and Power*, New York: Free Press.

Hayek, F.A., (1944), *The Road to Serfdom*, London: Routledge. Reprint 1956 with additional preface.

Hayek, F.A., (1960), *The Constitution of Liberty*, Chicago: University of Chicago Press.

Hayek, F.A., (1988), *The Fatal Conceit: The Errors of Socialism*, London: Routledge.

Hayes, R.H. & Abernathy, W.J., (1980), Managing our way to economic decline, *Harvard Business Review*, (July–August).

Hayes, R.H. & Garvin, D., (1982), Managing as if tomorrow mattered, *Harvard Business Review*, (May/June).

Henley, J., (2010), Inside the wonderful world of John Lewis, *The Guardian*, G2, 16th March.

Herrnstein, R., (1988), A Behavioural Alternative to Utility Maximisation, in S. Maital (ed.), *Applied Behavioural Economics*, Brighton: Wheatsheaf Books.

Hirsch, F., (1976), *The Social Limits to Growth*, Cambridge, MA: Harvard University Press, pp. 143.

Hopt, K.J., Kanda, H., Roe, M.J., Wymeersch, E. & Prigge, S., (1998), *Comparative Corporate Governance – the State of the Art and Emerging Research*, Oxford: Oxford University Press.

Hopt, K.J., Roe, M.J., Wymeersch, E., Kanda, H. & Baum, H., (eds), (2005), *Corporate Governance in Context: Corporations, States, and Markets in Europe, Japan, and the US*, Oxford: Oxford University Press.

Jensen, M.C. & Meckling, W.H., (1976), Theory of the firm: managerial behaviour, agency costs and ownership structure, *Journal of Financial Economics*, vol. 3, 305–360.

Jõnsson, S., (1996), Decoupling hierarchy and accountability: an examination of trust and reputation, in R. Munro & J. Mouritsen (eds), *Accountability: Power, Ethos & the Technologies of Managing*, Thomson Business Press.

Judt, T., (2010), *Ill Fares the Land*, London: Allen Lane.

Kanter, R.M., (2010), It's time to take full responsibility, *Harvard Business Review*, vol. 88, no. 10.

Kelemen, M. & Bunzel, D., (2008), Images of the model worker in state socialist propaganda and novels: the case of Romania, *Culture and Organization*, vol. 14, no. 1, 1–14.

Kester, C., (1993), *Japanese Takeovers: The Global Contest for Corporate Control*, Washington DC: Beard Books.

Kettle, M., (2010), The late, great Jimmy Reid left a legacy for our times, *The Guardian*, 12.8.2010.

Keynes, J.M., (1931), *Collected Writings, Vol. ix, Essays in Persuasion*, London: Macmillan.

Keynes, J.M., (1936), *The General Theory of Employment Interest and Money*, London: Macmillan.

Khurana, R., (2007), *From Higher Aims to Hired Hands*, Princeton: Princeton University Press.

Kotler, P., (1984), *Marketing Management: Analysis, Planning, Implementation and Control*, 5th edition, New York: Prentice Hall.

Lan, L.L. & Heracleous, L., (2010), Rethinking agency theory: the view from law, *Academy of Management Review*, vol. 35, no. 2, 294–314.

Lanchester, J., (2010), *Whoops! Why Everyone Owes Everyone and No One Can Pay*, London: Allen Lane.

Levitt, T., (1958), The dangers of social responsibility, *Harvard Business Review*, September-October.

López-Espinosa, G., Maddocks, J. & Polo-Garrido, F., (2009), Equity-Liabilities Distinction: the case for Co-operatives, *Journal of International Financial Management & Accounting*, vol. 20, no. 3, 274–306.

Lubin, D.A. & Esty, D.C., (2010), The sustainability imperative, *Harvard Business Review*, vol. 88, no. 5, 42–50.

McGregor, D., (1960), *The Human Side of Enterprise*, New York: McGraw Hill.

Macher, J.T. & Richman, B.D., (2008), Transaction cost economics: an Assessment of empirical research in the social sciences, *Business and Politics*, vol. 10, no. 1.

Maier, P., (1993), The revolutionary origins of the american corporation, *William and Mary Quarterly*, 3rd Ser., 51–84.

Maital, S., (ed.), (1988), *Applied Behavioural Economics*, Brighton: Wheatsheaf Books.

Marshall, A., (1922), *Principles of Economics*, 8th edition, London: Macmillan.

Marx, K., (1867), *Capital*, (1995 edition available, Oxford: Oxford World Classics).

Marx, K. & Engels, F., (1847), *The Communist Manifesto*, (2002 edition available with an introduction and notes by G.S. Jones, London: Penguin Classics).

Maslow, A., (1943), A theory of human motivation, *Psychological Review*, vol. 50, 370–396.

Matsusaka, J.G., (1995), The economic approach to democracy, in M. Tommasi & K. Ierulli (eds), (1995), *The New Economics of Human Behaviour*, Cambridge: Cambridge University Press.

Mill, J.S., (1848), *Principles of Political Economy*. The quotation at the end of Chapter 11 is from the 7th edition published in 1871. Currently available: (1973), Clifton, New Jersey: Augustus M. Kelly.

Milne, S., (2010), The strikes are good for China – and for the world, *The Guardian*, 1st July, p. 31.

Minsky, H., (1986), *Stabilizing an Unstable Market*, New Haven: Yale University Press.

Mises, von L., (1951), *Socialism: An Economic and Sociological Analysis*. English translation by J. Kahane, New Haven: Yale University Press. (Page numbering refers to that edition.) Originally published in German 1922.

Mises, von L., (1962), *The Free and Prosperous Commonwealth*, translated by R. Raico (ed.), A. Goddard, New York: Van Nostrand Co.

Mishel, L., (2007), *CEO to Worker Pay Imbalance Grows*, Economic Snapshots web site: www.epi.org/content.cfm/webfeatures_snapshots_20060621

Miwa, Y. & Ramseyer, J.M., (2005), Asking the wrong question: changes of governance in historical perspective. In K.J. Hopt et al. (eds), *Corporate Governance in Context: Corporations, States, and Markets in Europe, Japan and the US*, Oxford: Oxford University Press, pp. 73–84.

New Economics Foundation, see http://www.neweconomics.org/projects/ interdependence

Ostrom, E., (1990), *Governing the Commons: The Evolution of Institutions for Collective Action*, Cambridge: Cambridge University Press.

Pearson, G., (1999), *Strategy in Action: Strategic Thinking, Understanding and Practice*, Harlow: FT Prentice Hall.

Pearson, G., (2009), *The Rise and Fall of Management: A Brief History of Practice, Theory and Context*, Farnham: Gower.

Pierce, J.L., Rubenfeld, S.A. & Morgani, S., (1991), Employee ownership: a conceptual model of process and effects, *Academy of Management Review*, vol. 16, no. 1, 121–144.

Porter, M.E., (1980), *Competitive Strategy – Techniques for Analyzing Industries and Competitors*, New York: Free Press.

Read, A., (1971), *The Company Director: His Functions, Powers and Duties*, London: Jordan & Sons Ltd.

Ridley, M., (1996), *The Origins of Virtue*, Harmondsworth: Viking.

Roe, M., (1998), German co-determination and German securities markets, in K.J. Hopt et al. (eds), *Comparative Corporate Governance*, Oxford: Oxford University Press.

Roe, M., (2003), *Political Determinants of Corporate Governance*, Oxford: Oxford University Press.

Routh, G., (1975), *The Origin of Economic Ideas*, London: Macmillan.

Samuelson, P.A., (1948), *Economics: An Introductory Analysis*, New York McGraw–Hill.

Say, J-B., (1803), *Traité d'Economie Politique*.

Schein, E.H., (1984), Coming to an awareness of organisational culture, *Sloan Management Review*, Winter.

Schneider-Lenné, E.R., (1994), The role of German capital markets and the universal banks, supervisory boards and interlocking directorships, in Dimsdale, N. & Prevezer, M. (eds), (1994), *Capital Markets and Corporate Governance*, Oxford: Clarendon Press.

Schumacher, E.F., (1973), *Small is Beautiful: A Study of Economics as if People Mattered*, London: Blond & Briggs.

Seabright, P., (2004), *The Company of Strangers: A Natural History of Economic Life*, Princeton: Princeton University Press.

Sheard, P., (1991), The economics of interlocking shareholding in Japan, *Ricerche Economiche*, vol. XLV, 421–48.

Simon, H.A., (1956), Rational choice and the structure of the environment, *Psychological Review*, vol. 63, no. 2, 129–138.

Skapinker, M., (2010), Corporate plans may be lost in translation, *Financial Times*, 22nd November.

Skidelsky, R., (2009), *Keynes: The Return of the Master*, London: Allen Lane.

Smith, A., (1759), *The Theory of Moral Sentiments.* (Currently available in the Dover Philosophical Classics Series, New York: Dover Publications.)

Smith, A., (1776), *An Inquiry into the Nature and Causes of the Wealth of Nations,* a selected edition with introduction and notes by K. Sutherland, (1993), Oxford World's Classics, Oxford: Oxford University Press.

Solomon, J., (2007), *Corporate Governance and Accountability,* Chichester: John Wiley & Son.

Sternberg, E., (2004), *Corporate Governance: Accountability in the Marketplace,* The Institute of Economic Affairs.

Stiglitz, J., (2010), *Freefall: Free Markets and the Sinking of the Global Economy,* London: Penguin.

Sykes, A., (1994), Proposals for a reformed system of corporate governance to achieve internationally competitive long term performance, in Dimsdale, N. & Prevezer, M. (eds), *Capital Markets and Corporate Governance,* Oxford: Clarendon Press.

Tomasky, M., (2010), The money fighting health care reform, *The New York Review of Books,* vol. LVII, no. 6.

Tommasi, M. & Ierulli, K., (eds), (1995), *The New Economics of Human Behavior,* Cambridge: Cambridge University Press.

Veblen, T., (1899), *The Theory of the Leisure Class: An Economic Study in the Evolution of Institutions.* New York: Macmillan.

Wells, S., (2010), *Pandora's Seed: The Unforeseen Cost of Civilisation,* London: Allen Lane.

Wenger, E. & Kaserer, C., (1998), German banks and corporate governance: a critical view, in K.J. Hopt et al. (eds), *Comparative Corporate Governance,* Oxford: Oxford University Press.

White, J., (1984), Corporate culture and corporate success, *Management Decision,* vol. 22, no. 4.

Wilkinson, R. & Pickett, K., (2009), *The Spirit Level: Why More Equal Societies Almost Always Do Better,* London: Allen Lane.

Williamson, O.E., (19964), *The Economics of Discretionary Behaviour: Managerial Objectives in a Theory of the Firm,* Englewood Cliffs NJ: Prentice Hall.

Xiao, J.Z., Dahya, J. & Lin, Z., (2004), A grounded theory exposition of the role of the supervisory board in China, *British Journal of Management,* vol. 15, no. 1, 39–55.

Yafeh, Y., (2000), Corporate performance in Japan: past performance and future prospects, *Oxford Review of Economic Policy,* vol. 16, no. 2, 76.

Index

If you have found this book useful you may be interested in other titles from Gower

Complex Adaptive Leadership:
Embracing Paradox and Uncertainty
Nick Obolensky
Hardback: 978-0-566-08932-9
e-book: 978-0-566-08933-6

MisLeadership:
Prevalence, Causes and Consequences
Christopher Houghton Budd
Hardback: 978-0-566-09226-8
e-book: 978-0-566-09227-5

Strategic Review:
The Process of Strategy Formulation
in Complex Organisations
Robert F. Grattan
Hardback: 978-1-4094-0728-7
e-book: 978-1-4094-0729-4

GOWER

The Rise and Fall of Management:
A Brief History of Practice, Theory and Context
Gordon Pearson
Hardback: 978-0-566-08976-3
Paperback: 978-1-4094-4829-7
e-book: 978-0-566-08977-0

Rethinking Management:
Radical Insights from the Complexity Sciences
Chris Mowles
Hardback: 978-1-4094-2933-3
e-book: 978-1-4094-2934-0

Creating Collaborative Advantage:
Innovation and Knowledge Creation
in Regional Economies
Edited by
Hans Christian Garmann Johnsen and Richard Ennals
Hardback: 978-1-4094-0333-3
e-book: 978-1-4094-0334-0

Visit **www.gowerpublishing.com** and

- search the entire catalogue of Gower books in print
- order titles online at 10% discount
- take advantage of special offers
- sign up for our monthly e-mail update service
- download free sample chapters from all recent titles
- download or order our catalogue